Shattered
Assumptions

Shattered Assumptions

Towards a New Psychology of Trauma

Ronnie Janoff-Bulman

THE FREE PRESS
A Division of Macmillan, Inc.
NEW YORK

Maxwell Macmillan Canada
TORONTO

Maxwell Macmillan International
NEW YORK—OXFORD—SINGAPORE—SYDNEY

THE FREE PRESS
A Division of Simon & Schuster
1230 Avenue of the Americas
New York, NY 10020

THE FREE PRESS and colophon are trademarks
of Simon & Schuster Inc.

Manufactured in the United States of America

10 9 8 7 6 5 4 3 2 1

Library of Congress Cataloging-In-Publication Data

Janoff-Bulman, Ronnie.
     Shattered assumptions: towards a new psychology of trauma /
Ronnie Janoff-Bulman
        p.   cm.
     Includes bibliographical references (p.) and index.
     ISBN: 0-7432-3625-4
     1. Life change events—Psychological aspects.   2. Adaptability
(Psychology)   3. Psychic trauma. 4. Victims—Psychology.
     I.   Title.
     BF637.L53J36   1992
     155.9'3—dc20   91-34496
                                              CIP

For information regarding special discounts for bulk purchases, please contact Simon &
Schuster Special Sales at 1-800-456-6798 or business@simonandschuster.com

Credits

To the memory of my wonderful father,
whose gifts of love and learning
are always with me

Contents

Contents

Acknowledgments

I owe a deep debt of gratitude to many, many people who made this book both a possibility and a reality for me. I am fortunate to have colleagues and friends in my psychology department who are intellectually alive and stimulating, while at the same time emotionally supportive. Their willingness to listen, discuss, and encourage have helped me enormously. I am very grateful to my graduate school mentors and to my many superb students who, over the years, have kept me on my toes and helped me develop my ideas. The openness and insights of the Harvard Trauma Study Group are greatly appreciated; the group's participants have been more helpful than they know. It has truly been a pleasure to work with The Free Press; I never expected the publication process to be so hassle-free. With temendous respect and admiration, I especially want to express my deep gratitude to the many survivors who have taught me so much during these many years of research and writing.

Working in the area of trauma and victimization makes a person acutely aware of life's gifts, and there is no question that for me life's greatest gift is my family. I was raised—with my wonderful older brother—in a home filled with love, learning, joy, and respect, and I will be forever thankful for my very special parents. I miss my father, with his gentle, kind ways, his tolerance and integrity, his wisdom and warmth. I am incredibly fortunate to have a mother who has always been a great role model. She is the original supermom, and I thank her for her love of life, her generosity and caring, her enthusiasm and energy. Since my father's recent death my mother has taught me a great deal about coping and emotional strength, and she remains an extremely positive force in my life.

I give my greatest thanks to my husband, Michael, who as a partner and father demonstrates the true meaning of sharing. He has helped me with this book more than anyone, from discussing ideas and reading manuscript pages to successfully freeing me from any guilt when I needed time to write. I am deeply grateful for Michael's nurturance—both intellectual and emotional—and for his selflessness, creativity, responsibility, spontaneity, intelligence, and wit. Even after eighteen years of marriage I continue to find him endlessly fun and interesting.

Last, but certainly not least, I am incredibly grateful to our two terrific children, Jessica and David. I thank them for their thoughtfulness and sensitivity, their laughter and smiles, their pranks and serious discussions, their curiosity and intelligence, their imagination and humor, their understanding and encouragement. They give me more joy than they could ever know.

PART ONE

Background

1

Our Fundamental Assumptions

In a single day during the fall of 1989, I recall being struck by reports that nineteen high school students were killed when their school bus plunged into a forty-foot chasm in Texas, Hurricane Hugo lashed into the Carolinas, and a jet crashed at LaGuardia Airport in New York. Newscasts have since told us of the sniper death of a teenage girl on a school bus in Massachusetts, a disastrous train crash in London, cyclones and flooding in Bangladesh, earthquakes in California and the Philippines, the mass murder of fourteen women at the University of Montreal, war and devastation in the Persian Gulf, and the death of nine children when a tornado hit a school in upstate New York. These are catastrophes we read about in newspapers or hear about on television or radio. Yet every day countless more are victimized who do not receive such public attention.

Unfortunately, there is no dearth of such extreme events in our world today. Rape, incest, battering, other criminal assaults, the diagnosis of life-threatening disease, the sudden and untimely loss of a loved one, serious accidents, earthquakes, floods, other natural disasters, and combat are all too common. Increasingly, people are exposed to technological disasters such as Three Mile Island and Chernobyl; and we have witnessed mass atrocities in such forms as Nazi concentration camps and the atomic bombings in Hiroshima and Nagasaki. How can we understand the psychological impact and aftermath of these traumatic experiences? How do people come to terms with these events and go on with their lives?

3

The responses of survivors to extreme life events tell us a great deal about our common human needs, capacities, and illusions. The fundamental properties of a substance or object are often revealed through exposure to extreme conditions—for example, the familiar compound H_2O is more fully understood by its reactions to intense heat and cold. Just as the scientist attempts to understand the nature of elements by experimenting with them under extreme conditions, so, too, the child experiments with people and objects by exploring behavior at the boundaries. How much air can be inflated into the balloon? What are Mom and Dad's real limits? Traumatic life events involve reactions at life's extremes. By understanding trauma we learn about ourselves, victim and nonvictim alike, and begin to become aware of our greatest weaknesses and our surest strengths.

Certainly, extreme events differ in severity, and no two survivors will have identical reactions. Yet dramatically different victimizations may have psychological impacts that are similar in important ways. It is these similarities that both provide us with an understanding of those who survive trauma and enable us to draw conclusions about some basic aspects of human thought and behavior.

The survivor's experience tells us a great deal about the psychology of daily existence. A powerful lesson learned from working with victims is the extent to which we ordinarily rely upon—and take for granted—a few fundamental assumptions about ourselves and our world, assumptions that generally go unquestioned and unchallenged.

At the Core of Our Internal World

The philosophy which is so important in each of us is not a technical matter; it is our more or less dumb sense of what life honestly and deeply means . . . it is our individual way of just seeing and feeling the total push and pull of the cosmos.

—*William James*[1]

At the core of our internal world, we hold basic views of ourselves and our external world that represent our orientation toward the "total push and pull of the cosmos." Surely our basic assumptions may be more private and less elegant than theories that guide scientific observation and research; yet they are no less important as guides for our day-to-day thoughts and behaviors.

A few psychologists have explicitly discussed the importance of people's fundamental assumptions about themselves and their world. C. M. Parkes uses the phrase "assumptive world" to refer to people's view of reality, "a strongly held set of assumptions about the world and the self which is confidently maintained and used as a means of recognizing, planning and acting . . . Assumptions such as these are learned and confirmed by the experience of many years."[2]

Psychiatrist John Bowlby[3] writes of "working models" that people build of themselves and the world, which are used to perceive events, construct plans, and forecast the future. Sociologist Peter Marris refers to our "structures of meaning," basic principles that are abstract enough to be applied to any event we encounter and thereby make life continuously intelligible.[4] Similarly, psychologist Seymour Epstein writes that "everyone unwittingly develops a personal theory of reality that includes a self-theory and a world-theory. A personal theory of reality does not exist in conscious awareness, but is a preconscious conceptual system that automatically structures a person's experiences and directs his or her behavior."[5] From a very different perspective, psychiatrist Joseph Sandler describes a "representational world," the constellation of organized, enduring impressions culled from experience that serves as a cognitive map.

Although different terms are used, there is clearly congruence in these descriptions of a single underlying phenomenon. The reference is to a conceptual system, developed over time, that provides us with expectations about the world and ourselves. This conceptual system is best represented by a set of assumptions or internal representations that reflect and guide our interactions in the world and generally enable us to function effectively.

A network of diverse theories and representations constitutes our assumptive world; surely some are more central and basic than others. The assumptions "I am a good poker player" or "I am a good piano player" are different from the assumptions "I am a moral, decent person" and "I am a competent individual." Our theories are hierarchically organized, with our most fundamental assumptions being those that are most abstract and general, as well as most pervasive in their applicability.[6] Our fundamental assumptions are the bedrock of our conceptual system; they are the assumptions that we are least aware of and least likely to challenge. What are these core assumptions and why do they form the nucleus of our internal world?

Benevolence, Meaning, and Self-Worth

Most generally, at the core of our assumptive world are abstract beliefs about ourselves, the external world, and the relationship between the two. More specifically, and most simply, I propose that our three fundamental assumptions are[7]:

The world is benevolent

The world is meaningful

The self is worthy

Of course, not everyone holds these basic assumptions; yet it appears that most people do. If you are among those who are now responding, "But I know the world is bad and unfair. This certainly does not apply to me," I would ask that you do not yet discount the assumptions' role in your own life. Sometimes what we think we believe and what we really believe are not one and the same.

As an introduction to our fundamental assumptions, it is interesting to consider people's fascination, demonstrated generation after generation, with the biblical story of Job. Although this might be attributed to its literary qualities (e.g., Tennyson called it "the greatest poem of ancient and modern times"), it seems far more likely that the appeal of the story stems from its baffling sequence of events. Job is a good, righteous man who suffers catastrophe upon catastrophe, from the death of livestock and servants to the death of his seven sons and three daughters. Great thinkers, including Maimonides, John Calvin, Reinhold Niebuhr, Martin Buber, and Thomas Hobbes, have interpreted and reinterpreted the story of Job; theological and scholarly commentaries, old and new, abound. The attention this biblical story has received reflects the deeply disturbing nature of seemingly unwarranted human suffering; the attention it has received reflects our unwitting acceptance of the three fundamental assumptions.

Benevolence of the World. In general, people believe the world is a good place. The "world," in this context, is an abstract conception that refers to both people and events. When we assume other people are benevolent, we believe that they are basically good, kind, helpful, and caring. In assuming that events are benevolent, we believe in the preponderance of positive outcomes and good fortune over negative outcomes and misfortune. In my research, I have found that people's beliefs in the benevolence of people and events are very positive and highly correlated; the two seem to go together.[8] It appears that we maintain a kind of implicit base-rate notion about goodness and badness in the world; in general, we believe we live in a benevolent, safe world rather than a malevolent, hostile one.

In considering the benevolence of "the" world, people are actually considering the benevolence of "their" world. Generalizations move outward from experience, such that our own experiences with people and events form the basis for more general assumptions about the world. Things that happen to us are typically good, and thus the world that is relevant to us is characterized by positive outcomes. People around us are decent and caring, and thus people in general are good.

Maya Angelou attempted to capture the depth of our belief in the benevolence of others in the title of her book of poetry, *Just Give Me a Cool Drink of Water 'Fore I Diiie*. In explaining her choice, she discusses the remarkable "unconscious innocence" of human beings, which she feels is best illustrated by the belief that even a murderer, before putting the final wrench on our throat, would nevertheless have enough compassion to give us a sweet cup of water.[9]

One might ask how we maintain our assumption about the benevolence of the world in the face of so many obvious problems, both nationally and internationally. In this vein, it is interesting to note that individuals often distinguish between their own lot and that of the larger world. People are very optimistic about their own futures,[10] and this is the case even when they are pessimistic about political and economic conditions in the world at large. Thus, survey researchers have found a clear contradiction between how Americans view their personal lives, which has remained consistently positive over the years, and their far more somber views of the state of the nation.[11] Further, when asked to graph the past, present, and future for both their personal lives and the country on separate "ladders" (with top and bottom rungs representing the best and worst possible situations), survey respondents are extremely optimistic about their own lives and far less optimistic about the nation.[12]

We believe the world is benevolent because we see our own relatively limited world as benevolent. There is considerable research evidence demonstrating that people believe events in their lives have been predominantly pleasant. Margaret Matlin and David Stang, in their book *The Pollyanna Principle*,[13] review numerous studies in which people—children, college students, and older adults—classified many more of their life experiences as pleasant than unpleasant. Whether they actually experienced primarily pleasant events, or selectively recalled pleasant events more often than unpleasant ones, they nevertheless had positive perceptions of their world.

Like the caricatured Dr. Pangloss, who maintained a rose-colored view of the world despite a succession of negative outcomes, we view our world as a good, benevolent place. The monstrous calamities that befell Job are alien; to confront such unrelenting misfortune and evil is extremely disturbing. We also believe in a meaningful world, and thus how much more perturbed we are in recognizing that these catastrophes have struck Job, "a sound and honest man who feared God and shunned evil."

Meaningfulness of the World. Why is Job the victim of such catastrophes? We are puzzled and uncomfortable with the juxtaposition of Job's innocence and Job's sorry lot. We believe events in our world are meaningful, that they "make sense."[14] Our fundamental assumption about meaning involves not simply beliefs about why events happen in our world, but, more specifically, why these events happen to particular people. We seek to understand the "distribution" of good and bad outcomes, and in the service of meaning we recognize or impose seemingly natural contingencies between people and their outcomes.

A meaningful world is one in which a self-outcome contingency is perceived; there is a relationship between a person and what happens to him or her. People are able to make sense of the "selective incidence" of particular outcomes. This concern is reflected in the words of Brother Juniper in Thornton Wilder's *The Bridge of San Luis Rey* after the great bridge broke and five travelers fell to their death. He asked, " 'Why did this happen to *those* five?' . . . Either we live by accident and die by accident, or we live by plan and die by plan."[15] Brother Juniper then resolved to inquire into the travelers' lives so as to make sense of their deaths.

This concern with the seemingly selective incidence of events provides a way of understanding people's attempt to seek and impose meaning on events. Anthropologist Max Gluckman describes the belief in witchcraft among the Azande of the Sudan as a need to answer the question "Why misfortune to me and not others?"[16] Discussing the reactions of the Azande father whose son died when the boy's boat was overturned by a hippopotamus, Gluckman notes that the father is fully aware that the immediate cause of death was drowning, by water in the lungs; yet the parent believes that it was a witch or sorcerer who brought together the paths of the boat and the angry hippopotamus. According to the Azande, people are not harmed arbitrarily or haphazardly, and thus, through witchcraft, they are able to maintain a belief in a meaningful, orderly world.

Science attempts to address the how, but not the why, of events.[17]

Yet, in science, phenomena are comprehensible if they fit certain physical laws, accepted theories of physical events. In the case of events that happen to people, we typically turn to accepted social rather than scientific laws to understand the distribution of good and bad events in our world. In Western culture, the social laws most likely to be invoked to explain the "why" of events are those of justice and control; these enable us to believe that misfortune is not haphazard and arbitrary, that there is a person-outcome contingency.

According to popularly accepted conceptions of justice, the principle of personal deservingness determines which events affect which people.[18] From this perspective, the "goodness" of the individual becomes a primary factor to be considered in determining his or her lot in life. Thus, a good, decent, moral person deserves positive outcomes; conversely, misfortune should be most apt to strike the morally corrupt. The work of psychologist Melvin Lerner emphasizes the importance of this orientation in people's lives. Lerner's "just world theory" posits that people have a need to believe in a just world, one in which people get what they deserve and deserve what they get. We are deeply threatened by the possibility that negative events, if random, could happen to us. In a series of experiments, Lerner has demonstrated that innocent people are derogated and devalued by research participants, who are thereby able to maintain their own belief that the world is just, that people get what they deserve.[19] If we believe that the rape victim was an immoral woman or the accident victim was a reckless man, we can psychologically ward off the possibility that victimizations can be random and can strike the innocent.

When we view the world in terms of justice, negative events are viewed as punishments and positive ones as rewards. The lengths to which we might go in applying principles of justice are apparent in Brother Juniper's conclusions about the travelers on the fallen bridge. As Wilder writes, "He thought he saw in the same accident, the wicked visited by destruction and the good called early to Heaven. He thought he saw pride and wealth confounded as an object lesson to the world, and he thought he saw humility crowned and rewarded for the edification of the city."[20]

Often we understand events in our world not through a consideration of people's character but rather through an examination of their behaviors.[21] We are able to see a natural association between people and what happens to them, not only because of who they are (i.e., justice and deservingness), but also because of what they did. The assumption is that we can directly control what happens to us through our own behavior. Thus, if we engage in appropriate, precautionary behaviors, we will be protected from negative events; similarly, if we engage in appropriate positive behaviors, good things will happen to us.

From this perspective, the person who drives carefully can keep from getting in a car accident, the person who eats right and exercises regularly can stay healthy, and the person who knows the right "city survival tactics" can avoid being mugged on the street. And when negative events occur, the individuals involved are regarded as not having been careful enough—that is, they deserved it.

The recent health craze in the United States is in part a dramatic statement of our belief in control over negative outcomes. We believe that through our own behavior we can have tremendous control over our health, and thus people are running, climbing stairs, swimming laps, eating fiber, reducing cholesterol as never before. I recall the results of a national survey broadcast on the radio during the summer of 1988 in which more than 90 percent of Americans reported that they believed they could stay healthy if they just engaged in the right behaviors.

The work of Martin Seligman and his colleagues on learned helplessness suggests the difficulties that follow from a perception of no control.[22] The phenomenon of learned helplessness involves the perception that there is no contingency between one's actions and one's outcomes; nothing one can do will make a difference. Such helplessness involves "giving up" and loss of motivation and has been linked to forms of depression.

We generally believe in an action-outcome contingency, that we can control what happens to us, and such a belief provides us with one means of maintaining a view of the world as a meaningful place. In fact, we tend to perceive a contingency between what we do and what happens to us, even in situations when this is clearly inappropriate. Research by Ellen Langer has demonstrated that people believe they can control more than they actually can. Thus, because effort, exertion, practice, or planning generally have a positive effect on outcomes that we can control, the use of these same strategies often lead us to believe we can control chance outcomes as well.[23] Gamblers often fail to distinguish between chance and control-related outcomes and believe that their own behaviors, often ritualized, will lead to success. In the game of craps, for example, gamblers believe that they can control the dice by taking their time and concentrating, talking to the dice, snapping their fingers after a throw, and throwing hard for large numbers and softly for low numbers.[24] Most superstitious behaviors are also based on the belief that a contingency exists when in reality it does not; simply because you performed well on an exam or won an important game while wearing your red socks does not warrant the conclusion that this behavior and the outcome were at all related.

Although in Western society personal control is emphasized, people can nevertheless support their belief in a meaningful world by invoking justice-related religious beliefs.[25] Belief in a God who rewards a moral existence also reflects belief in a meaningful world, despite the fact that direct control does not rest with the individual performing the deeds but rather with a God responsible for making the ultimate judgment about one's outcomes.

The distributional principles of justice and control imply a sense of order and comprehensibility. Randomness essentially denies the meaningfulness of events. There is no way to make sense of why particular events happen to particular people; it is a matter of chance alone. In recognizing randomness, an individual must accept that ultimately there is nothing one can do or be that will serve as a protection from misfortune or a guarantor of good fortune; the person is not involved "in shaping one's own destiny as well as one's daily experience."[26]

Self-Worth. In addition to assumptions of benevolence and meaningfulness of the world, we maintain a third fundamental assumption, that of our own self-worth. This assumption involves a global evaluation of the self, and, in general, we perceive ourselves as good, capable, and moral individuals.

Just as a sense of meaning entails a belief in a person-outcome contingency that is reflected in conceptions about justice and control, the sources of self-worth often reflect parallel conceptions in the self domain. Thus, justice generally entails judgments of one's character, and one dimension of self-worth involves evaluations of one's essential goodness, decency, and morality. Similarly, control entails judgments of one's behavior, and another dimension of self-esteem involves evaluations of the wisdom and effectiveness of one's actions: whether we are doing things that will maximize successful outcomes for us. These self-evaluations include judgments of one's competence as well as of one's willingness to engage in appropriate behaviors. Thus, you may not have the necessary competence to control outcomes, such as someone who is simply not in good enough physical shape to successfully complete a long-distance race,[27] or you may have the ability but choose not to use it, such as an intelligent person who doesn't study when necessary or any person who decides not to use a seat belt in an automobile.

11

With very few exceptions, people evaluate themselves very positively. In study after study, people report themselves as better than others and certainly better than average in terms of their own abilities and personal qualities, and scores on self-esteem scales tend to be highly skewed towards the positive end of the scale.[28] In his classic paper on the self, Anthony Greenwald maintains that we use a number of information-control strategies in interpreting and organizing information about ourselves, and these strategies enable us to view ourselves in a particularly positive manner. Not only are our judgment and memory processes focused on the self, but we see ourselves as selectively responsible for positive, desired outcomes. As Greenwald points out, this selective responsibility is apparent in people's tendency to both recall and accept responsibility for successes far more than failures, to deny responsibility for harming others, and to identify with "winners" and disaffiliate with "losers."[29]

Thus, we believe we are good people who live in a benevolent, meaningful world. These three positive assumptions co-exist at the core of our assumptive world. They are not narrow beliefs, but broad, abstract conceptions that are also emotionally potent. Clearly, it feels good to believe that we are decent and the world is benevolent and meaningful. Our basic beliefs do not exist independent of emotions; rather, positive feelings are inextricably tied to our fundamental assumptions.[30]

An exploration of the origins of these core representations provides a basis for understanding their centrality and significance. An essential aspect of these beliefs is that they are the *earliest*—the very first—assumptions established in our internal world. More accurately, they are the verbal counterparts of our earliest, preverbal representations.

Origins in Early Experience

In his ever-popular book, *Baby and Child Care,* Dr. Benjamin Spock begins by telling parents to have confidence in themselves and their own common sense. He writes that what is most important is the

> natural loving care that kindly parents give their children. . . . It's taking care of your baby, finding out that you can feed, change, bathe, and burp successfully, and that your baby responds contentedly to your ministrations that gives you the feelings of familiarity, confidence, and love. A solid relationship and a mutual trust are established very early.[31]

From the present perspective, this same advice could be interpreted from the perspective of the child, not the parent. It is the "natural loving care" that infants receive that enables them to respond contentedly and develop "familiarity, confidence, and love," or, more generally, a sense of trust. It is this early development of trust, emphasized by Erik Erikson, that represents the preverbal elements of our three fundamental assumptions.

Erikson nominates a "sense of basic trust" as the most "fundamental prerequisite of mental vitality."[32] He defines it as a pervasive attitude towards both the world and oneself that is developed during the child's first year of life. For Erikson, the development of trust is based on the mutual regulation of the needs and abilities of infant and mother.[33] Thus, for example, the infant's inborn ability to "take in by mouth" must be met by the mother's ability to feed and welcome the child. The mother must coordinate the timing and intensity of sensory stimulation to meet the baby's needs as well. He argues that the amount of trust derived from one's earliest experiences does not depend on the quantity of care (e.g., amount of food or demonstrations of love), but the quality of care (for Erikson, the quality of the maternal relationship). According to Erikson, the presence of sensitive maternal care provides the infant with a sense of "friendly otherness." In an important way, however, a sense of trust involves not only the development of trust in others, but the development of trust in oneself.

The child's view of self, world, and their relationship originate in the infant's early experiences, which center around interactions with a caregiver (or caregivers), usually the mother. In these early preverbal interactions, we begin to establish expectations about our world, about the nature of our caregivers, the nature of ourselves, and the nature of the interaction between the two. These early representations are thus apt to be closely related and mutually dependent, a conclusion mirrored in Erikson's view of early development.

From the perspective of our fundamental assumptions, trust is actually the label for three intersecting representations derived from the child's earliest experiences. In the presence of a responsive caregiver, the child's earliest needs are met; the child's "world," represented by those caring for the child, is a benevolent one. A responsive caregiver is one who responds to the infant's behaviors (e.g., crying), and thereby provides the basis for the child's earliest understanding of person-outcome contingency. In the very act of providing care and meeting the child's needs, a responsive caregiver also provides the infant with the basis for self-worth, for the child begins to understand that he or she is worthy of care. Most simply, the infant begins to learn, "There is someone good who cares for me, and I can do certain things to bring about a caring response from this person . . . I must be worthy of care." The earliest interactions with sensitive caregivers provide a basis for preverbal representations about what the world and the self are like: The world is good and meaningful, and the self is worthy.

This emphasis on early social interactions is central in the work of object relations theorists, who have emphasized the importance of these interactions for the young child's internal, object world. For these theorists, the earliest object relations involve interactions between the needs of the child and caregiver.[34] As W. R. D. Fairbairn writes, children need to feel that their parents understand the world and are dependable and just in their caregiving.[35] D. W. Winnecott writes that the mother provides a "holding environment" for the infant and brings the world to the child.[36] He stresses the importance of maternal devotion and "empathic anticipation" of the baby's needs; these are qualities of the "good enough mother." Such a reasonably nurturant, dependable mother provides the child with an early sense of omnipotence, which, for Winnecott, is a basis for healthy development.

The adaptive role of "infantile omnipotence" is also discussed in the work of Heinz Kohut, who emphasizes the importance of the child's grandiose view of self, developed through responsive caregiving or "empathic parenting." According to Kohut, the infant's narcissistic fantasies, particularly the grandiose self and idealized parent, are not simply a waystation on the road to healthy object relations. Rather, they are transformed to more mature forms in the context of the parent-child unit and integrated as necessary, healthy parts of the personality.[37]

Of particular relevance to the early development of our positively biased basic assumptions is the work of John Bowlby,[38] who posits that children build working models of their world and themselves through their relationship with early attachment figures. His well-known theory of attachment emphasizes the importance of available, responsive caregivers during young childhood. A key feature of the child's model of the world is the attachment figure—who that person is, where that person may be found, and how that person may be expected to respond. A key feature of the working model of the self is acceptability in the eyes of the attachment figure. It follows that an available, responsive caregiver provides the basis for the child's positive representations of the world and the self.

How do these early models develop? What actually happens in the mind of the young child? The work of psychiatrist Daniel Stern provides some answers. Stern writes of the infant's subjective experience and focuses on the developmental progression of sense of self. He maintains that the infant has

> formidable capacities to distill and organize the abstract, global qualities of experience. Infants are not lost at sea in a wash of abstractable qualities of experience. They are gradually and systematically ordering these elements of experience to identify self-invariant and other-invariant constellations. And whenever any constellation is formed, the infant experiences the emergence of organization. . . .
> This global subjective world of emerging organization is and remains the fundamental domain of human subjectivity. It operates out of awareness as the experiential matrix from which thoughts and perceived forms and identifiable acts and verbalized feelings will later arise.[39]

Stern discusses how, specifically, the infant's experience becomes integrated into one organizing subjective perspective. For present purposes, this relates to the question of how the infant creates a coherent model of the self, of others (the world), and of their interaction. He argues that memory provides the answer, for memory is a process that integrates the diverse features of lived experience. In particular, he discusses episodic memory, our memory for "real-life experiences occurring in real time." Such memories range from trivial experiences (e.g., what I had for breakfast) to those that are more meaningful (e.g., what I felt when I was told of a friend's suicide). Perceptions, actions, and affects associated with the experience are the main ingredients of the episodic memory. Episodes enter into memory as indivisible units and generally stand as a whole.

According to Stern, when an infant experiences similar episodes, he or she begins to form a *generalized* episode, "an individualized, personal expectation of how things are likely to proceed on a moment-to-moment basis."[40] He uses the example of the "breast milk" episode: being hungry, being placed at the breast, rooting, opening mouth, starting to suck, getting milk. The generalized episode for "breast milk" is no longer a specific occasion, but rather an abstraction of many specific memories, each of which is slightly different. It is "average experience made prototypic."[41]

Stern is concerned with generalized episodes—involving sensations, actions, and affects—of the preverbal infant. More specifically, he is concerned with the interactive experience, and not simply interactive events. Citing research that suggests infants have some abilities to abstract, average, and represent information preverbally,[42] he argues that the episodic memories are also averaged and represented in the subjective world of the infant. Stern labels these higher-level generalizations RIGs—representations of interactions that have been generalized. RIGs constitute the basic units for the infant's representation of a core self.

Stern maintains that between the ages of two and seven months, the infant already gains enough experience with the major "self-invariants," and the ability to integrate episodic memories has advanced far enough, that the infant is able to form an organized, subjective perspective that he calls a core self. Stern believes that a sense of a core other emerges in a parallel fashion.

Episodic memories of particular interactions are combined into RIGs. In turn, RIGs are combined to form working models or theories. These models are generalized memories derived from particular episodes and are our earliest representations about ourselves and our world. We develop such working models of the self, the mother (or caregiver), and the nature of the interaction between self and mother, and these models are the origins of our later assumptions about ourselves, the world, and meaning.

The positively biased nature of our fundamental assumptions is largely accounted for by their origin in early interactions. Most infants receive "good enough caregiving," caregiving that is neither outstanding nor characterized by neglect or abuse. It is generally responsive to infants' early needs for physical care and contact comfort,[43] and enables them to develop positive views of others, positive views of themselves as recipients of this care, and positive views of their own agency in interactions. Also tied to these agreeable "thoughts" are positive affects, pleasant feelings associated with the satisfaction of needs and the expectation of continued care.

These earliest mental structures are refined and embellished with experience. With the onset of language, the young child begins to live in a world of shared meanings and new experiences. The early working models or representations can now be verbally represented (i.e., "The world is benevolent"; "The world is meaningful"; "I am a worthy person"), and the child begins to exist more fully within the larger cultural context. Within a society, people create a shared symbolic world that provides communal expectations about daily existence. The complex interweaving of individual and society suggests that, generally, each mirrors and strengthens the other, such that the beliefs held at the level of the individual psyche are also largely apparent at the level of the group or culture. Culture and society begin to both shape and reinforce the child's internal representations.[44]

The growing child begins to respond to new data and experiences, such that new people and occurrences begin to be incorporated within one's model of the world. New aspects of oneself become important bases for assumptions about the self. New experiences and outcomes, good and bad, become assimilated into our assumptions about the meaningfulness of events.

Although these assumptions may be modified throughout childhood and adolescence, fewer changes are apt to occur in adulthood. This perspective is consistent with that of Bowlby,[45] in his discussion of working models of attachment. These models are built up slowly during infancy, childhood, and adolescence, and what is developed during these years tend to persist relatively unchanged throughout one's life. Yet Bowlby also believes that between six months and five years, when attachment behavior is most readily activated, the child is optimally sensitive to the development of expectations about the availability of attachment figures. Although this sensitivity persists after five years of age, it does so in steadily diminishing degrees over time. Thus, Bowlby's perspective lies between the more extreme views that a high degree of plasticity to personality exists even through adulthood, and the view that such plasticity diminishes after the earliest months of infancy and is practically nonexistent after the first or second year of life.

The view espoused here echoes that of Bowlby. We begin to develop our models and assumptions quite early, and it is these early assumptions that are built upon and revised. Our earliest representations are extremely powerful, and although some change no doubt occurs throughout development,[46] changes are less likely over time. Thus, fewer changes are apt to be made in late childhood, and far fewer in adulthood. What comes first in general has a greater impact on the conceptual system than what comes later; for me, this view is derived not from clinical theories on psychopathology but from social psychological theories on information-processing, which will be explored in the next chapter. First, however, we need to consider the sense of invulnerability that the basic assumptions afford us.

Security, Trust, and Invulnerability

Human life is liable to many hazards. People are run over in the street, automobiles collide, travelers are injured or killed in train wrecks or airplane crashes. In the seeming security of one's home one may fall down stairs and break a leg. A child playing hide-and-seek may close himself in an old ice box and suffocate. One may fall prey to disease or something may go amiss with a vital organ—a heart attack, a brain hemorrhage. The cocktails and cigarettes which we enjoy may be working irremediable internal damage. And then there are the more large-scale dangers of fire, flood, earthquake, tornado, and the man-made destruction unleashed in war. As we consider this list, is not our first reaction apt to be one of smiling? Yes, we will say, and as you are walking down the street a tile may fall from a roof and hit you on the head. But who can worry about all these things?[47]

It is somewhat ironic that it is during their prolonged period of dependency (i.e., infancy) that human beings begin to develop the essential components of a lifelong sense of safety and security. Through early social interactions, we develop a view of the world and ourselves that enables us to continue to feel protected, even as our world expands far beyond its earliest, very limited boundaries. Our fundamental assumptions, rooted so deeply in our early experience, equip us with a sense of confidence and trust. This is not confidence in the narrow sense of being self-assured, for the focus is centered too much on the self. Nor is it trust in the narrow sense of expecting others to be honest and reliable, for the focus is centered too much on others. Rather, they refer to a general optimism that things will work out well, that we are safe and protected. Psychologist Aaron Antonovsky's "sense of coherence" largely describes this life outlook: "The 'sense of coherence' is a global orientation that expresses the extent to which one has a pervasive, enduring though dynamic feeling of confidence that one's internal and external environments are predictable and that there is a high probability that things will work out as well as can reasonably be expected."[48]

The expectation that the future will work to one's advantage or for one's pleasure is so common that anthropologist Lionel Tiger argues it has been central to the process of human evolution and is a part of human nature.[49] His point about the pervasiveness of this optimistic orientation is well taken, although I would locate its roots in early development rather than biology. As Ernest Becker asserts in his landmark work *The Denial of Death,* the young child who is loved and well nourished develops a "sense of his own indestructibility, a feeling of proven power and secure support."[50] From Becker's perspective, this responsive early environment simply makes it easier for the child to hide his or her innate fear of death. Whether or not one accepts the existence of a deeper, universal terror lying beneath our fundamental assumptions, the human tendency to perceive the self as indestructible and invulnerable remains the same. This perspective is most evident when people consider the likelihood of negative events happening to them; people feel protected from misfortune.

This sense of invulnerability is a logical outcome of our fundamental assumptions, reflected in the following internal dialogue:

> My world is benevolent. Even in such a good world negative events happen, even if relatively infrequently. Yet when they occur they are not random, but rather are meaningfully distributed. They happen to people who deserve them, either because of who they are or what they did or failed to do. I am a good, competent, careful person. Bad things couldn't happen to me.

Generally, we underestimate the likelihood of negative outcomes. Yet even when we recognize the possibility of misfortune—of crime, serious illness, accidents—we nevertheless feel more or less invulnerable. We believe in our own "goodness" and "behavioral wisdom," and thus if bad things happen, they won't happen to us.

There is considerable research evidence that people underestimate the likelihood of negative events happening to them and overestimate the likelihood of positive events; they appear to operate on the basis of an "illusion of invulnerability."[51] In an early exploratory study, my students and I found that college students consistently underestimated the likelihood that negative events—including mugging, cancer, car accident, senility, and natural disaster—would happen to them on the basis of studies of actual incidence in similar age groups.

More recently, "unrealistic optimism" has been demonstrated in a series of studies by Neil Weinstein and his colleagues.[52] The college students in Weinstein's sample regarded themselves as far less likely than their classmates to experience negative events such as having a heart attack or getting cancer, being fired from a job, and getting divorced. Older adults also underestimated the likelihood that negative events would happen to them.[53] In fact, regardless of age, gender, education, or occupational prestige, people are unrealistically optimistic in their assessments of the future.[54] As Soviet poet Andrei Voznesensky writes in his poem "My Achilles Heart,"

> Our destruction is unthinkable,
> More unthinkable what we endure,
> More unthinkable still that a sniper
> Should ever sever the quivering thread.

In general, we feel relatively invulnerable to misfortune. To a considerable extent, we simply do not think about threats and negative life events. But even if we recognize the possibility of such negative events as crimes, diseases, natural disasters, interpersonal losses, and serious accidents, we do not believe that we, personally, will be affected. After all, such events are meaningfully, not randomly, distributed.

We may tell ourselves that one out of four people gets cancer, and that crimes and accidents are common—even that we may be victims. However, this is probably no more than a verbal statement in the absence of true belief. At the gut emotional level—the level of raw experience—it appears that we do not truly perceive the risks. Just as we can experience strong emotions in the theater, when we know the events are not real, so we can recognize events as real without experiencing any emotions.[55]

This is what Martha Wolfenstein is referring to when she explains the state of mind of someone who acknowledges extreme danger but does not feel worried. She discusses the situation of many people in the United States in 1946 who considered it likely that an atomic bomb would be used against their country yet did not feel at all worried. She compares the case of Tolstoy's protagonist in *The Death of Ivan Ilyich,* who is dying and recalls a syllogism he had learned in school beginning with the words "All men are mortal." Ivan Ilyich notes that he never doubted this proposition, but it nevertheless did not seem to have any application to himself. It was only now, while facing death, that the simple sentence became filled with meaning. As Wolfenstein notes, a verbal statement that elicits no emotional response in some sense seems unreal. "Admission of a painful prospect on a purely verbal level may coexist with denial on a less conscious level, or with the implicit qualification: it does not apply to me."[56]

Despite occasional verbal statements to the contrary, we do not actually seem to believe that we will be the victims of misfortune. The virtual universality of the belief in invulnerability and the feeling that one is secure and protected is made particularly apparent by people's reactions to their own traumatic life events. Bad things do happen to people; the world is not wholly benevolent and meaningful, and we are not always competent and worthy. What are the implications of maintaining such positively biased assumptions?

Are Our Assumptions Illusions?

Given the positive biases characteristic of our fundamental assumptions, it appears that they might appropriately be described as illusions—false ideas or conceptions. To Sigmund Freud, the hallmark of illusions was wish-fulfillment.[57] Our assumptions are, in part, illusions; yet it would be inaccurate to portray people as naive optimists who simply believe what they want to believe and ignore their real experiences.

Rather, the illusory nature of our assumptions about benevolence, meaningfulness, and self-worth derives from their status as overgeneralizations. As the most fundamental assumptions in our conceptual system, they represent general expectations rather than discrete ones. First formed as representations in early childhood, they are generalizations across interactions and events during a particular developmental period as well as generalizations across time and different developmental periods. They are based on real experiences, beginning with relatively positive interactions with caregivers but, over time, are extended far beyond these specific episodes.

By way of useful comparison, it is worth considering our most familiar illusions: visual illusions. Two of the best known are the Muller-Lyer illusion and the Ponzo illusion. The Muller-Lyer is the arrow illusion, in which the length of two same-length lines appears different because of the angles set at the end of the lines; in one case the angles turn towards the line, in the other the angles turn outward. In the latter instance, the line looks longer. The Ponzo illusion is the railroad track illusion, in which two same-length line segments are placed at different points between two converging lines. The line segments appear to be different lengths, with the one set in the narrower portion of the converging lines appearing longer.

Despite the fact that the comparison lines are actually the same length in both cases, we perceive their lengths as different. Yet we are not simply seeing what we want to see. In perceiving the lines we use cues presented in the pictures that, in most instances of our lives, suggest depth and distance. Thus, the converging lines of the Ponzo illusion and angles in the Muller-Lyer illusion are perceived as depth cues. In each instance, one line is interpreted as farther and thus larger; for same-size lines would actually present different-size retinal images, and the retinal images in these instances are the same. We misperceive features of the visual presentation because we misapply perceptual principles that usually work and usually describe reality. It is an instance of overapplication or overgeneralization.

In a similar vein, in separate laboratory studies, Ellen Langer[58] and Camille Wortman[59] have demonstrated the extent to which people overgeneralize features from control-based settings to chance settings. Thus, for example, in settings where outcomes were, in fact, purely random, people bet less against a confident-looking opponent than one who seemed meeker; and people were less willing to turn in a lottery ticket that they themselves had chosen for one that offered them a better chance of winning. Environmental features that might have made a difference if the task had been skill-related were irrelevant in chance settings, and yet people nevertheless overestimated the amount of control they had over random outcomes when these features were present. People generalized from one situation to another, even when it was not appropriate.

Similarly, we may overestimate the benevolence and meaningfulness of the world and our own self-worth, and interpret our world and self in accordance with these "principles" even when inappropriate. But these are instances reflecting overgeneralizations rather than simply foolhardiness based solely on wishes.[60] We generalize from a preponderance of positive early experiences to abstract characterizations of our world and ourselves that are no longer directly tied to reality.

If these basic assumptions are positively biased overgeneralizations that may not always correspond to reality, are they maladaptive? Traditional views of mental health stressed the importance of accurate perceptions and close contact with reality. From this perspective illusions are maladaptive.[61] Recently, psychologist Shelley Taylor has argued that illusions are adaptive, and she posits a view of mental health based on personal happiness.[62] She maintains that the positive emotions fostered by illusions are associated with better mental functioning, better physical health, and better social interactions. Most simply, it feels good to hold illusions, and there are positive outcomes related to feeling good.

The question of adaptiveness requires a more complex response, for neither happiness nor accuracy can be considered wholly irrelevant to mental health. Rather, I would like to suggest that the adaptiveness of an illusion is related to its position in our conceptual system—that is, the hierarchical structure of our assumptive world must be considered. From this perspective, illusions can clearly be maladaptive; yet those at the broadest, most basic level of the hierarchy, such as our fundamental assumptions, are likely to be quite adaptive.

To recognize that illusions can be maladaptive we need only think of the person who believes he or she is a good swimmer, but who is actually unable to swim. The down side of illusions is generally discussed in terms of behaviors that are counterproductive, not only in terms of physical harm but also in terms of alienating others or, most often, maladaptively persisting at something without success. As Philip Brickman and I wrote, "The weak may drift irresolutely from goal to goal, but only the strong can destroy themselves in the manner of Captain Ahab."[63] This is the strategy of persisting at a task long after it would have been beneficial to quit, based on the illusion that one is more skilled at a particular task than is actually the case.

This negative view of illusions stems from the role of illusions in our narrower assumptions, those most directly tied to reality, those that can be confirmed and disconfirmed by direct reality tests. These are the assumptions about ourselves and our world that deal with more limited spheres of experience—one's specific abilities, the nature of specific tasks. Accuracy is optimal in these less abstract, narrower assumptions of our conceptual system. Accurate beliefs at this level maximally protect a person from physical harm and the possibility of looking foolhardy to others; they would enable a person to devote energies to those tasks that would provide the most satisfaction and success.

Our fundamental assumptions about the world and ourselves do not exist at this level of our hierarchical conceptual system. Rather, they are our most abstract, global beliefs about ourselves and the world. And it is at this basic level, I believe, that illusions are most adaptive, for their adaptiveness derives not only from the positive emotions directly tied to these assumptions but also from their implications for motivation.

Our positive illusions at this level afford us the trust and confidence that are necessary to engage in new behaviors, to test our limits. We need only think of secure children who are comfortable exploring their environment. Research by Mary Ainsworth and her colleagues has demonstrated that those young children who are able to use their mother as a secure base are able to explore freely in a strange situation, are not distressed by the presence of a stranger, and can best weather the temporary absence of the mother.[64] Over time, the internal representations that are built from this relationship with a sensitive caregiver can themselves provide a person with a sense of security, with the trust and confidence essential for exploring one's world.

In his inimitable fashion, William James is convincing about the benefits of such beliefs when he describes the situation of mountain climbing in the Alps and finds himself in a position from which the only escape is a terrible leap. He writes that he has had no similar experience before, and thus he is unaware of his abilities to make such a leap. He claims that hope and confidence in himself will help ensure a successful jump, whereas fear and mistrust would be devastating. He writes:

> In this case (and it is one of an immense class) the part of wisdom clearly is to believe what one desires. . . . There are then cases when faith creates its own verification. Believe, and you shall be right, for you shall save yourself; doubt, and you shall be right, for you shall perish. The only difference is that to believe is greatly to your advantage.[65]

The evidence necessary to evaluate a situation is not always available. It is better to have the trust and confidence to try, better to learn one's limits than never test them.

A key to the good life might well be illusions at our deepest, most generalized level of assumptions and accuracy at the most specific, least abstract levels. Most feedback we get relates to particular tasks and abilities and should be registered at the narrower level of assumptions. Illusions are least likely to exist here, primarily because of the numerous possibilities for direct behavioral feedback. To maintain them, illusions at this level would be maladaptive. Psychologically, the healthiest people probably have a good sense of their strengths and weaknesses, their possibilities and limitations. Those with more positive basic assumptions are apt to be those most likely to tackle new problems and situations with confidence and expectations for success.

Yet one's ability to receive feedback, and to be sensitive to environmental cues, will be crucial for maximizing one's successes over time. Perhaps surprising, research evidence suggests that there is no necessary association between illusions at the more global and specific levels of our conceptual systems. There is evidence, in fact, that those who have the most positive generalized assumptions about themselves are those who are best at reading themselves and their environment; they may be most sensitive to environmental cues.[66] It appears that we can think quite highly of ourselves and yet accept our own limitations and be self-critical when it comes to specific areas of our own behavior.[67] The ability to respond to feedback, to be self-critical and learn, is an important criterion for mental health. Yet such accuracy is not inconsistent with maintaining illusions at the most fundamental level of our assumptive world. Our core assumptions are positively biased overgeneralizations. Although not always accurate, they provide us with the means for trusting ourselves and our environment.

2

Cognitive Conservatism and Resistance to Change

Our core assumptions and the positive feelings of comfort and security associated with them provide the groundwork for understanding the psychological impact and aftermath of traumatic life events. To complete the background picture, however, requires some familiarity with the essential conservatism of our conceptual system. We tend to preserve already-established beliefs. Interestingly, the human animal is both extremely flexible, given its remarkable ability to learn, and yet highly resistant to change.

From a motivational perspective, our cognitive conservatism derives from our need for stability and coherence. As Prescott Lecky wrote:

> Immersed in an environment which he does not and cannot understand, the individual is forced to create a substitute world which he can understand and in which he puts his faith. He acts in consistency with that conception, derives his standards of value from it, and undertakes to alter it only when convinced by further experience that it fails to serve the goal of unity. Since this self-made scheme of life is his only guarantee of security, its preservation soon becomes a goal in itself. He seeks the type of experience which confirms and supports the unified attitude, and rejects experiences which seem to promise a disturbance of this attitude.[1]

Some semblance of this "unity principle" is at the heart of motivational analyses of our conservative tendencies. We need a stable, unified conceptual system in order to impose order on a complex, confusing, chaotic world.[2] Social psychological research has demonstrated that people are highly motivated to maintain cognitive consistency.[3] Recent studies of information-processing have provided strong evidence of our cognitive conservatism, as reflected in the biased manner in which we treat preexisting versus new information. We are heavily biased towards what we already "know" and believe, for these cognitions provide the lenses through which we perceive and interpret new information. Our prior theories or assumptions are insufficiently revised in the face of new, even contradictory, data.

In a very real sense, we are deductivists—not inductivists—in our approach to the world. We do not simply gather data and draw unbiased conclusions; rather, we have prior information and theories that guide data-gathering and interpretation. This latter perspective has recently been the focus of much attention in the philosophy of science, which has been influenced by the likes of relativity theory, advances in particle physics, and Heisenberg's Uncertainty Principle. Philosophers of science have begun to claim that there are no such things as objective facts but rather only theory-laden observations. Karl Popper clarifies this position when he writes:

> But in fact the belief that we can start with pure observations alone, without anything in the nature of a theory, is absurd; as may be illustrated by the story of the man who dedicated his life to natural science, wrote down everything he could observe, and bequeathed his priceless collection of observations to the Royal Society to be used as inductive evidence. This story should show us that though beetles may profitably be collected, observations may not. . . . Observation is always selective. . . . For the animal a point of view is provided by its needs, the task of the moment, and its expectations; for the scientist by his theoretical interests, the special problem under investigation, his conjectures and anticipations, and the theories which he accepts as a kind of background: his frame of reference, his "horizon of expectations."[4]

The well-known work of Thomas Kuhn expands this view of the theory-laden nature of observations within the scientific enterprise.[5] He emphasizes the primary role of prior theories or models, which he labels "paradigms," within the general scientific community. The reigning paradigm determines the activities that are engaged in during "normal science"; it influences not only what methods are acceptable but also what data are observed and regarded as meaningful.

Within the field of psychology, this theory-laden nature of our observations, perceptions, and interpretations is best reflected in recent work on the "schema" concept. "Schemas" also provide us with an alternative language for characterizing the nature of our fundamental assumptions about ourselves and the world.

The Schema Concept

Although few psychologists have specifically focused on people's basic assumptions or theories of reality per se, a substantial and growing number have devoted attention to the cognitive construct of "schema." A "schema" is a mental structure that represents organized knowledge about a given concept or type of stimulus.[6] The use of schemas implies an active construction of reality. As clarified by psychologist and journalist Daniel Goleman:

> Perception is interactive, constructed. It is not enough for information to flow through the senses; to make sense of the senses requires a context that organizes the information they convey, that lends it the proper meaning. . . . Schemas embody the rules and categories that order raw experience into coherent meaning. All knowledge and experience is packaged in schemas. Schemas are the ghost in the machine, the intelligence that guides information as it flows through the mind.[7]

Schemas are our preexisting theories and vary in level of abstraction and inclusiveness. They can refer to common categories such as dog, cat, rock, or table,[8] and thereby appear analogous to mini-theories. Schemas contain "knowledge" about the attributes of a concept as well as relationships among the attributes. Thus, in the case of our common categories, schemas provide us with information that enables us to determine, for example, whether a particular small, furry, four-legged animal is a member of the category dog or cat.[9]

Schemas underlie not only our common object categories but our social categories as well. Is Mr. Jones an introvert, eccentric, schizophrenic, sophisticate, or sage? We maintain organized knowledge structures about people, including ourselves, and categorize ourself and others along a number of descriptive dimensions. We hold schemas for social roles, too. In other words, we have knowledge structures for the behaviors and norms we believe are appropriate for membership in a particular social group, and familiarity with these schemas provides a basis for understanding the nature of stereotyping. Schemas also provide us with an understanding of event sequences in well-known situations (e.g., we know the order of events at baseball games, birthday parties, and restaurants), and these event schemas have been referred to as "scripts."[10]

There is little question that the schema concept is presently a fuzzy one. The specific types of information in a schema and how they are organized are not precisely known. Yet, in all instances, whether the organized knowledge is about a common object or a broad class of people, the relevant schema is essentially a theory that goes beyond the data given. A schema is not simply a straightforward accumulation of specific original instances and encounters but rather a generalization or abstraction involving organized knowledge about a stimulus or concept.[11]

Typically, research and theory on schemas have been concerned with categories and rules at low or middle levels of abstraction. There are generally clear, identifiable empirical referents for the categories or concepts involved; thus, research on schemas has not considered people's basic theories and assumptions about the world. The schema concept is nevertheless applicable to such levels of analysis. As David Rumelhart writes, "Just as theories can be about the grand and the small, so schemas can represent knowledge at all levels—from ideologies and cultural truths to knowledge about the meaning of a particular to knowledge about what patterns of sound are associated with what letters of the alphabet."[12] Our fundamental assumptions about the world are essentially our grandest schemas, our most abstract, generalized knowledge structures.

Given the applicability of the concept of schema to people's basic assumptions about themselves and their world, it is instructive to examine what has been learned about our tendency to preserve schemas rather than change them. Schema research demonstrates the theory-driven (rather than data-driven) nature of our perceptual and cognitive processes. Although a crystal-clear picture of the specific content of schemas still eludes psychologists, research presents a far clearer picture of the function and role of schemas in perception, memory, and the interpretation of information.

The Interpretation of Information

Jean Piaget[13] characterized assimilation as a process involving changes in the new, incoming information such that there may be a good fit with preexisting schemas. Accommodation, on the other hand, involves changes in these preexisting schemas so as to maximize the fit between the old and new. In responding to new information, we are biased towards assimilation rather than accommodation. Research points unequivocally to information processing that serves to maintain old schemas rather than change them. Schema-relevant information is more likely to be noticed and attended to; it is also processed more rapidly and easily.[14] We are also particularly good at remembering schema-consistent information. Thus, for example, we are very likely to remember individual behavior when it confirms a group stereotype, which then serves to perpetuate the stereotype.[15]

Support for our cognitive conservatism comes primarily from studies showing that people interpret information—both new information and information from memory—in ways that are consistent with their schema. In other words, our schemas guide our perceptions, memories, and inferences.[16] For example, people reconstruct biographies of friends and interpret the behaviors of others so as to be consistent with the schemas they hold for these people.[17] In a study on person perception, college students were shown a videotape of a woman having a birthday dinner with her husband. Some were told that the woman was a librarian; others were told that she was a waitress. Those who watched the supposed librarian remembered her wearing glasses and owning classical records, whereas those who were told she was a waitress remembered her drinking beer and owning a television. The students' memories, which were inaccurate, were clearly shaped by the social schemas they held for the two categories.[18]

A similar demonstration of misremembering occurred in a study in which people reporting having seen schema-consistent attributes they had, in fact, never seen. People read a list of adjectives describing a particular type of person, such as an extrovert. Later, when they were given a recognition task, they falsely recognized words that were schema-consistent—that is, they chose words that were not on the initial list but were consistent with "extrovert," such as spirited and outgoing.

In an interesting series of studies, Abraham Tesser[19] and his colleagues demonstrated the impact of schemas on people's judgments following mere thought. In thinking about a person we like, for example, we tend to polarize our judgments of the person in the direction of greater liking. In this sense, our attitudes become more extreme with thought because we think of the stimulus person in a schema-consistent manner.

This tendency to interpret information in a schema-consistent way accounts for differences in how we interpret the same behaviors when engaged in by members of different social groups. Thus, the very same behavior may be labeled as aggressive when the child involved is black, and assertive when the child involved is white.[20] This difference in interpretations of the same behaviors is apparent in the following joking comparison of men and women in the business world:

The family picture is on HIS desk:
Ah, a solid, responsible family man.

The family picture is on HER desk:
Hm-m-m, bet family will come before career.

HIS desk is cluttered:
He's obviously a hard worker and a busy man.

HER desk is cluttered:
She's obviously a disorganized scatterbrain.

HE's talking with co-workers:
He must be discussing the latest deal.

SHE's talking with co-workers:
She must be gossiping.

HE's having lunch with the boss:
He's on his way up.

SHE's having lunch with the boss:
They must be having an affair.

HE's getting married.
He'll get more settled.

SHE's getting married.
She'll get pregnant and leave.

HE's leaving for a better job.
He recognizes a good opportunity.

SHE's leaving for a better job:
Women are undependable.[21]

Our schemas for males and females guide our perceptions of the same behaviors, and may result in very different evaluations.

Within the field of clinical psychology, the work of Aaron Beck[22] on depression is particularly relevant to schema-consistent biases in information-processing. Beck emphasizes the importance of people's schemas in clinical work and suggests that negative schemas are involved in the distortions and inaccuracies associated with all types of psychopathology. Thus, Beck notes, people who believe everybody hates them will interpret the reactions of others on the basis of this belief. His work focuses primarily on depression and the idiosyncratic schemas he believes are associated with this diagnostic category. These schemas involve themes of personal deficiency, self-blame, and negative expectations about the future. Beck suggests that the depressed person selectively extracts features of the environment to fit these negative schemas.

> A highly successful research scientist had a chronic attitude, "I am a complete failure." His free associations were largely concerned with thoughts of how inferior, inadequate, and unsuccessful he was. When questioned regarding past performance, he was unable to recall a *single experience* that did not constitute failure to him.
>
> In this case, a schema with a content such as "I am a failure" worked over the raw material of his experiences and distorted the data to make it compatible with this content. Whether the particular cognitive process was recollection, or evaluation of his current status, or prediction of the future, his thoughts bore the imprint of this schema.[23]

The impact of schemas on information-processing is evident in the interpretations and misinterpretations all of us make, whether depressed or not. The schemas we use may differ, yet whatever the schema, we typically perceive and understand our world in schema-consistent ways.

Bringing About What We Already Believe: Self-Fulfilling Prophecies

Our cognitive conservatism is evident in how we interpret new information and reinterpret information stored in memory so as to be schema-consistent. Our preexisting theories exert undue influence and thereby tend to be further reinforced rather than changed. This self-perpetuating quality of schemas is apparent not only in our interpretation of information but in our behaviors as well. Our schemas provide us with expectations, and our behaviors are largely reflections of these expectations. In turn, our behaviors are apt to bring about the reality we expect. Thus, if I expect a person to be friendly and kind, I will act in a manner that is likely to elicit positive behaviors, for I will be friendly and positive. If I expect a person to be hostile and aggressive, I am likely to act in a suspicious, wary manner that is apt to elicit more negative behaviors. In other words, my own behaviors, derived from my schemas for others, will behaviorally confirm my preexisting schemas.[24]

This process of behavioral confirmation is essentially the same as the self-fulfilling prophecy popularized in the classic experiments of Robert Rosenthal and his colleagues. In a series of studies, teachers were told that certain students—whom the researchers had randomly selected—were quite capable and could be expected to do well in the class with the proper help and guidance. Although initially these students did not differ from their nonselected counterparts, several months later both their schoolwork and their IQs had improved. This effect has been found in numerous studies, with many types of expectations, people, and situations.[25] Teachers no doubt gave more attention, encouragement, and feedback to students who were expected to do well and, in the end, created the reality they expected.

In an intriguing social psychological experiment, Mark Snyder, Elizabeth Tanke, and Ellen Berscheid demonstrated the self-fulfilling prophecy with college men and women. Male college students were given a folder describing a female college student; included in the folder was a picture presenting the woman as either very attractive or unattractive. The men were asked to call the woman and talk to her for ten minutes; tape recordings were made of the conversations. The pictures were in fact bogus—that is, the men were not given pictures of the women they called; rather, the attractiveness of the picture was randomly determined. Yet when the women were independently judged through their recorded conversations, the "attractive women" were rated as friendlier and more likable. When judges rated the men on the basis of their recorded conversations, it became apparent that those who thought they were interacting with an attractive woman behaved in a warmer, friendlier manner on the phone. The men brought about the very behaviors they expected.

In our own interactions, we often confirm our expectations, not only by behaving in schema-consistent ways but also by selectively engaging in particular behaviors with particular people. Thus, consistent with our cultural stereotypes, if we expect women to be warm and nurturant, we go to women when we need comforting and emotional support. If we expect men to be knowledgeable about politics or finances, we go to men for advice in these domains. By doing so, we selectively elicit the very behaviors we expect, and do not allow for the possibility of learning that our needs might be equally well satisfied by men or women. We bring about expected behaviors and thereby reinforce what we already believe.

In their tendency to confirm our beliefs, our behaviors contribute to the essential conservatism of our conceptual system. There are times, however, when we are faced with information or experiences that do not confirm our preexisting theories but rather are clearly inconsistent with our schemas. What impact does this have on our schemas?

In the Face of Disconfirming Evidence

Research suggests that schemas persist even in the face of contradictory evidence. Often this is the case because we are able simply to discount the new information. Lee Ross, Mark Lepper, and their colleagues have conducted a series of studies that are vivid demonstrations of this "perseverance effect" involving the discounting of information. In these studies, college students are given the opportunity to formulate a theory based on information presented in the research setting. When the information that served as a basis for their theory is subsequently presented as false, students nevertheless persevere in maintaining their theory. Thus, in one study, people in the research setting were asked to distinguish between authentic and unauthentic suicide notes, and as they worked on the task they were provided with feedback about their performance. Some subjects were told they had performed very successfully (much above average), others at an average level, and others unsuccessfully (far below average). Following this feedback, subjects were debriefed—that is, they were told that the feedback they received was predetermined by the researcher and was not related to their actual performance. They were even shown the experimenter's instruction sheet that assigned subjects to the three feedback conditions. Yet when subjects subsequently completed a questionnaire asking about their actual performance, their ability to distinguish real from fake suicide notes, and their social sensitivity, their prior beliefs persevered. In spite of the clear discrediting of the information they received, subjects who had been told they were successful at the task rated their performance and abilities more positively than those who were told they were average, and subjects who were told they were unsuccessful rated themselves more negatively.[26]

Apparently, once told of their success (or lack thereof) on the suicide detection task, subjects mustered a great deal of other evidence to support this self-schema of social sensitivity. In other words, the feedback received by a person prompts a search for other information that is relevant to and supportive of the impression that is created.[27] The subsequent disqualification of only one piece of evidence—that specifically presented in the laboratory study—is then not sufficient to alter the schema. To the extent that these studies largely involve the development and perseverance of new theories or schemas rather than preexisting ones, it becomes apparent how much more difficult it would be to change older, deeply embedded schemas; the supportive evidence would be far more impressive.

The process of discounting a particular disconfirming instance or specific contradictory evidence in the face of long-accepted schemas is well recognized in work on stereotypes. Stereotypes are schemas that organize our expectations and knowledge about people who fall into a socially defined category; such a category might be based on age, race, religion, or gender.[28] Once a person is categorized as a member of a particular socially defined group, the content of the schema is likely to be applied. Members of out-groups (i.e., those groups to which we do not belong) are perceived as less variable—more similar to one another—than are in-group members, or insiders.[29] And the content of stereotypes is difficult to change; as with all schemas, stereotypes are self-perpetuating, even in the face of clearly disconfirming instances.

It is interesting to note that often the traits that constitute our stereotypes are not easily proven false. Psychologists Myron Rothbart and Oliver John[30] argue that traits and settings differ in how readily they lend themselves to disconfirming instances. Thus, it may be clear what types of behaviors might contradict a belief that a person is talkative or messy, but it is less clear what specific behaviors would disconfirm a belief that a person is suspicious or treacherous or sly. Interestingly, Rothbart and Bernadette Park[31] have shown that groups in conflict are most apt to ascribe to each other traits that are least disconfirmable—that is, they have the least clear behavioral implications (e.g., untrustworthy and devious). Similarly, Rothbart and John also maintain that certain behaviors, such as talkativeness or friendliness, can be expressed in a large number of social settings. Other traits, such as bravery or heroism, may have an opportunity for expression in rare instances. Thus, even if the behaviors that would disconfirm a stereotyped belief are clear, the occasions available for such disconfirmation may not be available. They suggest, for example, that role relationships that are highly structured, such as that between an employer and employee, are less likely to provide information about such traits as warmth and generosity than are less structured interactions.

Yet research suggests that even is those instances when disconfirmation of a stereotype is, in fact, quite clear, the consequences for the stereotype are likely to be minimal. Work by psychologist Susan Fiske has demonstrated that with sufficient motivation people may cease to consider a person in terms of group membership; we may consider a person as an individual and combine information in a "piecemeal" rather than category-based fashion.[32] Yet even when we consider individuals in a unique way, the stereotype appears to remain unaffected. In other words, even if the individual is regarded as not fitting the stereotype, the outcome at the level of the schema or stereotype is not very heartening.

When a member of a category—such as "black," "woman," or "elderly"—does not fit the category, the person can readily be regarded as an "exception" and the schema content can remain wholly intact. The specific instance is simply regarded as irrelevant to the stereotype and is discounted. Alternatively, we may engage in a process of isolating the contradictory evidence so that it has minimal impact on our stereotypes. Research has shown that disconfirming information, even numerous disconfirming instances, can lead to the creation or use of a subordinate or lower-level category rather than the superordinate or group-level stereotype. Thus, very competent, dominant women may not fit the superordinate category "woman" used to initially categorize people. Instead, a less inclusive category of "assertive woman" may be created to provide easy processing of information about this "new" instance. The broader stereotype thus remains relatively immune to disconfirmation. As Rothbart and John write:

> For example, when a white (who is familiar with blacks) first meets a black person, "blackness" (an attribute associated with a superordinate category) may be the most salient feature, and the one that becomes most strongly associated with relevant behavioral episodes. With increasing familiarity, the black person becomes "individuated" and is encoded under more specific categories (*Artist, Scientist, Extrovert,* etc.) with "blackness" losing its salience. The interesting implication, however, is that as the person loses his or her "blackness" s/he is less likely to be stored under the category *Black People,* and his/her counterstereotypic attributes may therefore become isolated from the stereotypic category.[33]

The difficulty of producing stereotype change becomes apparent as one realizes that instances of disconfirmation are minimally associated with the stereotypic category. To change stereotypes, disconfirming instances must become associated with, or "attached to," the category or group label. This is unusual, and may entail a combination of traits in individuals, such that some fit the superordinate category well, despite the existence of others that do not. A woman who is both assertive and nurturant might represent such a combination of traits. Her stereotypic nurturance may keep her "tied" to the group-level category "woman" and, by also being assertive, ultimately help to change the content of the category.

It is also possible that with an increasingly large number of subordinate categories, a particular superordinate, group-level category will no longer be regarded as a valuable guide to category members. However, as Rothbart and John[34] argue, such a possibility may be unrealistically optimistic; awareness of a few, even nonrepresentative instances of the superordinate category is likely to disproportionately reinforce the stereotype, and the existence of even slight amounts of stereotyped behaviors from a group (elicited by social expectations) is likely to lead to the persistence of stereotypes. As with other schemas, stereotype change is difficult. Cognitively, we are conservative. We tend to maintain our theories rather than change them; we interpret information so as to be schema-consistent, we behave in ways that serve to confirm our preexisting beliefs, and we discount or isolate contradictory evidence so that our preexisting schemas remain intact.

Basic Assumptions and the Primacy Effect

If what we already believe influences how we act and how we interpret new information, it naturally follows that our earliest beliefs or theories may exert an inordinate impact on our judgments and evaluations. Popular lore implicitly acknowledges this principle when it tells us that "first impressions are important." Work on schemas provides a basis for understanding the psychological process of interpreting new information in light of preexisting beliefs. Research that has more directly addressed how order of information affects judgments provides strong support for "the primacy effect," the finding that information that is presented early exerts an undue influence on people's final judgments.[35]

In a classic early study by Solomon Asch,[36] this effect was demonstrated through the simple presentation of an adjective list. One group of subjects was asked to evaluate a person who was described as "intelligent-industrious-impulsive-critical-stubborn-envious," whereas a second group was asked to evaluate a person who was "envious-stubborn-critical-impulsive-industrious-intelligent." Although the only difference between the two lists was order of adjective presentation, subjects presented with the first list evaluated the person more positively. Asch argued that the early adjectives altered the meaning of those presented later.[37] In the first instance, a more positive impression was formed first, and later adjectives such as critical and stubborn could be understood within the context of this relatively favorable view (i.e., "Smart people sometimes cannot help being critical and stubborn sometimes; after all, their views are probably the correct ones"). The opposite adjective sequence no doubt created an unfavorable impression, with undue emphasis placed on the early adjectives "envious" and "stubborn." Later adjectives were then made to fit this more negative view, with industrious and intelligent providing additional support for an unpleasant, hostile overall impression.

In a different experiment, psychologists asked subjects to watch a person solve thirty multiple-choice analogy problems.[38] Subjects were told the problems were equally difficult. Although the target always solved fifteen problems, in one condition of the experiment many more problems were solved early in the series (i.e., descending condition), whereas in a second condition a disproportionately greater number was solved later in the series (i.e., ascending condition). Again, early performance was unduly influential. Primacy effects were found; subjects who saw more problems solved early evaluated the target person as more intelligent and predicted the target would perform better on a subsequent series of similar problems.

These experiments are simple illustrations of the primacy effect, which emphasizes the undue influence of early thoughts and beliefs. The implications of the primacy effect are particularly relevant to our fundamental assumptions, whose potency is largely attributable to their early development in our conceptual system. We generalize from our earliest interactions in the world, and these representations serve as guides and selective filters for our subsequent experiences. Psychoanalysts have long argued for the importance of our first few years, particularly unresolved conflicts during this period, for understanding adult psychopathology, and object-relations psychoanalytic theorists, in particular, have focused on the importance of our early introjects, or internal objects derived from our earliest social interactions, for understanding adult psychopathology.

Whether one agrees or disagrees with central tenets of psychoanalytic thought, it is nevertheless interesting to note that the emphasis on early development—on what comes first—readily follows from recent models of information-processing. As we will see, one would not want to conclude, as a result, that one's later experiences are therefore psychologically unimportant, for they can have a major impact on one's mental health and well-being. Nevertheless, to fully understand the impact of these later events, it is instructive to know what came before. Thus, an appreciation of our fundamental assumptions about reality represents an attempt to provide a sense of our broadest preexisting theories, so that we may better understand the psychological impact and aftermath of traumatic life events.

These fundamental assumptions or theories of reality are at the core of our conceptual system and are cognitively and affectively quite potent. They shape our subsequent interactions in and interpretations of our world. In doing so, they are in turn reinforced. If we are biased against change in our narrower beliefs, even those formed within the context of an experimental study, imagine how much more resistant to change we must be at the level of our fundamental assumptions.

Resistance in Clinical Work

The clinical concept of "resistance" is particularly appropriate when discussing change in our broadest schemas. A pervasive phenomenon in the therapeutic process, resistance is not puzzling but rather natural, expected, and completely comprehensible when viewed from the perspective of schema change. At a meta level, psychotherapy can be regarded as an attempt to effect change in people's fundamental beliefs about themselves and the world.[39] Certainly, the techniques or mechanics for evoking such change differ greatly across modalities; therapists may attempt to teach new behavioral repertoires, may use insight and interpretation, may directly challenge specific cognitions, or may establish some paradoxical intervention. Regardless, these different orientations can all be considered attempts to get the client to question and change old assumptions and construals of reality.

The pervasiveness of resistance in clinical work was noted by Freud when he wrote:

When we undertake to cure a patient, to free him from the symptoms of his malady, he confronts us with a vigorous, tenacious resistance that lasts during the whole time of treatment. This is so particular a fact that we cannot expect much credence for it. . . . Just consider, this patient suffers from his symptoms. . . . And yet he struggles, in the very interests of his malady, against one who would help him. How improbable this assertion must sound![40]

If resistance is considered in terms of therapeutic goals to make the client feel or function better, resistance seems surprising, as indicated by Freud's reaction. Yet if considered in terms of people's tendency to resist change in their conceptual system, resistance is no longer surprising; it is, in fact, expected.

Resistance actually reflects our powerful tendency to maintain rather than change the fundamental beliefs that have enabled us to make sense of ourselves and our world. Rather than bear an association with any particular school of thought such as psychoanalysis, it can be considered a transtheoretical concept that describes numerous all-too-familiar phenomena in therapy.[41] Clients may reject or devalue therapists and their advice; they may stop coming to therapy sessions or may come late; they may not do their homework assignments; they may fill sessions with superficial, irrelevant information; they may engage in denial or rationalization, or intellectualization. In all cases, the client is indicating his or her resistance to change in preexisting theories of reality.

Even when our fundamental assumptions are not associated with positive feelings, and even when they lead to dysfunctional behaviors, change in these assumptions is nevertheless resisted. Change in these core beliefs threatens an individual's sense of stability, his or her way of knowing and interacting in the world. The known is familiar and conceptually comfortable; the unknown is threatening. In this vein, W. R. D. Fairbairn noted, with reference to one's object relations, having a bad internal object is better than having no object at all.[42] And behavior therapists emphasize the importance of creating and reinforcing new, positive behaviors when trying to eliminate old, maladaptive ones. Our tendency to preserve the old—particularly our higher order beliefs and assumptions—is reflected in the client's resistance during the therapy process. Ultimately, for change to occur, such resistance must be overcome, and thus in the case of therapeutic change such resistance, or cognitive conservatism, appears maladaptive, even if comprehensible. Yet this should not lead us to conclude that our cognitive conservatism is generally or even typically dysfunctional.

The Case for Cognitive Conservatism

Although our penchant for maintaining preexisting theories may seem unfortunate, the possible advantages of such conservatism should nevertheless be acknowledged. Political biases aside, there are reasons, both logical and psychological, why cognitive conservatism may be advisable.

From a logical perspective, one must consider the question of how much evidence is needed to overturn a theory that has seemingly served us well. Apart from any issue of information-processing capacities, or question of time constraints that may preclude the careful search for and integration of all new information, there is the real question of when a theory should logically be overturned. As Richard Nisbett and Lee Ross,[43] among others, have argued, our theories and schemas stand us in good stead most of the time. They are generally well founded, based on our own experiences or those of others, and typically serve us well as effective, automatic guides to behavior. We should not simply trade in these theories when confronted with disconfirming evidence.

Such arguments have been made by several major figures in the philosophy of science. Thus, Karl Popper[44] argues that we should maintain old theories far longer than might otherwise seem appropriate, suggesting a strong conservative bias in evaluating new versus old theories. Old theories should be clung to, even in the face of new, conflicting evidence. Only after a great deal of contradictory evidence has been accumulated, and the old theory has been pushed to its limits, should it be exchanged for an alternative theory.

The psychological significance of cognitive conservatism is suggested by British sociologist Peter Marris, who discusses our "structures of meaning" in terms of our basic "conservative impulse," which he regards as necessary for our survival as adaptability.

> The continuing viability of this structure of meaning, in the face of new kinds of experience, depends on whether we can formulate its principles in terms abstract enough to apply to any event we encounter; or, alternatively, on whether we can ignore or prevent experiences which could not be comprehended in terms of it (experiences where our expectations would be repeatedly and bewilderingly unfulfilled). The first is an extension of learning, the second a constriction of experiences: both seek to make life continuously intelligible.[45]

Our theories serve as guides that enable us to make sense of our world, to understand and integrate events in our world. These basic assumptions provide us with coherent pictures of our world and enable us to efficiently and effectively organize our experience. We have a need for stable knowledge structures in order that we may function in a complex, changing world.[46] Our fundamental need for stability in our conceptual systems is largely reflected in our tendency to maintain rather than change our theories about the world and ourselves. Given our need for stability, schema change is apt to be shunned most at the deepest levels of our knowledge structures, the level of our most fundamental assumptions about benevolence, meaning, and self-worth.

The Nature of Change

Our basic cognitive conservatism is a relatively uncontroversial postulate in current psychology. As we have just seen, we do tend to maintain old theories. We attempt to assimilate new information into preexisting knowledge structures. Although most recent work on schemas has stressed the extent to which schemas do *not* change, it would be inaccurate to suggest that our schemas or assumptions never change, for they do, even outside of special cases such as clinical settings.

In light of our very clear biases to conserve our cognitive structures, how can we best understand the changes in our assumptive worlds or schemas that do commonly occur? Two characteristics seem to define them. First, change most often occurs at the level of our narrower schemas or mini-theories rather than our most fundamental assumptions. Second, change is gradual and incremental rather than sudden and swift.

The very process of learning involves changes in our conceptual systems, and thus we do alter our schemas. Piaget's complementary conceptions of assimilation and accommodation both operate, even if our overall preference is for one over the other. As we move from infancy to adulthood, we no doubt learn about ourselves and our world. We learn how to act in particular situations, how to conduct ourselves socially; we may become adept at playing sports or instruments, may acquire new knowledge about history or science. Certainly, these changes are reflected in our theories about the world. Every time we learn something new, some schema is changing, and thus schema change is likely to be more common than one might suppose. However, these changes are most likely represented at the level of our narrower assumptions about the world and ourselves. The acquisition of knowledge and skills involves schemas about specific stimuli and abilities. They are not our fundamental assumptions, which are abstract generalizations, but far more specific theories that

42

are largely tied directly to particular interactions in our world. These are the schemas that are subjected to the "direct test of experience."[47]

Change in our mini-theories is often the rule rather than the exception, and it is likely to occur in an incremental manner. Just as the gradual changes in a child's physical growth are rarely noticed on a day-to-day basis, changes in our narrower schemas are unlikely to be noticed as they occur. Rather, they, too, must be compared with some distant marker to be recognized as substantial. The changes are small and gradual, adding up over time; they represent real learning. When Thomas Kuhn[48] discusses the "additive adjustment of theory" in science, he is referring to this type of gradual, incremental change. There is no crisis in science, but rather cumulative contributions to theory. Paul Watzlawick and his colleagues[49] are referring to this type of change when they write of "first-order change," which involves change in a system without any fundamental alteration of the system. Myron Rothbart,[50] too, in his work on stereotyping, discusses the "bookkeeping model" of schema change, in which minor adjustments are made slowly over time, in the face of new information.

"Normal" change is apt to occur slowly and gradually, and is represented by small, incremental adjustments in our narrower schemas. The stability of our conceptual system is not jeopardized by such change. The changes are not only gradual, but they are not occurring at the level of our most fundamental assumptions, the bedrock of our conceptual systems. We are learning animals and therefore acquire new information and strategies that enable us to function more effectively. Although we are cognitively conservative and attempt to assimilate new information rather than alter our schemas, gradual, incremental change is not unusual in the mini-theories of our assumptive worlds, in the knowledge structures that correspond to specific aspects of our reality.

While these schemas may commonly change through learning and experience, the core of the system is nevertheless likely to stay intact. Even with altered narrow schemas, we can choose to emphasize what we want, overvalue things we excel at, and overemphasize the positive, benevolent, meaningful aspects of our world. Although change in basic assumptions may occur in response to pervasive change in more restricted schemas, such a situation is the exception rather than the rule, for our cognitive conservatism is strongest and most influential at the deepest levels of our assumptive worlds. Nevertheless, as the level of conceptual change gets less and less narrow, the importance of a gradual, incremental process increases.

Role transitions that occur as we move through our lives—entering kindergarten, high school, and college, getting a job, getting married, becoming a parent—typically involve life changes that could affect more general, abstract views of ourselves and our world. Although most often these transitions add to and confirm already existing assumptions (e.g., the world is good, or I am a worthy person), they have the potential to have a more major impact. However, the process of change involved in these transitions is typically a relatively gradual one, for there is generally some type of psychological preparation that eases one into the new role: the young child is provided with lots of preparatory information about school, the pregnant woman is already learning about the responsibilities of motherhood, and the college student anticipates life in the working world. The possibility for stability and continuity in our conceptual system is maximized and preexisting assumptions are minimally disrupted.

Fundamental change in our most basic assumptions about the world and ourselves is the rarest of all conceptual change. Certainly such change does occur, yet when it does the process is generally a gradual, lengthy one. An illustrative case is that of the brilliant writer and philosopher Voltaire, whose basic beliefs changed over the course of his life. In his early adult years, Voltaire's poetry and prose reflected an incredible optimism; he believed life was good and sang its praises and mocked the regrets others espoused for a golden age. Over time, Voltaire's view of the world and people began to change, such that in 1738 he suggested that good and evil were balanced in the world. In 1747, he wrote *Zadig,* and though some protest is evident, in the end all works out well in the parable. Yet Voltaire became increasingly impressed by the amount of human cruelty, meanness, and selfishness in the world, and by 1751, he was portraying God as a capricious being trying to keep boredom at bay. The Lisbon earthquake moved him even closer to pessimism and the belief in a totally indifferent God. In 1758–59, he wrote *Candide,* which presented an extremely negative view of people as cruel and corrupt, and a totally pessimistic view of the human condition. By this time he retained little or nothing of the positive assumptions that characterized his earlier views; they had not changed overnight, but rather over the course of a lifetime.[51] Whether or not such fundamental change through deliberation and reflection is associated with a particular type of intellect is not the issue. What is important is the gradual nature of the change represented by the course of Voltaire's beliefs over his adult life.

Psychotherapy represents an attempt to alter fundamental assumptions, and it, too, takes time and involves a gradual process, though usually not a lifetime. Nevertheless, it is important to remember that the success of psychotherapy in altering our core assumptions remains an open question. Despite well-meaning attempts, psychotherapy often has little impact on an individual's fundamental beliefs.[52] And despite the dysfunctional nature of preexisting assumptions, individuals who seek therapy nevertheless resist change.

We are cognitively conservative; from both motivational and information-processing perspectives, we are heavily biased towards the old rather than the new, our preexisting theories rather than new data. When we do experience schema change, it is apt to occur in our narrowest, most restricted assumptions. In the normal course of events, the rarer instances of change in our most global, abstract assumptions involve a slow, gradual process, such that our fundamental assumptions never cease to provide us with an intelligible, comfortable, known universe. Yet there are times that this known universe is suddenly and powerfully threatened. These are times marked by trauma.

PART TWO

Impact

3

Trauma and the Terror of Our Own Fragility

Criminal victimizations such as rape and assault, natural disasters such as earthquakes and floods, life-threatening illnesses such as cancer, serious accidents such as automobile and airplane crashes, human-induced disasters such as military combat and bombings, torture, and concentration camps are overwhelming life experiences[1] that exact an enormous psychological toll. Until recently, the impact of traumatic events was only understood within the framework of a particular type of victimization. However, a study of type-specific reports and analyses reveals commonalities in the psychological experiences of a wide variety of victims, a conclusion reflected in the appearance in 1980 of a new diagnostic classification—post-traumatic stress disorder (PTSD)—in the *Diagnostic and Statistical Manual* (DSM-III) of the American Psychiatric Association.[2] Later revised in DSM-III-R[3]:

> The essential feature of this disorder is the development of characteristic symptoms following a psychologically distressing event that is outside the range of usual human experience. . . . The stressor producing this syndrome would be markedly distressing to almost anyone, and is usually experienced with intense fear, terror, and helplessness. The characteristic symptoms involve reexperiencing the traumatic event, avoidance of stimuli associated with the event or numbing of general responsiveness, and increased arousal. The diagnosis is not made if the disturbance lasts less than a month.[4]

To a considerable extent, the significance of the PTSD classification lies in the implications of a single category for traumatic events. Such a single classification for responses to all events "outside the range of usual human experience" recognizes inherent similarities in the psychological experiences of victims. Further, contrary to a long-standing mental health tradition that focuses on preexisting pathology in understanding psychological difficulties, there is explicit acknowledgment of the fact that PTSD "can develop in people without any such preexisting conditions."[5] We are confronted with a psychological disorder that can strike psychologically healthy individuals. What is clear is that there are extreme life events that will produce psychological difficulties not in a vulnerable few, but in large numbers of people exposed to them.[6]

The specific PTSD criteria established in DSM-III-R remain somewhat controversial, and unfortunately the depth and complexity of the psychological responses of victims to traumatic events are lacking in the description of this post-trauma syndrome. Anxiety and depression, for example, are extremely common responses to overwhelming life events and yet are not presented as PTSD criteria. Clearly, anxiety and depression are also symptomatic of a large number of other psychological disorders.[7] As psychologists Lisa McCann and Laurie Pearlman conclude, PTSD is simply a "slice of the pie," which is "not meant to incorporate the complex psychological phenomena associated with trauma but rather represents the most parsimonious view of post-trauma sequelae that differentiates it from other disorders."[8] From this perspective, the PTSD classification serves as an aid to diagnosis rather than as a description of the victim's psychological experience. Yet an understanding of trauma lies in grappling with the totality of the survivor's psychological experience.[9] How can we understand the responses of victims in the aftermath of extreme life events? The term *trauma* was first used in medicine, yet the defining features of physical trauma also characterize psychological trauma: "a violent shock, the idea of a wound and the idea of consequences affecting the whole organisation."[10]

Over the past fifteen years my students and I have studied a number of victimized populations, including individuals who have experienced rape, battering, and other crimes; life-threatening illnesses, particularly cancer; severe accidents resulting in paralysis; and premature, unexpected deaths of parents and spouses. We have attempted to understand the responses of trauma survivors through both intensive interviewing and through quantitative measures of their reactions. For some survivors, the trauma is relatively short-lived, for others it lasts years. Yet regardless of population, and regardless of research approach, we have found remarkable similarities across different victim populations. The basis for these similarities is apparent in the words and responses of survivors: The traumatic event has had a profound impact on their fundamental assumptions about the world.

Shattered Assumptions

We typically move through life without considering or examining the fundamental assumptions discussed in Chapter 1. Our broadest schemas seem to serve us well, providing us with the means for making sense of our world and for tackling new experiences with relative confidence. There are also pleasurable emotions associated with their positively biased content, for at the core of our psyche we feel safe, secure, protected.

Our penchant for preserving rather than changing knowledge structures suggests the deeply embedded, deeply accepted nature of our beliefs about the benevolence and meaningfulness of the world and our own self-worth. As we saw, in our world bad things happen infrequently, and when they do, they don't happen to us; they happen in accordance with certain principles, and we are personally protected because of who we are or what we do. We are able to maintain an "illusion of invulnerability."[11] We take for granted our own indestructibility and assume the continuity of a secure existence. Consistent with our cognitive conservatism, we interpret our experiences such that our fundamental assumptions are essentially unaffected.

In his work on the philosophy and sociology of science, Thomas Kuhn[12] discusses instances when paradigms—the broad schemas that drive scientific activity—are stretched too far and an "additive adjustment of theory" is impossible. In most cases, the data of scientific investigations, even anomalous data, can be readily assimilated. In some instances, the scientific community adjusts its dominant paradigm or scientific theory so that the basic paradigms are not called into question. Yet there are times when a new paradigm is needed to account for anomalous data. These are times of extreme crisis in science, periods characterized by scientific revolutions.

Similarly, within the mind of a single individual, there are times when one's guiding "paradigms"—one's fundamental assumptions—are seriously challenged and an intense psychological crisis is induced. These are times of trauma. The new data of experience do not resemble the grist for the mill of "normal change," which typically involves gradual and incremental accommodation at the level of our narrowest schemas. The assault on fundamental assumptions is massive. These traumatic events do not produce the psychological equivalent of superficial scratches that heal readily, but deep bodily wounds that require far more in the way of restorative efforts. The injury is to the victim's inner world. Core assumptions are shattered by the traumatic experience.[13]

Characterizing Events that Produce Trauma

There are times when reality comes closer . . .

—*Theodore Roethke*[14]

What is the nature of life events that actually shatter core assumptions? In the face of our cognitive conservatism and the solidified, consolidated nature of our fundamental assumptions about benevolence, meaning, and self-worth, what is it about these events that leads them to rupture the core of our conceptual system? One response to these questions is simply to list extreme life events, such as rape, criminal assaults, natural disasters, life-threatening illnesses, serious accidents, combat, and torture. Clearly, however, it begs the question. What is it about such stressors that forces us to objectify and question our most deeply held assumptions?

At the outset it is imperative to recognize that the response to any particular life event must be understood in terms of the particular victim or victims involved. In other words, there is always an appraisal process[15] that occurs, and it is how an event is understood that ultimately determines whether it will be traumatic or not. All stimuli and events must first be interpreted as a threat in order to be perceived as threatening. One student may appraise an exam as very stressful and threatening, whereas another may not. Certainly, people respond differently to potentially threatening situations, and this is also the case with life events. Those events that seem most overwhelming do not produce a traumatic response in every survivor, and other life events that may not be considered very threatening may, in fact, produce a traumatic response in some survivors. It always comes down to a question of interpretation and meaning. What does this event mean to the victim?

The recognition that events are always subject to personal appraisal might suggest that we throw in the towel and simply conclude that a traumatic event is one that shatters a victim's fundamental assumptions. In other words, it is an event that is appraised in such a way that it shatters the core of our conceptual system. I do, after all, believe this to be the case. Yet this is circular and unsatisfactory; clearly, some events are more likely than others to produce trauma, to shatter fundamental schemas. Can we say anything about them? I would suggest that we agree that the meaning of an event for any particular individual is important and then move beyond to consider the nature of events that are most likely to produce a traumatic response. Personality and social psychologists generally take what they call an interactionist perspective and agree that any particular response is a function of both the person and the situation. Nevertheless, they recognize that there is typically a trade-off between the power of a situation and the degree of individual differences that presumably reflect personality. Very powerful situations are least likely to provide much information about personality, for variability in response is minimized.

Traumatic life events are "powerful situations" and therefore justify reframing the question as a probabilistic one: What types of events are most likely to produce a traumatic response? We are thus able to acknowledge that there are some events that are more apt than others to result in trauma. Rape and criminal assaults are far more likely to shatter peoples' assumptions than an intensely anxiety-provoking exam. Simply stated: Traumatic events—those that are most apt to produce a traumatic response—are out of the ordinary and are directly experienced as threats to survival and self-preservation.

Out-of-the-Ordinary Events

Traumatic events are unexpected in the normal course of daily life; they are extreme, unusual crises. As the American Psychiatric Association writes, such events are "outside the range of usual human experience" and "would be markedly distressing to almost anyone."[16] The very fact that these are atypical events means that psychologically we are unprepared for them; they are not represented in our assumptive world. In defining traumatic events as "out of the ordinary," there is a recognition of the possibility of important cultural differences in what would be experienced as traumatic. Thus, for example, in a culture where parents are aware of and experience considerable infant mortality in their communities, the death of an infant may be less devastating than in a culture that has very little infant mortality. There are certain ongoing victimizations, such as incest and battering, in which the initial occasion is generally unexpected, but subsequent instances may not be entirely unexpected to the victim.[17] Although there may be a general expectation of future occurrences, the victim is rarely certain of precisely when they will reoccur. Further, there may be a general expectation of an earthquake in earthquake-prone areas, or of death and losses in military combat, but to suggest that people are truly prepared, psychologically, for the reality of the events is likely to be quite a different matter. From this perspective, the non-normative nature of events defines our typical failure to actually consider these extreme experiences in our cognitive-emotional worlds.

In discussing traumatic events, the American Psychiatric Association specifically rules out certain common, yet extremely negative, experiences as candidates: simple bereavement, chronic illness, business losses, and marital conflict.[18] These are regarded as within the range of normal experience; they are not unusual. Nevertheless, we could readily imagine instances of bereavement or chronic illness, for example, that would clearly qualify as traumatic. The thirty-five-year-old who is diagnosed with cancer or the forty-year-old whose spouse dies suddenly would both be having statistically unusual experiences that could readily be regarded as traumatic events. Certainly, it is not possible to draw a sharp distinction between ordinary and out-of-the-ordinary events; in most instances, there would be general agreement about them, and the fact that certain cases might be problematic (i.e., When is bereavement not "simple bereavement"? When is the diagnosis of a chronic illness extreme and unusual?) does not preclude the significance of the criterion for understanding traumatic events.

Directly Experienced Events

Given our need for stability, our cognitive conservatism and resistance to change, anomalous data must be particularly powerful to challenge preexisting assumptions. This is the case for theories in science as well as for our own theories of reality. To a considerable extent, within science the convincingness of data is determined by the "validity" of the data.[19] Scientists use rationally generated criteria to attempt to establish such validity, and the beliefs of qualified, respected authorities are of particular significance to the final outcome. The convincingness of anomalous data is largely directed and resolved by consensus.

In the case of traumatic life events, the "validity" of disconfirming data is readily apparent through the power of personal experience. The distinction between the ways of assessing validity in science and in the individual corresponds to two types of knowing: argument and experience—discussed by Roger Bacon over seven hundred years ago.[20] More recently, psychologist Philip Brickman[21] distinguished between two types of validity—inferential and phenomenological—that correspond to ways of knowing in science (i.e., careful calculation, typified by experiments) and in personal experience. Similarly, Seymour Epstein[22] maintains that we have both a rational and an "experiential" mind. The former expresses itself in numbers and words and is logical and analytical, whereas the latter is connected with emotions and represents reality largely through images.[23]

This important difference between rational thought and direct experience was noted by Charles Darwin in a firsthand report he provided after witnessing a devastating earthquake in February 1835, a disaster that killed more that five thousand people in Concepción and Santiago, Chile. Darwin wrote that this earthquake in "one second of time has created in the mind a strange idea of insecurity, which hours of reflection would not have produced."[24]

It is interesting to speculate about the significance of the experiential mind for changes in our fundamental assumptions. The power of one directly experienced, negative event is "real" in a way that the written word, for example, cannot approach.[25] Such traumatic events no doubt involve some type of emotional encoding, in addition to any rational, more verbal encoding, of the experience. In fact, visual imagery is often regarded as the most important part of a traumatic memory, and is typically associated with very powerful emotions.[26] This imagery no doubt reflects in part the direct experiential nature of the traumatic event.

The experience that challenges an individual's basic assumptions almost always involves the person as the direct victim of threat or attack. However, it is also possible to experience trauma following a serious threat or harm to people very close to us, particularly close loved ones. Our emotional attachment to these people essentially makes the traumatic event directly felt. Further, witnessing physical violence to another person, even a stranger, as in torture or combat, also involves direct experience. The witness directly perceives the events; the experience is powerful and immediate.

Events That Threaten Survival

What is it that is directly experienced? The answer to this question lies at the very heart of the determination of a traumatic life event. It is implicit in the use of the word *survivor*. As Robert J. Lifton defines it, a "survivor is one who has encountered, been exposed to, or witnessed death, and has himself or herself remained alive."[27] In our lifetimes, we may directly experience a number of unusual events that are nevertheless not traumatic. Winning a lottery, for example, may present difficulties in adjusting to one's new economic status, but it is not a stressor that would induce a traumatic response. Similarly, unexpected failures at certain tasks (e.g., in school or work) at which most others succeed are apt to lead to very negative feelings and difficulties, but they, too, are unlikely to induce a traumatic reaction. It is not simply any negative or difficult experience that induces trauma, not simply any occasion that taxes our resources. There is something unique about traumatic events that assaults our most fundamental assumptions about the world and ourselves. They are extremely powerful and their potency is not fully accounted for by their out-of-the-ordinary, directly experienced nature. Rather, traumatic events involve perhaps the most basic of threats, that to our very survival.

We have built our lives on assumptions that enable us to feel safe and secure; we tend not to concern ourselves with our physical existence as much as our psychological existence. And yet our fragility as physical beings becomes painfully obvious through traumatic events. These are occasions when we are forced to recognize the real possibility of annihilation, of serious injury, and our own mortality. Our own survival—or that of those we care deeply about—becomes seriously questioned.

A group that has recently been the focus of extensive study is Vietnam veterans. Research consistently has shown that combat exposure is associated with trauma; those with high combat exposure were most likely to experience PTSD.[28] More specifically, being wounded, being involved in the deaths of noncombatants, and exposure to atrocities have been regarded as critical factors in the development of PTSD.[29] Veterans with PTSD were exposed to the annihilation of others and were also at great personal risk; they were most apt to directly experience their own mortality.

Lifton recognizes the significance of this basic survival threat in trauma when he discusses the "death imprint" as the key to the survivor experience. This imprint differs somewhat depending on the nature of the traumatic event; thus, for Hiroshima survivors there was a total "death saturation" as well as the taint of death associated with continued radiation and the fear of nuclear extermination. For concentration camp survivors, the death imprint involved "generalized psychic and bodily assaults—including exposure to starvation, suffocation in crowded box-cars, extreme heat and cold, beatings, forced labor, epidemic diseases, and medical and surgical experimentation."[30] For both of these groups, there was also a grotesqueness that surrounded the death imprint. Yet Lifton claims that less intense forms of the death imprint are of great importance in all disasters, whether they are natural or produced by people. He writes: "But what needs also to be emphasized is the survivor's having experienced a *jarring awareness of the fact of death* . . . he has been disturbingly confronted with his own mortality."[31]

The confrontation with one's own survival is a defining feature of traumatic events, whether the victimizations are the result of natural disasters, serious accidents, diseases, or criminal attacks. Research by Bonnie Green and Goldine Gleser has demonstrated that life threat was a predictor of traumatic stress reactions following the Beverly Hills Supper Club fire and the Buffalo Creek dam collapse of 1972.[32] Regarding the latter, Kai Erikson wrote that virtually everyone on Buffalo Creek had a very close encounter with death, either because they felt doomed themselves, because they lost relatives and friends, or because they came in contact with dead bodies. As in many other mass disasters, the faces of death at Buffalo Creek were frequently grotesque and disfigured; bodies were often unrecognizable.

As a thirty-eight-year-old survivor of Flight 232, the DC-10 plane that crashed on its flight from Denver to Chicago in July 1989, put it: "Someone asked me if I feel invincible now. It's just the opposite. I feel very mortal now. If I'd been seated ten rows back I'd be a dead man right now. It's not something I ever expect to forget, and I don't think I should. I'll never forget the smell of the burning plane."[33]

In the case of life-threatening illness, the confrontation with mortality is an integral part of the victimization. One's survival is abruptly challenged by the diagnosis of disease. In the words of Rose Kushner, who had been diagnosed with breast cancer: "Cancer had always been a scare word to me, an automatic signal to order a cemetery plot and a tombstone. . . . While there was no breast cancer in my own family, as far as I knew, I kept remembering the close relatives on Harvey's side of the family who had breast cancer, none of whom had survived."[34]

Based on her own reaction and that of a sample of women she surveyed, Kushner is adamant in stressing that the primary concern of women following a diagnosis of breast cancer is that of survival. "The single biggest psychological adjustment a woman must make is to the sudden knowledge that she has a chronic, potentially fatal disease. . . ."[35]

Awareness of the possibility of death or serious injury is made painfully obvious in violent victimizations such as rape. The words of a robbery victim who was badly beaten attests to the sudden awareness of possible annihilation:

> While the crime was in progress, my overall feeling was that I was going to die and it was the greatest fear I've ever known. It was just a sick kind of fear and then, at the same time, I was to do whatever I could to get out of the situation. I was feeling for my life. After the assailant left, the feeling was, "I just can't believe it. It's just not real." I think it was too awful to think about. I might have been dead. It drove me crazy.[36]

These examples of the "death imprint" represent victimizations in which there are clear instances of physical injury or death. One's physical integrity has clearly been compromised. There are numerous traumatic events that do not seem to involve explicit instances of injury and death, and yet the threat of survival nevertheless underlies their power to strike our fundamental assumptions about the world and ourselves. Thus, certainly: "Robbery is not as devastating as rape, but it *is* a defilement. As in rape, the robbery victim has the feeling of being close to death. 'I could have been killed,' is a common response to a robbery experience."[37]

As Morton Bard and Dawn Sangrey note in their work on reactions of crime victims, any face-to-face encounter with a criminal makes victims all too painfully aware that their survival is on the line.[38] Further, similar words are heard from individuals whose homes have been destroyed by fire. Certainly, material extensions of themselves have been destroyed; most important, though, for these victims the fragility of human survival has become all too apparent.

The confrontation with possible annihilation is also evident in the experiences of child trauma victims. A well-researched and particularly gruesome incident involved children in Chowchilla, California, in 1976. A school bus, with twenty-six children, was kidnapped and a twenty-seven-hour ordeal followed in which the children were hijacked at gunpoint, driven about eleven hours in blackened vans without food, water, or bathrooms, and were buried alive for sixteen hours in an interred truck-trailer. Lenore Terr, who later conducted extensive research with these children, found that even four years after the event, they were still showing signs of post-traumatic stress and, in particular, were preoccupied with self-preservation.[39]

Although threats to survival are most apparent when the possibility of serious physical injury or death are present, such threats may also be engendered in events that entail abandonment and separation. Real or threatened abandonment may mean personal annihilation; this is particularly the case for children, for whom survival is intimately tied to care by others. The child is dependent on others for survival, and real or threatened abandonment by or separation from those close to the child can therefore produce a confrontation with annihilation. Interpersonal betrayal through such experiences as incest are likely to involve threats of abandonment, whether implicit or explicit, whether or not they also involve real or threatened physical injury as well.

The terror of being abandoned—of being left alone—has particular survival value for children, but may still be real for adults as well. Certainly, the more dependent one person is on another, the more likely abandonment will strike fundamental fears about survival. The battered woman not only confronts real physical injury but also the possibility of being left, often with little or no resources of her own. The woman or man who has lived for and through a spouse and then experiences his or her death or divorce is apt to confront frightening questions of self-preservation. We were all children once, and thus we learned that close ties to others are associated with security, safety, and self-preservation. Being left alone is traumatic for children, and certainly may continue to be traumatic into adulthood.

Extreme negative events that induce trauma are unique in that they force victims to come face to face with their vulnerability, with their essential fragility. They are abnormally stressful, not the stuff of our daily lives. They tell us that survival can no longer simply be assumed or ignored, and this threat to our biological integrity serves to undermine our psychological integrity as well.

The Dualism of the Human Condition

As flies to wanton boys, are we to the gods.

—*Shakespeare*[40]

An understanding of trauma lies in fully recognizing the duality of the human condition, people as both biological and symbolic creatures, because overwhelming life events pose intense threats to both biological and symbolic survival. The threat to symbolic survival should not be trivialized, in the sense that death would obviously put an end to psychological existence as well. Rather, the threat should be understood in terms of the massive disintegration of the individual's symbolic world that frequently follows the survivor's confrontation with mortality. It is the recognition of our fragility as physical creatures that threatens our psychological integrity.

The two sides of our existence—physical and symbolic, body and self—are typically not considered with equal ease or fervor. Our positively biased assumptions about the world and ourselves enable us to maintain illusions about our safety and security. We take for granted our biological existence and dwell primarily in the world of symbols. We are not always comfortable confronting the biological side of human survival. Thus, Sartre sees us as hopelessly confused and deluded about our true condition; each of us wants to be a god with only the equipment of an animal, and thus we exist on fantasies. As Kierkegaard argues, it seems like some hoax that we can have consciousness, deep feelings, and self-expression, yet also be creatures that die.[41]. This is the paradox of the human condition. This is the existential problem that Ernest Becker has labeled the "condition of *individuality within finitude*":

> Man has a symbolic identity that brings him sharply out of nature. He is a symbolic creature, a creature with a name, a life history. He is a creator with a mind that soars out to speculate about atoms and infinity, who can place himself imaginatively at a point in space and contemplate bemusedly his own planet. This immense expansion, this dexterity, this ethereality, this self-consciousness gives to man literally the status of a small god in nature, as the Renaissance thinkers knew.
>
> Yet, at the same time, as the Eastern sages also knew, man is a worm and food for worms. This is the paradox: he is out of nature and hopelessly in it; he is dual, up in the stars and yet housed in a heart-pumping, breath-gasping body that once belonged to a fish and still carries the gill-marks to prove it. His body is a material fleshy casing that is alien to him in many ways—the strangest and most repugnant way being that it aches and bleeds and will decay and die.[42]

This is an impossible situation according to Becker, and thus our symbolic world is an attempt to overcome and deny our biological fate.[43] Clearly the assumptions we hold about ourselves and our world provide us with illusions about our own invulnerability. Although I believe these assumptions derive from our earliest experiences with "good enough" caregivers and are not simply constructed as defenses from early on, the ultimate impact of these illusions is the same: we approach the world with optimism and trust; we believe in our safety and security; we fail to truly appreciate the reality of our fragility as physical creatures.

Filmmaker Luis Buñuel attempts to remind us of our fragility in the midst of the mundane. He introduces a mad dog into each of his films as a reminder that no matter what illusions we hold about our security and safety, we are only one chance bite away from annihilation.[44] Yet, as a filmgoer, to recognize the dog is to briefly note our existential paradox from a distance. To experience a traumatic victimization is to powerfully, experientially, confront mortality, danger, and our "creatureliness." The result is terror.

"It can't be stressed, one final time," says Becker, "that to see the world as it really is [is] devastating and terrifying . . . it makes *routine, automatic, secure, self-confident activity impossible*. It makes thoughtless living in the world of men an impossibility. It places a trembling animal at the mercy of the entire cosmos and the problem of the meaning of it." In writing this, Becker was not referring to trauma and victimization but rather presenting a philosophical position to account for our denial of death. Yet this terror is the lot of trauma survivors, who have been forced to "see the world as it really is," or can be.

The Psychological World of the Survivor

The night I awoke to discover a strange man in my bed, I completely lost my sense of security. . . .

—*Rape victim*[45]

In the immediate aftermath of traumatic events, victims experience the terror of their own vulnerability. The confrontation with real or potential injury or death breaks the barrier of complacency and resistance in our assumptive worlds, and a profound psychological crisis is induced. What generally begins as a threat to victims' physical integrity becomes an overwhelming threat to their psychological integrity as well. Suddenly survivors become dramatically aware that "bad things can happen to them." They are not protected, safe, and secure in a benign universe. Rather, as Martha Wolfenstein writes, the victim experiences a sense of "helplessness against overpowering forces . . . [and] apprehension that anything may now happen to him."[46]

Overwhelming life events force victims to confront their own fragility at a deep experiential level. Their vulnerability is glaringly exposed. Psychologically, they are unprepared, for at the core of their being they believed in their own security and protection. Intense shock, disbelief, and confusions are immediate reactions to the survivor's tragic victimization. "No! How could this happen to me?"

The scripts victims wrote for their personal life dramas did not acknowledge the real possibility of victimization and serious misfortune. How could this happen? Where did things go wrong? Victims are frequently preoccupied with questions about how and why they were victimized. "Why me?" is a particularly common question following traumatic life events.[47] The question is not why there is rape or cancer or serious accidents or personal disasters of any sort, but rather why these extreme negative events happened to them.

Thus, the rape victim might account for the general occurrence of rape by pointing a finger at society and the way it socializes men and women, but this does not provide a satisfactory response to why she, in particular, was raped. The automobile passenger who is paralyzed because another car jumped the median and crashed into the car in which he was riding comprehends the mechanics of the collision but not why it happened to him. The person who understands the biology of cancer in terms of cell growth is nevertheless at a loss to explain why he or she, in particular, developed cancer. Why me? The very source of this question is the victim's shock and bewilderment, the recognition that what has happened does not readily fit one's long-standing, comfortable and comforting views of oneself and the world.

Nothing seems to be as they had thought, their inner world is in turmoil. Suddenly, the self- and worldviews they had taken for granted are unreliable. They can no longer assume that the world is a good place or that other people are kind and trustworthy. They can no longer assume that the world is meaningful or what happens makes sense. They can no longer assume that they have control over negative outcomes or will reap benefits because they are good people. The very nature of the world and self seems to have changed; neither can be trusted, neither guarantees security.

This view is evident in the words of a woman diagnosed with cancer: "I thought I was a well-cared-for, middle-class woman who chose her doctors carefully and who was doing everything right. I was rather pleased with myself. I had thought I could handle pretty much what came my way. And I was completely shattered."[48]

Psychologists Camille Wortman and Christine Dunkel-Schetter describe the reactions of individuals who have been diagnosed as having cancer. The person "is likely to be profoundly fearful and uncertain about many things. An environment that was formerly at least tolerable has now become unpredictable and threatening. . . . He or she is confronted with a web of fears, including fear of pain, of recurrence, or progressive deterioration, of dependency on others, and of death."[49]

Victims of natural disasters, such as the 1972 Buffalo Creek flood, no longer perceive their environment as "life-sustaining"; they now look upon it as "threatening and lethal."[50] Similarly, victims of crime report a sudden recognition of a frightening environment. They report an extreme awareness of themselves as target. Bard and Sangrey discuss the responses of mugging victims. In a matter of minutes, the mugging changed what had been familiar and nonthreatening into an environment that was unfamiliar and threatening. The words of a rape victim are instructive in suggesting the importance of her prior belief in personal control: "I feel ashamed, embarrassed, and stupid . . . I have always said women could prevent being raped. I never thought this would happen to me. . . ."[51]

In her short story "Madame Zilensky and the King of Finland," Carson McCullers[52] presents the plight of Madame Zilensky, whose life largely revolves around a grand and cherished illusion about her close relationship with the king of Finland. A neighbor decides to challenge the illusion as an untruth and forcefully confronts Madame Zilensky. The description of her reaction brilliantly captures the psychological response of trauma victims, who are also forced to confront their most fundamental illusions. McCullers writes: "In her eyes there was astonishment, dismay, and a sort of cornered horror. She has the look of one who watches his whole interior world split open and disintegrate."[53]

The essence of trauma is the abrupt disintegration of one's inner world. Overwhelming life experiences split open the interior world of victims and shatter their most fundamental assumptions. Survivors experience "cornered horror," for internal and external worlds are suddenly unfamiliar and threatening. Their basic trust in their world is ruptured. Rather than feel safe, they feel intensely vulnerable. For victims, the "Under Toad," as Garp called it,[54] is all too strong, powerful, and threatening; traumatic life events provide powerful evidence that the world is a frightening place in which they are not protected.

Suddenly the victim's inner world is pervaded by thoughts and images representing malevolence, meaninglessness, and self-abasement. They are face to face with a dangerous universe, made all the more frightening by their total lack of psychological preparation.

The Double Dose of Anxiety

The predominant emotional experience of trauma victims is intense fear and anxiety.[55] Their psychological world is one filled with terror. Survivors are dealt a double dose of anxiety, one associated with the realization that one's survival is no longer secure, that their self-preservation can be jeopardized in a world that is frightening and unsafe. The other is associated with the survival of their conceptual system, which is in a state of upheaval and disintegration. The very assumptions that had provided psychological coherence and stability in a complex world are the very assumptions that are shattered.

This double dose of anxiety occurs in addition to the initial fear that is experienced as a direct response to the extreme event. An immediate response to the traumatic event is apt to be fear associated with the possibility of one's own annihilation. There is a primitive, fundamental fear associated with our recognition of personal injury or death through disease, accident, disaster, or design of another person. As biological beings, survival is the name of the game. A realization that one's survival is no longer secure in an immediate sense—that self-preservation has been jeopardized—produces what might be regarded as an instinctual emotional response associated with the organism's physiological arousal, that of fear. Fear arises from the perception of danger and is associated with a readiness to flee the danger.[56]

Subsequently, fear and anxiety may be signaled by features of the environment that resemble some aspect of the traumatic event. The fear may be conditioned to other stimuli that are somehow linked to the initial experience. Thus, following their victimization, rape victims often exhibit extreme fear in response to cues associated with their rape (e.g., darkness, being alone, genitals, knives). Further, combat sounds and particular odors often evoke intense anxiety in Vietnam veterans.[57] Work by psychologist Terence Keane and his colleagues suggest the importance of a second learning factor—instrumental avoidance learning—in the aftermath of trauma. Victims learn to avoid these anxiety-provoking situations and stimuli, and thus avoidance and escape behaviors are reinforced.[58] In the words of a rape victim several years after her brutalizing experience:

> I'm still afraid and will be for the rest of my life. It took me until last year to really learn to be alone. I never drive my car with the doors unlocked. There is always a feeling of terror when I have to get out of my car in an empty parking lot or walk into an empty house. And the first thing I do in a hotel is check every closet. I

have so many alarms and locks at my home in New York that anyone who got in could never get out. And there are two special locks on my bedroom door. Every night I lock them all.[59]

Following the actual traumatic event, tremendous anxiety becomes the emotional lot of survivors. Suddenly the world is a threatening, dangerous place. They are vulnerable. Anxiety involves an expectation of danger, a danger that is neither immediate nor necessarily well defined. In its simplest form, "Anxiety is fear mediated by images" and involves cognitive symbolic processes.[60] Suddenly, victims are living in a world they perceive as dangerous and threatening, in which one's own survival cannot be guaranteed. The cognitions of anxious individuals center on themes of threat, danger, unpredictability, and uncertainty, and these are central to the emotional experience of victims. Pervasive anxiety is apparent in the words of a woman after the October 1989 California earthquake: "Once you know what can happen, every little thing terrifies. I'm exhausted and nothing feels the same."[61]

A similar anxiety is reflected in the decision of a San Franciscan father who, several months after the earthquake, noted that he was still unable to leave his children with a baby-sitter. Acknowledging that this might appear paranoid, he said that he couldn't bear to be separated from his children.[62] Victims appear to experience the "basic anxiety" discussed by Karen Horney: feeling helpless in a hostile world.[63]

Yet it is not only the external world that is perceived as threatening, but the internal world as well: It is in a state of chaos. Victims cannot derive any equilibrium from prior assumptions, for they are no longer adequate guides to the world. The result is cognitive disintegration, which, according to James Averill, is the defining characteristic of anxiety.[64] This double dose of anxiety, which occurs on top of the initial fear in direct response to the victimization, is the psychological counterpart of physiological arousal. The intense anxiety of victims is paralleled, physiologically, by intense arousal.

Physiological Responses: Hyperarousal and Hyperreactivity

Physiologically, trauma is represented by hyperarousal. Extreme threat produces increased autonomic arousal that prepares the organism to respond with fight or flight responses. Survival is the name of the game. Based on his work with combat soldiers during World War

II, Abram Kardiner coined the term *physioneurosis* to describe post-traumatic stress. He suggested that the autonomic nervous system continues to prepare survivors for action, thereby accounting for the high levels of autonomic arousal and the tendency to physiologically overreact. It is as if the body is in a constant state of preparation to respond to threat.

In a recent review of psychophysiological laboratory studies of Vietnam veterans, researchers concluded that regardless of the stimuli presented (i.e., audiovisual, auditory, or imaginal), veterans with PTSD were consistently found to be more physiologically reactive than controls to trauma-related cues.[65] Thus, for example, in a study comparing reactions of combat veterans diagnosed with PTSD and combat veterans without PTSD, only the PTSD group exhibited an increase in heart rate in response to combat sounds.[66]

Recent research has begun to specify, more precisely, the nature of biological responses to extreme threat, although a clear, complete picture has not yet emerged. Increased autonomic arousal occurs in response to intense stressors, and research has suggested that this arousal is mediated by changes in the central neurotransmitter systems, particularly the noradrenergic system.[67]

> Neurochemical systems are influenced by stress as both *responders* and *effectors,* that is, they are both stimulated by stress, and in turn act upon other systems to provoke secondary and tertiary responses. The result is a cascade of biochemical and neuronal responses. . . . In between, a multitude of physiologic responses has been provoked, each of which acts in some way to mobilize the organism: secretion of hormones, acceleration of heart rate, vasoconstriction and rerouting of blood flow, contraction of muscles, immunologic responses, alerting and arousal reactions, and alterations in mood and emotional state. In each of these, and in probably others as well, neurotransmitters, and particularly the catecholamines, play an important role.[68]

Catecholamines are "emergency-mobilizing" chemicals—specifically norepinephrine (noradrenaline), epinephrine (adrenaline), and dopamine—that are synthesized in neuronal cells of the brain, adrenal medulla, and sympathetic nervous system. In response to extreme stressors, catecholamine levels are increased. One result is intense stimulation of (noradrenergic) neurons in the central nervous system. According to Bessel van der Kolk and his colleagues, there is evidence that with prolonged or repeated exposure to traumatic life events, the use of catecholamines may exceed production, and catecholamine depletion may result. This depletion is believed to produce changes in the sensitivity of neurons, such that they become overly sensitive to later stimulation. Chronic depletion of central nervous system norepinephrine, in particular, may result in norepinephrine receptors in the brain that are hypersensitive to subsequent norepinephrine stimulation that occurs in response to threat.[69] The trauma victim is thus left in a state of hypersensitivity and decreased tolerance for subsequent arousal. Even minor stress and stimulation can trigger major autonomic arousal.

In a recent study of trauma victims, John Mason and his colleagues found that levels of norepinephrine and epinephrine were at or near the extreme high end of the range, but, perhaps somewhat surprisingly, cortisol levels were at extremely low levels.[70] Low cortisol levels have been found in other studies as well, though not consistently.[71] Mason and his colleagues attribute these low levels to the chronic nature of the victim's psychological stress. They maintain that under such conditions, cortisol levels are lowered not because of glandular exhaustion but because of the suppressive influences of coping mechanisms and psychological defenses, such as denial.[72]

High levels of norepinephrine levels combined with low levels of cortisol suggests a dissociation between the sympathetic–adrenal medullary system and the pituitary–adrenal corticol system, a "cortisol-catecholamine dissociation" in trauma.[73] There is apparently high sympathetic nervous system activity and reactivity coupled with some form of psychological defense, a situation that directly parallels the biphasic nature of psychological responses to traumatic events, which will be explored in Chapter 5.

Recently, the locus coeruleus, which essentially regulates brain hormones that prepare for emergencies, has been implicated in trauma. In fact, it has been suggested that this may be a "brain trauma center" where arousal, responses, and memories are integrated.[74] Autonomic hyperarousal and increased norepinephrine production have suggested that this part of the brain is overactive and hyperreactive. As a result, it secretes catecholamines even in situations involving little or no threat, thereby keeping the body mobilized for emergencies even when there is none.

A central role for the locus coeruleus is also suggested by recent findings showing increased production of CRH, corticotropin-releasing hormone. Research has found that CRH stimulation of the locus coeruleus produces anxietylike symptoms.[75] Further, investigators have posited an imbalance between opioid production, which can blunt the feeling of pain, and norepinephrine production in the area of the locus coeruleus as well.[76]

There is now some evidence that a single case of overwhelming terror may be capable of changing brain chemistry such that some survivors are more sensitive to adrenaline surges even decades later. Increasingly, there is a suggestion that traumatic stress may result in permanent structural changes in the brain. Nevertheless, it is important to bear in mind that "The plasticity and resilience of the brain, with its redundancy of systems and remarkable capacity for compensation and adaptation bodes well for the possibility of good outcomes."[77]

In the face of overwhelming life events, the organism responds, physiologically, by preparing to deal with extreme threat. Unfortunately, the mammoth proportions of the stressor results not simply in a temporary state of arousal but in a continued state of hyperarousal. "Persistent symptoms of increased arousal" represents one of the DSM-III-R criteria for PTSD and is often manifested in sleep disturbances, difficulties concentrating, outbursts of anger, hypervigilance, and an exaggerated startle response.[78]

The trauma victim remains in a state of readiness to respond, a state of preparedness in response to extreme stress. Victims are hyperreactive; they are set to respond physiologically to certain stimuli as if they remained threatened with death and destruction. In their state of increased arousal and readiness to respond physiologically, survivors have difficulties modulating the intensity of their affects and warding off their anxiety. Thus, for example, relatively benign stimuli can result in intense fright. For the crime victim, everyday sounds and experiences can produce a total panic response; every footstep is a signal for danger, of the possibility of another crime: "I'm afraid when I hear a sudden noise behind me on the street; when my dog jumps up on me from the back I go into sudden, instant shock/fear; when I hear a noise from below going up the stairs to my apartment; . . . I am afraid when going into my apartment building and turn around and go in backwards."[79]

Or, as a rape victim reported two months following the rape:

I keep jumping when I go anywhere. People really frighten me. So many things scare me. I never used to be frightened; didn't fear things. Now I can't stand it. I moved to a fourth-floor apartment and when it is locked I wish it had bars on the windows. . . . One night I went to bed and my roommate was out. I started hearing sounds. I was certain someone was there. My heart was beating so fast and I was trembling. My roommate came in and suddenly everything was okay. I thought I'd die till she came in.[80]

For the disease victim, the slightest symptom can similarly produce a panic response. Every physical symptom is a signal for danger, of the possibility of a recurrence or another disease.

Those who have been through a natural disaster are also hypersensitive to a recurrence. Thus, a survivor of the Buffalo Creek flood noted:

> My nerves is my problem. Every time it rains, every time it storms, I just can't take it. I walk the floor. I get so nervous I break out in a rash. I'm taking shots for it now.
>
> I live up on a hill now, but that doesn't take away my fear. Every time it rains or goes to come up a storm, I get my flashlight—if it's two o'clock in the morning or if it's three. Now it's approximately five hundred feet from my house to the creek, but I make me a round about every thirty minutes, looking at that creek. And then I come back to the house, light me a cigarette or maybe get me a cup of coffee, and carry my coffee cup with me back down the hill to see if the creek has raised any.[81]

The response to threat or potential threat is difficult to modulate. The body is primed to respond with hyperarousal. There is a major disruption in the physiological equilibrium of the organism. There is also a major disruption in the psychological equilibrium. Thus, it is not solely physiological arousal that provides an understanding of the victim's terror in the face of new symptoms or reminders of the victimization. When a person no longer feels protected, but instead feels unsafe in a world that is no longer benign, the possibility of recurrence—of disease, crime, accidents, or disaster—seems very real. Once an individual has confronted his or her own vulnerability, it is difficult to believe that "lightning never strikes twice in the same place." Traumatic events rupture the trust necessary for such a belief.

In the end, it is a rebuilding of this trust—the reconstruction of a viable, nonthreatening assumptive world—that constitutes the core coping task of victims. There is now evidence that the long-term impact of trauma may be represented physiologically. There may be enduring changes that affect how survivors react to stressful events in their lives. There appear to be enduring changes that occur psychologically as well. These, too, can be considered structural, not in the sense of biological structures but rather mental structures. These are changes in the victim's fundamental schemas about self and the world.

4

Disillusionment and Change in the Assumptive World

Fear and anxiety are dominant early responses to overwhelming life events; represented physiologically as arousal and cognitively as the perception of threat, these emotions can persist months and even years after the traumatic event. Yet a very different psychological reaction typically co-exists with the fear and anxiety, and this is the experience of profound disillusionment, a response that often outlasts a victim's fear and anxiety. Victims' inner worlds are shattered, and they see their prior assumptions for what they are—illusions. In the end, the adjustment of survivors rests largely on whether they experience profound disillusionment and despair or, ultimately, minimal disillusionment and hope.

Experiencing Disillusionment

Rob the average man of his life illusion, and you rob him of his happiness at the same stroke.

—*Henrik Ibsen*[1]

In literature, the destructiveness of disillusionment is a well-worn theme. One need only be reminded of the pipe dreamers in Harry Hope's bar. In *The Iceman Cometh*, Eugene O'Neill[2] presents Hickey's attempts to dash their varied illusions. Hickey's efforts do not bring comfort and satisfaction but rather reduce the patrons of Harry

Hope's bar to utter despair. The joy of illusions and the pain of disillusionment are also powerfully portrayed in Cervantes's masterpiece, *Don Quixote*.

Traumatic events force a sudden realization of the Pollyannaish nature of victims' fundamental assumptions. They cannot account for the trauma. Victims experience the loss of old, deep, positive views of the world and themselves. This loss is experienced primarily as depression, a common psychological response in the aftermath of victimization.[3] No longer is the world viewed through rose-colored lenses. Joy and happiness seem emotions of the past. Victims are no longer able to sustain their prior optimism; their worldview is pervaded by pessimism, the element that turns simple sadness into depression.[4]

Interestingly, psychological research has suggested that depression, particularly mild depression, is often associated with more accurate views of self, the world, and the future.[5] I am reminded of a T-shirt I saw on which an optimist was defined as someone who doesn't have all of the facts. The term *depressive realism* has been coined to suggest the accuracy of those who are depressed. Compared with their nondepressed counterparts, they are less likely to describe themselves in positive terms, to believe they have control over outcomes, and to believe their future is bright. Unfortunately, as depression becomes more severe, their greater accuracy metamorphoses into a marked negative bias. They become overly pessimistic and negative about themselves and all aspects of their lives, manifesting "unrealistic pessimism."[6]

To begin to understand the sadness and pessimism of victims involves not simply recognizing that they may now see the world and themselves differently and more negatively but also that, underlying these new views, is the experience of loss. Psychologically, the shattering of fundamental assumptions produces a state of both loss and disintegration; the known, comforting old assumptive world is gone, and a new one must be constructed.

The loss of old illusions is not a gradual, easy process but one that is unanticipated, sudden, and dramatic.[7] It is thus likely that the process of living one's life in part involves slowly coming face to face with reality, a process of some gradual disillusionment. Growing up and getting older may entail slowly coming to terms with one's own vulnerability; after all, with time we are likely to experience poorer health, the loss of family and friends. Judith Viorst writes of the "necessary losses" that all of us experience, such as leaving our parents, letting go of children, and growing old. These involve essentially universal losses of expectations, dependencies, and illusions.[8] Psychiatrist Roger Gould has also written of people's movement away from "childhood consciousness," which entails gradually giving up some illusions about one's absolute safety.[9] Yet as in the case of traumatic versus "normal" change, the process of disillusionment following traumatic life events is powerfully accelerated. The trauma victim's confrontation with human fragility and mortality is direct and sudden. What might take some a lifetime to confront is suddenly thrust upon the victim prematurely in one fell swoop.

Survivors now know all too well that bad things happen, and that bad things can happen to them. They know that the world is not a safe haven, that they are not protected, that they are fragile beings. Suddenly things look different. They can no longer maintain an illusion of invulnerability. Consider the response of a rape victim who told me: "It's like I've walked through a door. An event like rape separates you from the mainstream. It forces you to develop a personal philosophy; you have to do thinking and searching. The world is dangerous to me now. I know that really anything could happen. I could die tomorrow."

Victims no longer feel they have the luxury of maintaining illusions, for their traumatic experience removed their rose-colored glasses. The disillusionment of victims is reflected in their basic assumptions about themselves and their world.

The World Assumptions Scale

Over the past fifteen years, my students and I have attempted to study the psychological responses of a variety of victims. We have conducted intensive interviews that have provided us with vivid information about their experiences. The victims talked openly and in great detail about the traumatic event, their reactions, their difficulties, their enduring strengths, their questions. In particular, they spoke at length about their views of themselves and the world and the extent to which they believe these changed as a result of their experiences. These data are powerful and compelling, although they are no doubt subject to the criticisms of qualitative research, not the least of which is the subjectivity and potentially biased perceptions of the interviewer.

In an attempt to complement these intensive interviews, and to provide some data that would allow me to make direct comparisons with nonvictimized populations, I developed a scale to explore the basic assumptions of individuals. The World Assumptions Scale is a questionnaire that taps our three core assumptions: the benevolence of the world, the meaningfulness of the world, and self-worth. Respondents indicate the extent of their agreement with each of thirty-two statements.[10] Examples of items that tap benevolence of the world are: the world is a good place; people are basically kind and helpful; if you look closely enough, you will see that the world is full of goodness. Included are statements about the world in general as well as statements about people.[11]

Meaningfulness of the world includes questions that measure beliefs in justice, control, and randomness. Examples are: misfortune is least likely to strike worthy, decent people; through our actions, we can prevent bad things from happening to us; the course of our lives is largely determined by chance (reverse-scored). Self-worth questions include: I am very satisfied with the kind of person I am; I usually behave so as to bring about the greatest good for me; I have reason to be ashamed of my personal character (reverse-scored).

Do victims view themselves and their world more negatively than nonvictims? As a first step, we were interested in determining whether victims and nonvictims differ on one or more of the three assumptions. If victims are more pessimistic and feel less safe and more vulnerable, this should be reflected in basic assumptions. They may believe that bad events are far more common than they had thought, or that misfortune is random and meaningless. Perhaps they continue to see the world as meaningful but see themselves as deserving of misfortune. In exploring survivors' assumptive worlds, we first looked across victimizations to explore differences between victims as a broad category and nonvictims. We then looked more closely at particular types of victimizations.

Looking Across Victim Populations

In study after study—whether with college students, a broad community sample of middle-aged adults, or selected samples obtained through doctors, hospitals, or crisis centers—we have found that the assumptive world of trauma victims differs from that of nonvictims. Whether victimized by crime, life-threatening disease, serious accident, or the untimely loss of a loved one, victims' basic assumptions about the benevolence of the world, the meaningfulness of the world, and their own self-worth are generally more negative than those of their nonvictim counterparts.[12] And this is the case even ten to fifteen years after the event.

In studies first conducted with college students, we used the World Assumptions Scale to tap students' basic assumptions about themselves and their world. In a typical study of this sort, several hundred male and female undergraduates were asked to indicate which, if any, of the following extremely negative events had happened to them during their lives: death of a parent, death of a sibling, incest, rape, fire that destroyed their home, an accident that resulted in their own serious disability. These six events were chosen because they were all regarded as extremely negative in a prior pilot study that included fifteen stressful events that might have happened to college students.

We collected data of this sort several times, from several different student populations. Typically, 20 to 30 percent of each sample experienced one of the extreme negative events. Further, both men and women are generally highly represented in each category.[13] In analyzing the data initially, we were interested in common effects across victimizations. In these studies, we found differences between those students who had experienced an extreme negative event and those who had not for all three categories of assumptions.[14] In all cases, the assumptions of victims were more negative than those of nonvictims. (The victimized and nonvictimized college students in these studies did not differ in socioeconomic status, religion, race, parental income, or parents' education.) Although the traumatic life events occurred at all ages—from early childhood to late adolescence and early adulthood—we did not find differences in assumptions that could be accounted for by the victim's age at the time of the extreme event. Even years later, victims differed from nonvictims in their basic assumptions.

In a representative study at the other end of the age spectrum, we found similar results. Respondents were several hundred individuals between the ages of fifty and sixty-five, whose names had been randomly selected from published lists (by street) of town residents.[15] Respondents completed the World Assumptions Scale and indicated which of a number of events they had experienced—the list of events included rape and other serious crimes, cancer and other life-threatening illness, death of a spouse, and serious accident. The basic assumptions of individuals who had experienced an extreme negative event again looked quite different from those who had not experienced these events. They saw the world as less benevolent, less meaningful, and perceived themselves more negatively.

Generally, then, those who had survived a traumatic life event generally viewed the world and themselves less positively than those who had not been victimized. They recognized that bad things happen more often than they had thought, that people can be monstrous, that events may be more random, less just, and less controllable than they had thought. They realized that being a decent person was not protection against bad outcomes, or they maintained a belief that the world is just but no longer perceived themselves as decent and good. Regardless of the particular pattern of basic assumptions affected, to them, the world was no longer unquestioningly regarded as safe and secure. They had "walked through a door," and what they found on the other side was threatening.

Looking for Differences

When viewed from the perspective of people's assumptive worlds, the impact of trauma, regardless of the specific type of victimization, is essentially the same. A common process, involving the shattering of the assumptive world, results in basic beliefs that are more negative— either with regard to the benevolence of the world, meaningfulness of the world, or self-worth. This is a general picture of survivors, yet once painted, it suggest the need to look more closely at trauma victims and traumatic events.

The results of studies that look across traumatic events, such as those reported above, give the impression that the assumptions necessarily change together, for typically we have found that differences are found between victims and nonvictims in all three assumptions. Our basic schemas about the benevolence of the world, meaningfulness of the world, and self-worth have intertwined roots in the earliest social interactions of the child. One might thus suspect they would necessarily change as a unit. However, though interconnected, over time they nevertheless appear to exist independently; though all may be questioned in the aftermath of overwhelming life events, one may change without another. Unfortunately, a breakdown of any single assumption is sufficient to eliminate feelings of security and safety, be it because the world is now seen as hostile and malevolent, or events are randomly distributed, or one is unable to be protected through character or behavior.

Often a survivor reports changes in all of these basic schemas. Yet any individual victim may report changes in only one or two assumptions. Ultimately, the meaning of the event for the survivor—how the experience is interpreted in light of the victim's prior assumptions— determines which assumptions are most affected. Nevertheless, a closer look at some of our data has suggested the possibility that the specific changes experienced may also, in part, reflect the nature of the victimization.

There are numerous ways to consider victimizations, to draw distinctions between types of events. One could distinguish between discrete and chronic events, for the former—such as rapes, robberies, serious accidents, fires, earthquakes, and floods—differ from ongoing experiences—such as life-threatening illnesses, internment in concentration camps, and repeated child and spouse abuse. In the latter instances, the victim is forced to continue to respond directly to the stressor itself (e.g., the disease, dangerous people inflicting harm) rather than to the traumatic images, memories, and emotions associated with an earlier traumatic event.[16]

One might distinguish between individual and group victimizations, with most crimes and diseases falling in the former category, and natural and technological disasters in the latter. Single victimizations are apt to lead to more self-questioning because of the perceived selective incidence of the event. Why did this happen to me in particular? When traumatic experiences are kept secret, as has often been the case with rape and incest, for example, survivors lack any real awareness of the extent to which these horrors happen to others. Thus, as breast cancer has become openly discussed in the media, it is likely that there is a decreased sense of "deviance" and the feeling of being singled out for misfortune among women diagnosed with the disease.[17] In general, group victimizations are less likely to produce self-questioning.

Perhaps the most fundamental distinction that can be drawn between victimizations is that between events that involve a perpetrator with malicious intent and, at the other end of the spectrum, overwhelming life events we refer to as "acts of God." The latter is our culturally accepted term for those events that are, ostensibly, not human-induced. Criminal victimizations are, by definition, brought about by another person; the individual who has been raped, sexually or physically assaulted, or whose home has been burglarized has suffered directly because of the actions of another person or persons. There is a perpetrator who has intentionally subjected the victim to harm.

Victimizations considered "acts of God" include natural disasters such as earthquakes, tornadoes, and floods. There are no perpetrators. Serious diseases also fall at this end of the spectrum, reflecting the belief that illnesses are generally not caused by another person and do not reflect harmful intent. In the cases of cancer, heart disease, and diabetes, there are no perpetrators; they are not caused by another. Yet, there are no doubt exceptions in the case of disease. To some, AIDS may seem to be such an exception; yet the rapid, early spread of AIDS was due to ignorance rather than malice.

Similarly, there are "fuzzy" instances—usually involving negligence rather than intent—in the case of some natural disasters. The Buffalo Creek disaster was a flood that at first appeared to be a straightforward "act of God." Yet the flood apparently resulted from corporate negligence. Coal waste had been dumped into a mountain stream in a manner that created an artificial dam that eventually gave way. The resulting disaster killed 125 people and left five thousand homeless.[18] Although the company was clearly negligent in its concerns for the people of Buffalo Creek, one might nevertheless question whether the company acted out of a malicious intent to harm. Similarly, serious auto accidents often involve other people, often very careless, negligent others, but they generally do not operate with the specific intention of harming another. This type of negligence typically defines technological disasters as well; human error or carelessness may have contributed, but generally specific intent to harm was not involved.

To be the victim of rape or other criminal victimizations, including incest and battering, involves an awareness that another person has intentionally harmed you. These victims have been singled out for injury (physical, psychological, or material) by another person, and this fact presents particular challenges to the victim's assumptive world. In an attempt to look more closely at natural versus human-induced traumatic events, we have gone over past interview transcripts with a variety of victim populations, looked more closely at different groups within our larger survey samples, and reexamined our studies that focused specifically and more intensively on survivors of particular victimizations, including life-threatening disease (i.e., cancer), rape victims, accidents victims, and young adults who have experienced the premature death of a parent. It appears that some victimizations are more likely to affect particular assumptions than others.

In particular, our research suggests that survivors of human-induced victimizatons are most apt to hold more negative assumptions about themselves and the benevolence of the world. The meaningfulness of the world is a core concern of these survivors in the aftermath of victimization, but the question often seems to be reframed and reconsidered in terms of questions about the perpetrator and the self.[19] Although many see the world as less meaningful, the greatest impact is seen in assumptions about self-worth and the perceived benevolence of the world. In general, for these survivors, these two assumptions seem to move in concert; the world is viewed as more malevolent and the self is viewed more negatively, as if one mirrors the other.

To be the victim of natural disasters, diseases, or accidents—victimizations that do not involve intentional harmdoers—presents difficult challenges as well. The words and responses of these survivors reflect an acute awareness and concern about randomness and chance in their lives. Many also view themselves more negatively, having lost confidence in their autonomy and strength, or see the world as more malevolent. Yet our data suggest that the greatest differences in the assumptive worlds of these survivors and those of nonvictims lies in the perceived meaningfulness of the world.

Survivors, regardless of type of victimization, feel more vulnerable. They have lost their sense of safety and security. They experience disillusionment; earlier assumptions are no longer so positively biased. Certainly, there is no single, uniform response to different types of traumatic events. Nevertheless, it appears that some types of victimization may present unique challenges to survivors' assumptive worlds.

Surviving Human-Induced Victimizations

Rape, battering, incest, other criminal assaults, robbery, torture, terrorism, and atrocities in war are all victimizations that involve perpetrators who intend to harm. This defining characteristic is crucial for understanding the unique psychological challenges posed by these traumatic events. Although the ruthlessness of the perpetrators may differ, survivors of intentional, human-induced victimizations suddenly confront the existence of evil and question the trustworthiness of people. They experience humiliation and powerlessness and question their own role in the victimization.

"Evil" is a term reserved for human interactions. It describes something that is morally bad or wrong, and the world of morals is the world of people, their conduct and character. Human-induced victimizations make one directly aware of utter immorality in a way that "acts of God" cannot. They involve understanding, at a deep experiential level, that one's terror and pain were intentionally caused by another human being. These survivors are forced to acknowledge the existence of evil and the possibility of living in a morally bankrupt universe.

The world is suddenly a malevolent one, not simply because something bad has happened to the victim but because the world of people is seriously tainted. Trust in others is seriously disturbed. As Morton Bard and Dawn Sangrey write about crime victims:

Because crime is an interpersonal event, the victim's feeling of security in the world of other people is seriously upset. The crime victim has been deliberately violated by another person. The victim's injury is not an accident; it is the direct result of the conscious, malicious intention of another human being. Some people can't be trusted—again, we all know that, but the victim is confronted with human malevolence in a very graphic way.[20]

Such human malevolence is now part of the victim's own world; it is not simply "out there," a part of other people's world.

For survivors who have been victimized by a person they know and have trusted, such as a parent, spouse, or friend, this breakdown in interpersonal trust is particularly acute. The victim feels utterly unsafe and unprotected. This is the lot of the incest victim abused by a family member or family friend; this is the lot of the rape victim abused by a spouse, friend, or partner.

Yet even the individual victimized by a stranger is likely to experience a breakdown in interpersonal trust, a newfound perception of the interpersonal world as hostile and dangerous. The victimization represents a dramatic recognition that people can be malevolent. The entire world of people becomes suspect. Who can be trusted? Who is completely safe? As Constance Fischer concludes, based on her detailed study of crime victims' stories, the foundations of their social harmony are fractured; their sense of community and social order are radically disturbed.[21] Unfortunately, as will become apparent in Chapter 7, these perceptions of a hostile, untrustworthy world are all too often reinforced rather than reversed by the responses of other people and institutions in the aftermath of the victimization.

Based on the recognition of the perpetrator's injurious intent, one might expect anger to be a primary response to human-induced victimizations. Anger is not wholly absent; many crime victims experience anger, rage, and an intense desire for revenge.[22] Yet this response is complicated and often compromised by the victim's self-questioning, which, perhaps surprisingly, may be particularly apt to follow human-induced victimizations.

Typically, we view human behavior as rational. In human interactions, we do not see people's actions as whimsical but rather as largely dependent upon cues from other people. In the case of human-induced victimizations, there is likely to be considerable scrutiny of the victim, by both the victims themselves and others.[23] Why was this particular individual *selected* as the target of injury? It is as if there is an implicit assumption that the perpetrator was responding to the victim's behavioral cues or actions.

Victims struggle to make sense of the event: "Why did this happen to me?" often becomes "Why did he/she/they do this to me?" Randomness and uncontrollability are reframed in terms of human intent. Human-induced victimizations exist within the domain of human interaction, though forced, unwanted interaction. As a result, the victimization is generally not seen as the chance intersection of two independent causal paths—that of the victim and that of the perpetrator—but rather as a single path in which events are causally related.

Survivors are likely to engage in a great deal of self-questioning, and this self-focus is underscored by their sense of powerlessness and helplessness at the hands of another human being. When an individual is victimized in a natural disaster or is diagnosed with a serious illness, powerlessness and helplessness are also experienced. Yet these are felt in the face of impersonal forces, a situation that forces a recognition of the weakness and powerlessness of people in general rather than in oneself in particular.[24] Victimizations that do not involve perpetrators are apt to be humbling, whereas human-induced victimizations are more appropriately characterized as humiliating.[25] These survivors have experienced helplessness before another person; they have been overpowered by another, a malevolent perpetrator. The victim's autonomy has been violated, and a self-perception of competence and independence is replaced by weakness and dependence.

The victim not only feels helpless, but sullied and tarnished in the process. This is very evident in the case of victimizations involving physical penetration, such as rape, in which sexual acts are used specifically to humiliate and degrade the victim. Yet even burglary victims speak of their homes as having been "penetrated, desecrated, and dirtied."[26] Human-induced victimizations affect survivors' core beliefs about themselves. Personal autonomy, strength of will, pride of self-possession are broken, and in their place are personal violation, loss of self-respect, and lingering doubts about one's self-worth.

Before looking more closely at victimizations that are not of human design, it is interesting to consider one further response that may occur in victimizations involving human interactions. During their victimization, individuals sometimes respond in kind, harming others and engaging in violent acts. These are responses born of rage and powerlessness, and yet are often devastating once the victims perceived what they have done. The response to these acts in the aftermath of the victimization is often not a feeling of strength but a sense of betrayal of oneself. Could I really have done that? What kind of person could behave so violently? Can't I even trust myself?

Although this situation has been reported by some victims of violent crimes, it is particularly characteristic of the responses of many Vietnam veterans, who are sometimes appalled by their own past behaviors. War places incredible stresses on soldiers, and the nature of the Vietnam War made it particularly stressful and problematic for soldiers. This was an unfamiliar guerrilla war in which there were no front lines. It was often difficult to tell friend from foe, and support troops were always at risk of an attack on their base camps.[27] It has been estimated that the risk of being killed in combat in Vietnam was seven times greater than that in World War II.[28] In the context of this war, soldiers sometimes engaged in "nonmilitary" actions, such as the deliberate killing of civilians, that often resulted in intense self-questioning and self-derogation. These veterans often feel shame, humiliation, personal distrust, and a distancing from themselves. In the end, they are uncertain about whether they can even trust themselves.

In general, those who have been intentionally victimized by another human being feel unprotected and unsafe. They live in a world in which people can be terribly malevolent. Even their own sense of self-worth, which had previously afforded them a sense of security, is severely challenged and often derogated.

Surviving "Natural" Disasters

The world isn't what it was to me. I don't see things the same way. I know about chance now, that bad things happen when you don't expect them.

—Cancer survivor

In the absence of a perpetrator who intends to harm the victim, survivors are more apt to turn to questions of meaning and the rules governing the universe. Life-threatening diseases, serious accidents, and natural disasters are not understood as the result of willful acts of others. The very term acts of God, most often used to describe natural disasters, suggests our culturally shared inability to truly understand the seeming arbitrariness of the traumatic events. Unlike human-induced victimizations, accidents, natural disasters, and disease are generally threats that come from outside the social system.

All survivors recognize that bad things can now happen to them, that invulnerability is an illusion. Those victimized by disease, accidents, and natural disasters may believe in a more malevolent world and a decreased sense of self-worth. However, they are most likely to experience changes in their assumptions about meaning. These victims are confronted with a less-than-benign universe, yet the world of people is not suspect. They have not experienced interpersonal betrayal. These survivors are also more likely to receive social support following their victimization; such support is far less forthcoming in the case of survivors of crimes and other human-induced victimizations.[29]

Regarding assumptions about the self, victims of disease, accidents, and natural disasters often report feeling powerless. Many report having lost confidence in themselves, in their ability to take care of themselves, or in the integrity of their bodies. Further, societies can culturally define some diseases in moral terms that include regarding the victim as tainted. Susan Sontag makes such a case for tuberculosis in the last century and cancer in our own.[30] Yet survivors of accidents, disasters, and diseases typically do not report the extreme humiliation that is commonly the lot of victimizations that are the ruthless design of another. Despite the considerable self-questioning that may occur in the immediate aftermath of extreme life events, over time these survivors seem to exhibit minimal negative change in self-views. It is as if the helplessness they feel is recognized not as unique but as the common lot of people. Our own findings are supported by a recent study of cancer patients by Shelley Taylor and her students. They found that these survivors perceive the world as far more frightening, but they do not perceive themselves more negatively.[31]

Victims of disasters that are not human-induced experience tremendous disruption in their assumptive worlds, and the changes they experience appear most dramatic in their beliefs about meaning. In a recent study of young adults who experienced the untimely death of a parent, for example, we found that it was assumptions about the meaningfulness of the world, and not benevolence or self-worth, that differentiated this group from a matched sample of young adults.[32] As one respondent noted: ". . . The world's not fair. I used to think that justice and goodness would always come through in the end. It was a very idealistic belief, and a very stupid one."[33]

A whimsical universe is extremely threatening; bad things can happen to good people, horrors can be the lot of careful people. The world can no longer be trusted to operate along our human constructions of justice and control. These victims are forced to confront the real possibility of randomness and chance in people's lives, a realization discussed by many of the cancer patients we've spoken with over the years. Most speak with acceptance, though with some anxiety and sadness, of chance and fate. Note the philosophically similar, though more playful, reaction of the cancer patient who told me that her newfound recognition of the role of chance and random events in her life has made her consider playing the lottery.

The world is less controllable, less subject to our manipulation than these victims would ever have chosen to believe. Misfortune can be the lot of anyone. It is difficult to maintain a belief in a wholly meaningful world in which events make sense and happen in accordance with our accepted social laws. It is all too obvious to these survivors that they are unprotected and unsafe in a universe too often defined by random events.

Childhood Versus Adult Victimization

The present perspective on trauma emphasizes the victim's shattered assumptive world and long-term changes in survivors' core assumptions. What are the implications of such a model for differences between traumatic events that occur in childhood versus those that occur in adulthood? Just as human-induced versus natural represents a fundamental distinction between traumatic events, children versus adults is a fundamental distinction between trauma victims. In recent years, there has been a growing interest in post-traumatic stress in children. Although it appears that PTSD exists in this population,[34] some debate about its presence should alert us to the difficulties in making such a diagnosis with children.

There is little question, however, that following traumatic life events, children can and often do experience considerable difficulties,[35] manifested in a range of symptoms, including fear, hypervigilance, nightmares, apathy in a variety of behaviors (from eating to schoolwork), and physical complaints. Often, the trauma is reenacted and represented in game playing, which is generally considered a part of recovery, an attempt to master the threat. Lenore Terr, for example, noted that the victims of the Chowchilla school bus kidnapping often played such games as "traveling Barbie," in which a Barbie doll is taken somewhere in a bus and comes back safely.[36] What are the implications of the present model for understanding the effects of trauma on children?[37]

A major impact of traumatic events is their assault on the assumptive world of the victim, and this world is apt to be different for the child and the adult. The assumptive world of the adult is more solidified than that of the child. The adult has had many more years to use and confirm his or her basic assumptions, which are apt to be more deeply embedded in the conceptual system, and more unquestioningly accepted.

The child, too, has an assumptive world to serve as a coherent guide to the world and self, but it is more pliable. The rudiments of this system begin in the preverbal years and are typically built upon and validated over the years of childhood. An extreme negative event will disrupt the assumptive world of a child, but its less solidified nature is bound to make an important difference.

This is apparent in research that has explored the impact of sexual abuse on male victims.[38] Compared with adults, child victims are far more likely to struggle with questions of gender self-perceptions. Researchers have found that boy victims of sexual abuse often become very aggressive, even later perpetrators of abuse. With few exceptions, these boys have been sexually abused by men. This not only results in the perception of self as helpless victim, but it also raises questions about one's masculinity and heterosexuality. These young male victims appear to spend years acting out a super-male script so as to reestablish their own maleness.

The child's inner world is a more open system, more capable of accommodation in response to new inputs. Paradoxically, the relative plasticity of the child's inner world provides the possibilities for both greater psychological protection from trauma as well as for greater psychological devastation.

The Possibilities for Protection

Maximal protection is afforded the child by the emotional investments and interpretive efforts of close, caring adults, particularly parents. For children, the meaning of an extreme event is more subject to inputs by close others. In responding to such events as serious accidents, diseases, and natural disasters, for example, the child is apt to be exquisitely sensitive to parental interpretations and definitions. Those very close to the child can potentially reframe and transform the event so that it is less frightening and less likely to challenge the child's inner world.

When an event nevertheless disrupts the child's existing core schemas, the continued input of caring others may foster a relatively smooth and healthy resolution to the psychological trauma.[39] Violent victimizations and those that force the separation of children from parents (e.g., kidnapping) are particularly likely to shatter the child's sense of safety and security. Yet in the aftermath of these traumatic life events, the child is apt to be particularly sensitive to the empathic, caring responses of parents or other attachment figures, whose inputs will also be incorporated into the child's assumptive world. The possibility of constructing an integrated, stable, and still positive assumptive world are maximized for such children, even in the face of extreme life events.

The crucial role of parents in determining children's reactions to extreme events is evident in studies of children in extreme situations. Research on air raids during World War II found that persistent psychological disturbances among children typically appeared when there was also a very nervous parent.[40] Studies of children in war have shown that children's responses are primarily determined by the behavior of parents, guardians, and other significant adults.[41] Further, researchers who investigated the long-term impact of the Buffalo Creek disaster found that the degree of psychological impairment among children was associated with that of their parents.[42]

The important role of the family in childhood victimization was also apparent in a study of Cambodian children who had survived the horrors of the Pol Pot regime. Pol Pot controlled Cambodia (Kampuchea) from 1975 to 1979, during which time there were mass executions, forced labor, starvation, and separation of families. The mental health community in the United States has become increasingly aware of the extreme psychological distress and trauma characterizing large numbers of Cambodian refugees as a result. In a recent study of forty Cambodian adolescents who had been in concentration camps for four years (typically between the ages of eight and twelve), researchers found that virtually all of those who lived in a foster home had sufficient psychological symptoms to warrant a psychiatric diagnosis (generally, PTSD or major depressive disorder), whereas approximately half of those who lived with a nuclear family member warranted a diagnosis.[43] Number of family members killed and other indices of the severity of their traumatic experience were not associated with a psychiatric diagnosis. It was very apparent that living without a member of the nuclear family dramatically increased the risk of psychological disturbance.

The Possibilities for Greatest Harm

Parents or trusted, caring others provide a protective environment within which the child can understand and integrate extreme life events. In the absence of such an environment, the long-term effects of trauma are apt to be very negative. The most extreme, devastating effects of negative life events on children are likely to be those that involve victimization by the very people who are looked to for protection and safety. These are instances of child abuse by close family members, cases of violence between the child and trusted adults; in the most severe victimizations, the child has no one to turn to for care and protection.

In these cases, the traumatic experience is apt to become fully incorporated into the child's inner world; the basic building blocks of this world are still in the development stage, and the victimization is likely to define the world and self-assumptions of the child. These children are apt to have negative assumptions in all domains, for core beliefs are less likely to be disentangled at an early age. The trust and optimism, the sense of safety and security, the feeling of relative invulnerability that are afforded the person with positively biased assumptions are absent in the psychological world of these children. Instead, their world is largely one of anxiety, threat, and distrust.

For such children, the core sense of self and others is powerfully affected. Such total disruption is often manifested, psychologically, in a basic personality disorder. Researchers are becoming increasingly aware of the high incidence of character disorders among adults who were abused as children. Recent research by Drew Westen and his colleagues has shown significantly higher rates of both physical and sexual abuse among patients diagnosed as having borderline personality disorder than among other inpatients.[44] In a review of the literature on borderline personality disorder, Judith Herman and Bessel van der Kolk concluded that childhood trauma plays a significant role in the development of this character disorder. Data suggest that histories of childhood physical and/or sexual abuse can be found in the majority of borderline patients, and the incidence is greater than that which appears in a general psychiatric patient population.[45]

Borderline personality disorder is characterized by disturbances in self-concept, affect regulation, interpersonal relationships, and impulse control. Borderlines have an unstable, diffuse sense of self, and under certain types of stress they experience a disintegration of the self and "annihilation panic."[46] They have poor affect tolerance, report feeling empty and bored, and overreact to relatively mild stimuli. Borderlines also have difficulty with interpersonal relationships; although they cannot tolerate being alone and actively seek involvement with others, their relationships are intensely conflictual and unstable. They manifest very poor impulse control and often engage in behaviors that are harmful to themselves or others. Suicide attempts and self-mutilation, particularly wrist-cutting, are extremely common among borderline patients.[47]

Interestingly, recent studies have also implicated severe childhood abuse in the development of multiple personality disorder (MPD),[48] and Herman and van der Kolk noted the marked resemblance between borderline patients and those with multiple personality disorder.[49] Both have extreme reactions to relatively mild stimuli in the environment, reactions that include the emergence of alternate personalities in MPD. Further, the use of dissociation and "fragmentation of the self" commonly seen in borderlines is carried to the extreme in patients with multiple personality disorder.[50]

Severe child abuse can result not only in dysfunctions in personality, but in cognitive dysfunctions as well.[51] Abused children frequently show cognitive delays in the development and use of age-appropriate problem-solving operations. Cognitively, they appear extremely inflexible, unable to accommodate to new situations and data. They also have poorer verbal abilities. These children manifest a great deal of cognitive disorganization, which is typically attributed to the intensity of their anxiety and, in turn, interferes with their ability to organize information. Perhaps not surprisingly, then, the child victim of severe abuse is often diagnosed with learning disabilities. Clearly these problems may require far more than remedial education; the traumatic experience, which is interfering with the child's cognitions, must be addressed.

The cognitive-emotional system of the child is not nearly so firmly ensconced in the psyche as that of the adult, and the more fluid state of the child's inner world is both a blessing and a bane. Although the impact of an extreme event will be minimized by a loving, caring environment, it will be magnified by an uncaring, abusive one. Children who have been victimized by the very people they trust, who cannot be comforted in a secure, protective environment, will carry negative views of the self and the world into adulthood. These become the fundamental schemas of their assumptive world, their core psychological structures.

Impact Versus Recovery: The Role of Prior Assumptions

Popular wisdom suggests that those who have the greatest psychological problems prior to a victimization will have a particularly difficult time in the aftermath of a traumatic event. More simplistically, those who are extremely anxious or depressed before a victimization are apt to look even more troubled after being victimized. In the well-established psychiatric vulnerability model, prior stressors and psychological history predispose people to further problems. Research has, in fact, shown that preexisting psychological problems are associated with chronic psychological symptomatology postvictimization. Thus, rape victims who had not recovered after five years were more poorly adjusted prior to the rape than those who had recovered after six months.[52]

Survivors of severe childhood victimizations are likely to overreact to new stressors, even mild ones. Extreme traumatic events present particular difficulties for this group. To a considerable extent, their personality continues to reflect their traumatic experience, and a revictimization is apt to be tremendously disruptive. Physiologically, these victims are "primed" to respond with hyperarousal, and psychologically with cognitive-emotional disintegration.[53] The new situation will be perceived as intensely threatening and the impact of the extreme event is apt to be particularly traumatic.

The difficulties these victims are likely to experience are not, however, wholly accounted for by the powerful impact of the new traumatic event. These victims are also likely to possess minimal coping resources. Severe childhood victimizations may seriously hinder the development of cognitive and emotional abilities that facilitate recovery. Thus, even in adulthood, both the initial impact of a subsequent victimization and the process of recovery are apt to be harsh and difficult; there will be considerable short-term and long-term distress.

We could imagine, however, that there are victims for whom impact and recovery are not parallel. Consider the adult trauma victim who experiences intense difficulties in the immediate aftermath (i.e., impact phase) of the victimization but who has the coping capacities to readily resolve the trauma and recover. In such cases there will be considerable short-term distress but good long-term adjustment.[54] This best describes the survivor who had very positive assumptions prior to the victimization; he or she felt relatively invulnerable to misfortune and thereby has great difficulty in the immediate aftermath of an overwhelming life event. This is the quintessential mismatch of expectations and reality.[55]

It is those with the most positive preexisting assumptions whose core schemas are most deeply violated. Extreme negative events produce tremendous psychological upheaval and anxiety, for their inner worlds are shattered. The intense impact of victimization, however, does not imply a similarly difficult recovery process. In fact, these survivors may have a relatively easy time rebuilding a stable, comfortable assumptive world, the essence of the recovery process. The same psychological makeup, history, and social environment that provided these optimistic people with their prior positive assumptions are also likely to have provided them with the psychological resources to cope successfully postvictimization. Thus, positive core assumptions may be a risk factor for initial psychological disruption, but they may also be associated with long-term recovery.[56]

Work by psychologist William McGuire[57] on attitudes and persuasion provides a useful analogy to the breakdown of extremely positive, unquestioned basic assumptions in the immediate aftermath of victimization. McGuire's research has demonstrated that cultural truisms—beliefs that are so widely accepted we are unpracticed in defending them—are highly vulnerable to influence and persuasion. People have no counterarguments to use in resisting them. In order to inoculate attitudes against influence, they must be challenged so that counterarguments can develop.

Our fundamental assumptions are least subject to the direct test of reality and typically go unquestioned; they are likely to be relatively rigid and inflexible. Traumatic life events challenge these core schemas; we have no "counterarguments," and they come tumbling down.

It follows, however, that to the extent that fundamental assumptions have already been questioned, they may be less likely to shatter. There are a number of research studies that suggest such a conclusion. Ann Burgess and Lynda Holmstrom, for example, found that rape victims who experienced the loss of a significant person prior to the assault had fewer difficulties.[58] Researchers who studied the life changes of rape victims in the year prior to the rape found that a moderate amount of change (as compared to no change) was associated with better adjustment immediately following the rape, as judged by social workers in an emergency room.[59] Studies have also shown that people over age sixty-five may be minimally at risk for psychological impairment following natural disasters, a finding that may be attributable to the increased recognition of personal vulnerability that may occur as one grows older.[60]

Recent research by Zahava Solomon found that Israeli soldiers with no prior war experience were more likely to exhibit a combat stress reaction (i.e., shell shock) following the 1982 Lebanon war. Further, those who had fought and were exposed to the stresses of war but did not previously develop a combat stress reaction were least likely to manifest such trauma symptoms.[61] In a study of Vietnam veterans, those with a stressful childhood history were found to be less likely to develop PTSD symptoms than a control group.[62]

There is some evidence, then, that prior stressors may inoculate an individual against extreme trauma following negative life events. Generally, these appear to be stressors of moderate magnitude, sufficient to challenge and even slowly change some assumptions in the direction of decreased naivete.

The role of prior experiences with extreme life events that have resulted in trauma—that have shattered the victim's assumptive world—depends largely on whether the survivor has reestablished a stable, nonthreatening, integrated inner world. To the extent that this has not happened, the victim is likely to be more vulnerable to psychological disintegration in the face of future extreme life events. A very tenuous, fragile assumptive world is likely to have been constructed, with memories and images of the victimization always threatening. The victim is likely to remain hyperreactive to stress, particularly that associated with the prior trauma. It would not take much in the way of an extreme event to shatter this fragile inner world.

To the extent that the survivor has reestablished a stable, nonthreatening, integrated inner world, it is conceivable that the traumatic experience may itself serve as a psychological inoculation against future breakdown. These survivors' core schemas would already include a recognition that "bad things can happen to me," that people cannot always protect against misfortune, that the world is not always benevolent or meaningful.[63] Some degree of personal vulnerability would already be acknowledged.

The coping task for survivors of traumatic life events is that of reconstructing fundamental schemas in the face of psychological breakdown and cognitive-emotional disintegration. The search for equilibrium involves efforts to reestablish a coherent set of basic assumptions following the shattering of the victim's old assumptive world. For some survivors, this takes weeks, for others months, and still others years. In the end, their inner world is different from that of individuals who have not experienced an extremely negative life event. They recognize their vulnerability and are less Pollyannaish in their perceptions of the world and themselves. Yet their self- and worldviews are often surprisingly positive. How can survivors create an inner world whose fundamental schemas are not wholly negative? How do they arrive at a new assumptive world?

PART THREE

Coping

5

Processing the Powerful New Data

Psychologically, victims are between a rock and a hard place. They are in a state of conceptual disintegration because the nature of the world and the self implied by the traumatic victimization—a helpless, weak self in a malevolent, meaningless world—contradicts the old, positively biased assumptions. To accept these new views entails embracing a wholly threatening impression of self and environment, as well as catastrophic rather than gradual change. The victim is stuck between two untenable cognitive-emotional choices: preexisting assumptions that are no longer viable in describing the world and oneself and new assumptions that not only involve a total reworking of prior views, but are themselves extremely negative and threatening.

Somehow survivors must resolve this intense dilemma. In the aftermath of serious crimes, disease, bereavement, accidents, combat, and natural disasters, victims must rebuild their assumptive worlds and integrate their new, negative experience. This is no small effort. Given the very fundamental nature of the challenged assumptions, given people's tendency to persevere in the maintenance of their theories, given the powerful "experiential reality" of their new experience and the frightening world implied by the traumatic event, the coping task facing victims is overwhelming.

Integrating the Old and the New: Cognitions and Emotions

How can survivors reconcile their prior outlook and existence and their powerful victimization? The possibilities for a new assumptive world are framed by two extremes: maintaining the old assumptions unchanged or accepting the new assumptions implied by the victimization.

The old assumptions were so comfortable, yet now seem naive. Only those who began with negative assumptions can easily maintain them, experiencing minimal trauma and requiring little change. For most survivors, old assumptions have been shattered. Though the same assumptions can be restored and are emotionally attractive, conceptually they seem invalid.

The other extreme involves the rebuilding of an assumptive world based on threatening views of the world (malevolent and meaningless) and/or negative views of the self (helpless, unworthy). Once again the emotional and conceptual evaluations seem at odds; yet now these new assumptions may seem valid, relatively apt descriptions of reality, but emotionally they are extremely unattractive. The anxiety associated with experiencing the disintegration of one's inner world may be dissipated, but the anxiety and depression associated with living in a threatening universe remain.

Attempts by victims to rebuild their assumptive worlds post-trauma illustrate the powerful interplay of both cognitive and emotional factors in adjustment. It would be wrong to conclude that conceptual stability is the sole motivational force driving the coping effort post-trauma. Certainly, victims need to rebuild their inner conceptual worlds to restore psychological equilibrium, but the crucial motivational role of emotion cannot be overlooked.[1] The full acceptance of new, threatening assumptions would provide survivors with a stable conceptual system that might seem quite valid in light of their victimization. Nevertheless, the survivor avoids it because of the intensely negative feelings associated with these assumptions.

Although framed largely as a cognitive dilemma, the victim's coping task involves two evaluative systems, the cognitive and the emotional, the rational and the experiential. When coping is successful, both cognitive and emotional evaluative systems are "satisfied." The now conceptual system is regarded as valid, a reliable guide for future interactions. It is also affectively "agreeable enough"; emotional pain has been minimized, even though the new inner world is likely to be less pleasant and positive than one's prior conceptual system. This is apt to involve some integration of the old and the new, such that the newly created assumptive world can be characterized as falling between the two extremes. How is this accomplished?

The rebuilding task is a difficult one, but is generally facilitated by three distinct categories of coping processes. The first are automatic routines for processing new, powerful data. These, particularly denial/numbing and intrusive reexperiencing, will be discussed in this chapter. The second are efforts to reinterpret the new data, to "massage" them so that they fit better—these will be considered in Chapter 6. The third are interactions with others that assist (or impede) recovery—these will be analyzed in Chapter 7.

Automatic Coping Processes: More than Meets the Eye

Two seemingly contradictory sets of processes constitute the primary psychological responses to traumatic life events. One set, characterized by denial and emotional numbing, represents efforts to avoid painful thoughts, images, and feelings. A second set, characterized by intrusions and reexperiencing of the trauma, represents efforts to confront them. Victims alternate between the need to approach the trauma and to avoid it, to confront their experience and protect themselves from it.[2] Indeed, denial/numbing and reexperiencing are generally regarded as the sine qua non of traumatic stress; with arousal, they are the psychological symptoms that are diagnostic of post-traumatic stress disorder according to DSM-III-R.[3]

Unfortunately, in considering denial and intrusive recollections as indicative of trauma, we have too often considered them abnormal responses to stressful events, rather than adaptive responses to abnormal events. Both have frequently been regarded very negatively, as responses that interfere with successful coping and recovery. We have overpathologized denial and intrusion as problematic symptoms and have too often failed to recognize their considerable adaptive value. From the present perspective, however, they are automatic efforts by survivors to come to terms with and integrate their traumatic experience. While they may be symptomatic of trauma in that they so commonly occur in the aftermath of extreme events, they are nevertheless, also efforts to facilitate recovery.

Denial/numbing and intrusive recollections represent the exquisite interdependence of emotions and cognition, denial representing the need to emotionally protect the individual, and intrusions reflecting the need to conceptually process the event. The two processes complement one another and operate in tandem, and thus their overall facilitative impact can best be appreciated when they are considered together. First, however, we must arrive at an understanding of each phenomenon and its individual contribution to the survivor's coping efforts.

Denial and Numbing: Modulating the Onslaught

I was diagnosed with breast cancer. In those early days I just kept waiting for results of all sorts of medical tests. It was a bit like being on a roller coaster. But all through that time, including the mastectomy itself, I never even considered the possibility that I could die, that I wouldn't make it and recover.[4]

—*Cancer patient*

The definition of denial is as controversial as its adaptiveness. A useful working definition, however, has been provided by Leo Goldberger:

Stated succinctly, denial is a term for almost all defensive endeavors which are assumed to be directed against stimuli originating in the outside world, specifically some painful aspect of reality. Perhaps even more succinctly, one might define it as a refusal to recognize the reality of a traumatic perception. Though denial can be direct, because of its unconscious status it is more often than not *inferred* by indirect evidence through behavior that is said to mask, bolster, or maintain denial.[5]

There is disagreement in the psychological literature as to whether denial pertains to intrapsychic or external "events," and whether it is a conscious or unconscious process. Nevertheless, Richard Lazarus has convincingly argued that the negation of a problem or situation, the defining characteristic of denial, can involve the negation of an impulse, feeling, or thought, or of an external demand or reality.[6] Further, he has distinguished denial from the more conscious process of avoidance, which involves the deliberate refusal to think or talk about the stressful event but does not deny its existence.

Following overwhelming life events, trauma-related thoughts are intensely painful and distressing and survivors often engage in conscious processes of avoidance. They use instrumental behaviors to avoid people, places, and things associated with the traumatic event. The cancer patient may quickly flip past articles about the disease, the rape victim may intentionally avoid passing the building in which she was raped, the car accident victim may take an alternate route home so as to bypass the site of the crash. They actively choose not to be reminded, for they can then avoid the pain of remembering. To keep their emotions from being too overwhelming—to avoid the pain—survivors sometimes use alcohol and/or drugs. These are efforts to self-medicate, to modulate their intense affect and arousal.

Although survivors may decide to engage in these avoidance behaviors, they alone are unlikely to successfully ward off the victim's psychic distress. Automatic denial processes, involving cognitions and emotions, are set in emotion by an organism that seeks to protect itself. By turning off awareness of the event or its implications, or by shutting down the capacity to feel, survivors maximize the possibility, ultimately, of successfully integrating their experience.

Denial processes are "chosen" as an automatic response to overpowering new data. The choice is neither conscious nor voluntary in the ordinary sense of the word. Consistent with Lazarus's analysis, denial operates outside of people's awareness—that is, people do not know they are engaged in these processes. Further, people can deny both external reality as well as internal feelings and thoughts, with the latter representing perceptions or emotions related to the occurrence of a painful external event.

Certainly, the question of external reality is, perhaps, a philosophically sticky one, as are the related issues of truth and accuracy. How are we to know what really happened, what a person is truly denying? Rather than claim ontology is completely knowable, I would argue for a consensual criterion in determining whether an individual is engaging in denial. We could reach a shared consensus, based on cultural expectation, that particular events have occurred, and that certain types of events (e.g., serious illness with the possibility of imminent death) would be threatening to most people. When people disavow such consensually validated events, or the consensually validated implications of these events, we could reasonably maintain denial is operating.[7]

Definitional issues aside, how have psychologists evaluated denial? It has often been viewed as a maladaptive mechanism, one that interferes with an accurate perception of reality. Traditionally, Western psychiatry and clinical psychology have regarded the accurate perception of reality a primary criterion of mental health, and coping strategies have generally been regarded as adaptive if they emphasize or facilitate accurate reality testing. Thus, Freud[8] defined denial as a "disavowal" of external reality and assumed it occurred only in psychosis.

Much of the psychiatric writing on denial describes, in particular, its use by psychotics. Perhaps as a result of these descriptions, psychologists have tended to regard denial as a sign of underlying psychopathology.[9]

The description of denial as a defense mechanism originated with Anna Freud,[10] who viewed it as a unifying concept for a variety of defenses whose common goal is to reduce some threatening aspect of reality. For both Anna and Sigmund Freud, denial was distinguished from repression, and as has generally been the case in psychoanalytic theory, denial was viewed as a more primitive, earlier defense used by small children before the mechanism of repression has matured. It is regarded as an elemental component of all outer-directed defenses, including projection, displacement, and isolation. Generally, psychoanalytic theorists agree that it is usually succeeded by more sophisticated defense mechanisms and coping methods. In the case of psychosis, however, it remains the central defense mechanism.[11]

It is probably an understatement to conclude that, psychologically, denial has been underappreciated. From the present perspective on trauma, denial is far from a maladaptive mechanism suggesting psychopathology. Rather, it is a useful and valuable process that reflects the survivor's extraordinary psychological predicament postvictimization.[12] For most people, who view the world as benevolent and meaningful and themselves as worthy and effective, the initial impact of traumatic events is nothing short of overwhelming. Trauma-associated images and thoughts reside within the victim's inner world. They are powerful, intensely painful, and threaten to completely overwhelm the survivor. It is the process of denial that prevents a steady, unmodulated attack on the victim's cognitive-emotional world. Denial enables the survivor to more gradually face the realities of the victimization and incorporate the exeeprience into his or her internal world.

In evaluating denial, much depends on whose perspective one takes. Certainly, from the perspective of an outside observer, the disavowals—either of the victimization or, more typically, of the implications of the extreme event—may appear odd or pathological. For example, to deny that one's loss is permanent, that one has a dread disease, or that death is a likely outcome of one's life-threatening illness, may seem very strange. Observers match the victim's words and actions against a consensually validated view of the loss or disease. Although not accessible to the observer, the denier's internal reality—the world of basic assumptions—is every bit as real to the victim. When the words and acts of the victim are matched against this internal world, which has been maintained over years of experience, the denier's behavior no longer seems odd or pathological.

As we saw in Chapter 2, people generally resist change in their schemas, and such change is apt to be most resisted in their most basic assumptions. When "normal" change does occur, it reflects a slow, incremental process. In essence, denial serves to transform a massive onslaught of powerful, incongruous, threatening data into a more gradual, manageable confrontation. As Seymour Epstein has written of anxiety, "Not until an acute state of arousal has somewhat dissipated can the work of mastery begin, and even then pacing is important, as excessive increments in arousal will tend to reverse the process."[13] The initial impact of the traumatic event is likely to be overwhelming. Denial enables the victim to reestablish some equilibrium and confront the threatening experience in smaller, manageable doses.

Denial and Emotional Numbing

After great pain, a formal feeling comes—
The Nerves sit ceremonious, like Tombs—
The stiff Heart questions was it He, that bore,
And Yesterday, or Centuries before?

. . . . .

This is the Hour of Lead—
Remembered, if outlived,
As Freezing persons, recollect the Snow-
First- Chill-then Stupor-then the letting go-

—*Emily Dickinson*[14]

Typically, there are two aspects of denial, one involving thoughts and ideas related to the victimization, the other involving feelings and emotions. The "turning off" of cognitions has more generally been discussed in terms of denial and the "turning off" of emotions has generally been discussed in terms of numbing, particularly psychic numbing or emotional anesthesia.[15] These two types of automatic avoidance are often considered together, two sides of one coin; thus, psychiatrist and stress researcher Mardi Horowitz treats ideational denial and emotional numbness as a single phenomenon, and writes of "denial numbness."[16]

In order to minimize the threat posed by the traumatic event, the victim typically disavows information and feels little or nothing in response to this information. The initial onslaught is so massive, the cognitive upheaval and emotional responses (e.g., fear and anxiety) so intense, that the cognitive-emotional system largely shuts down; denial processes are invoked, and the victim acknowledges and feels little.

Based on his work with victims of Hiroshima, Robert J. Lifton wrote: "Human beings are unable to remain open to experience of this intensity for any length of time. Very quickly—sometimes within minutes or even seconds—*hibakusha* began to undergo a process of 'psychic closing-off'; that is, they simply ceased to feel."[17]

The words of one of these survivors, a physicist who walked among the corpses searching for relatives, are particularly powerful:

> As I walked along, the horrible things I saw became more and more extreme and more and more intolerable. And at a certain point I must have become more or less saturated, so that I became no longer sensitive, to what I saw around me. I think human emotions reach a point beyond which they cannot extend—something like a photographic process. If under certain conditions you expose a photographic plate to light, it becomes black; but if you continue to expose it, then it reaches a point when it turns white. . . .[18]

Emotional numbing was also extremely evident in concentration camps. To survive, inmates appeared to automatize functions that were dedicated solely to survival; such "robotization" involved feeling nothing yet going through the motions of daily existence. The extreme stage of numbing involved complete withdrawal into a "musselman," an individual characterized by extreme apathy, lack of any response to the environment. Virtually all concentration camp inmates had brief periods of "semi-musselman" behavior, in which they ceased to feel and ceased to struggle to survive. This was particularly common when the inmates arrived at the camp and there was a masssive onslaught of a new, terrifying reality.[19]

This sense of feeling emotionally detached, of being unable to feel anything, is reported by victims who have experienced all types of traumatic events. It is often reflected in survivors' reports that they feel detached from others, are unable to feel any sense of intimacy following their victimization, and feel uninterested and unmoved by previously enjoyable activities.

Denial—involving both cognitive and emotional numbing—enables survivors to pace their recovery; excessive amounts of anxiety are reduced and the requisite cognitive-emotional work required to rebuild a viable assumptive world can proceed gradually. In essence, the survivor undergoes a reversible, symbolic form of death in order to avoid a more permanent psychological or physical one.[20]

Given the massive attack of traumatic events on victims' inner worlds, one would expect a great deal of denial immediately following the victimization, followed by less and less denial over time as the victim works to integrate the experience. This expectation is supported by empirical evidence; denial is very common in the immediate aftermath of victimizations, including serious illness, loss of a loved one, accidents, and crime.[21]

Early in the recovery process, victims resist the emotional pain of traumatic images and thoughts; they resist the intensely threatening implications of their victimization through denial. For some, this period is one that takes on the qualities of "pseudoadjustment," for the denial allows the victim to return to normal life patterns;[22] some throw themselves busily into work or some activity unrelated to the victimization and appear consistently busy.[23] Most apparent in the early periods of recovery, the frequency and comprehensiveness of denial and numbing processes typically decrease over the course of the healing process.

Extreme Denial: The Case of Dissociation

There are, however, instances of extreme denial that do not abate over time. These are most often represented by various forms of dissociation, in which large aspects of trauma-related experience are split off and completely disowned. Psychologist Ernest Hilgard's interest in hypnosis led him to explore consciousness and dissociation. He argued that our beliefs about the unity of consciousness are illusory, for we are always doing more than one thing at a time and yet our conscious representation of our actions is never complete. Typically, we "pay attention" to only some things going on, although attention can shift to other aspects of our thoughts and actions. He noted, however, that sometimes a part of our ongoing thought and action is *dissociated* from consciousness, in that it is concealed and outside of awareness.

From this perspective, the denial and emotional numbing experienced by trauma victims represent a form of dissociation. When the traumatic event is not remembered—when the victim exhibits continued, total amnesia for the overwhelming experience—the dissociation is regarded as more extreme. This is the rape victim who has no memory of the attack, or the accident victim who has no memory of the crash. Such amnesia is regarded as an extreme form of denial; it is an extreme response to a massively painful event. However, it does not fully capture what many psychologists think of as dissociation. Perhaps the most extreme instances are represented by the separate, split-off existence of a distinct personality.

In his historical account of dissociation, Hilgard notes that the beginning of the concept is commonly attributed to Pierre Janet in 1889.[24] In these earliest writings, it is this form of dissociation that is most apparent:

> Janet's interpretation is that systems of ideas are split off from the major personality and exist as a subordinate personality, unconscious but capable of becoming represented in consciousness through hypnosis. . . .
>
> Janet's term dissociation derived from the prevalent doctrine of association. If memories were thought to be brought to consciousness by way of the association of ideas, then those memories that are not available to association must be disassociated.[25]

Thus, a set of coherent ideas could be separated from one's primary personal consciousness. These dissociated systems are evident in fugue states and, particularly, in multiple personality disorder. Some "amnesic" barrier prevents this relatively coherent subsystem from being integrated. As Hilgard maintains, this is the difference between alternating normal roles and alternating personalities, as found in extreme cases of psychopathology. Sometimes system X may be aware of system Y, without Y being aware of X; apparently one-directional amnesia is sufficient to constitute dissociation.

Dissociation has been associated with trauma. In fact, "except when related to brain injury, dissociation always seems to be a response to traumatic life events."[26] Thus, as noted in Chapter 4, there is considerable evidence that multiple personality disorder (MPD) results from severe child abuse.[27] Dissociation—through amnesia, fugues, or multiple personality—represents a defensive, self-protective response to traumatic life events.[28] Much of the survivor's personality is left unaffected, and the victim is able to continue to function. For such survivors, any confrontation with the trauma would be psychologically devastating, and thus the immediate adaptive response is to wall off any awareness of the trauma.[29]

To the extent that these forms of dissociation—or any extreme levels of denial—are maintained over time, the processes are likely to become maladaptive. Although, as psychiatrists Bessel van der Kolk and

William Kadish note, it is at least conceivable that "amnestic dissociation" can remain adaptive throughout a person's lifetime, without
further indices of psychopathology, they, like Freud, are not optimistic.[30] From the perspective of the victim's cognitive and emotional
world, it is not as if the trauma does not exist; it is that the trauma does
not exist in consciousness or the consciousness of one's primary personality. Although the original distress is walled off, the person is left
"with a tendency to react to subsequent stess as if it were a recurrence
of the trauma. The patient experiences the emotional intensity of original trauma without conscious awareness of the historical reference."[31]
The traumatic experience is likely to continue to affect the survivor;
unexplained panic experiences, reenactments of the trauma, poor social and emotional functioning are possible consequences.

The traumatic material continues to exist and, ultimately, must be
integrated. Extreme denial and dissociation interfere with mastery of
the event,[32] for processing of the traumatic experience is precluded. It
is this crucial processing of the traumatic experience that is represented
by a second set of commonly experienced symptoms, those related to
reexperiencing the trauma, particularly intrusive images and recollections of the event.

Intrusive Reexperiencing: Confronting the Data

I have trouble keeping the whole thing from coming into my
mind. There are just so many thoughts running through. Once at
work the thought came into my mind and hit me and I lost my
breath, the feeling was so intense.

—Rape victim[33]

What I went through on Buffalo Creek is the cause of my problem. The whole thing happens over to me even in my dreams,
when I retire for the night. In my dreams, I run from water all
the time. The whole thing just happens over and over again in
my dreams.

—Flood disaster victim[34]

Sometimes my head starts to replay some of my experiences in
Nam. Regardless of what I'd like to think about it, it comes creeping in. It's so hard to push back out again. It's old friends, their
faces, the ambush, the screams, their faces. . . . You know, every

time I hear a chopper or see a clear unobstructed green treeline, a chill goes down my back; I remember.

—Vietnam veteran[35]

Following victimization, survivors commonly reexperience the traumatic event through intrusive recollections or distressing dreams. Even as they "try" to avoid trauma-related thoughts and feel little, victims suddenly feel or act as if the traumatic event were recurring, as if they are reliving the experience. During the day, or in their dreams, survivors reexperience their trauma.[36] These thoughts and memories are involuntary, persistent, recurrent, and psychologically disturbing, and they are virtually universal among those who have experienced extreme, negative life events. Why do these intrusive ideas and images occur? Are they simply symptomatic of the victim's distress, or might they serve some adaptive function?

Freud's Death Instinct

It is interesting to note that these intrusive recollections, particularly recurrent nightmares, led Freud to reconsider his own theory and propose what is probably regarded as his weakest theory, that of the death instinct. Freud wrote *Beyond the Pleasure Principle* at the age of sixty-four, largely as a way of making sense of the repetitive dreams reported by World War I soldiers suffering from traumatic neuroses. He was impressed by the intensity and duration of these soldiers' symptoms, particularly the recurrent nightmares they reported. In their dreams, these soldiers reexperienced the terror of their war experiences, and it was apparent to Freud that these unbidden images were not wish fulfillments.

Freud posited a "compulsion to repeat which overrides the pleasure principle,"[37] a compulsion that could account for the repetitive dreams of the traumatic neuroses as well as the impulse that leads children to play. In the middle of his book, Freud claimed that repetitive dreams serve a mastery function:

But it is not in the service of that principle [the pleasure principle] that the dreams of patients suffering from traumatic neuroses lead them back with such regularity to the situation in which the trauma occurred. We may assume, rather, that dreams are helping to carry out another task, which must be accomplished before the dominance of the pleasure principle can even begin. These dreams are endeavouring to master the stimulus retrospectively, by developing the anxiety whose omission was the cause of the traumatic neurosis.[38]

Freud believed that the absence of anxiety left people unprepared for the excitation that followed from a traumatic event, and thus the individual's "protective shield" could be most easily breached. Yet Freud did not stop here, satisfied with any mastery function of repetitive dreams.[39] Instead, he went on to write that there "was also a time before the purpose of dreams was the fulfillment of wishes," and finally, he proposed his now-famous "death instinct." For Freud, life and death instincts were now regarded as primary human motives. He attributed the repetition compulsions, apparent in the nightmarish, repetitive dreams of the traumatic neuroses, to the death instinct.

In the end, the soldiers' recurrent nightmares led Freud to reevaluate his theory and to arrive at an extremely questionable, generally poorly respected resolution. Ernest Becker's evaluation of this piece of Freudian theory seems quite appropriate: "Freud's tortuous formulations on the death instinct can now securely be relegated to the dust bin of history."[40] Yet we are left with the problem of accounting for the intrusive, repetitive thoughts and images so often found among those who have experienced a traumatic event.

In the Service of Integrating the Traumatic Experience

In reliving the traumatic event, the victim once again is forced to confront two aspects of the experience: the actual ideas and images, and the fear and anxiety associated with these cognitions. Psychologists have suggested that intrusive recollections have a curative effect because the distressing emotions are gradually extinguished through repeated exposure; the victim is provided with the "possibility of gradually inuring oneself to an initially overwhelming experience."[41] This perspective is also reflected in the view that such intrusive recollections provide for an opportunity to master anxiety by setting up counterphobic defenses. These views suggest that intrusive thoughts and images are adaptive because they result in a diminution of distressing emotions.

Unfortunately, the intrusions often evoke extreme levels of fear and anxiety that may preclude any natural process of habituation. Past psychological research, for example, has demonstrated that a stimulus such as a loud tone will result in habituation if it is not too intense, but sensitization if it is too intense,[42] suggesting that reliving high levels of emotional distress may not facilitate recovery. There may be some building of tolerance or mastery over anxiety over the long run, and psychological benefits may derive from directly confronting the emotional intensity of the traumatic experience.

Nevertheless, a more complete understanding of this curious repetitive phenomenon lies in recognizing the role of the actual images and recollections in light of the victim's coping dilemma postvictimization. The survivor must rebuild shattered assumptions; from prior assumptions and new, threatening data, the victim must arrive at a viable, assumptive world. Reexperiencing the event through unbidden thoughts and images is primarily in the service of this crucial cognitive reconstruction process.[43]

Each time the event is reexperienced, the new data can be "worked on," such that gradually the complementary processes of assimilation and accommodation can effectively meld the old and new. Representations of the traumatic event—through intrusive thoughts and images—provide a means for rendering closer and closer approximations of the new, threatening data and the old assumptions, such that ultimately assimilation of the traumatic experience and accommodation of prior assumptions can be successfully completed.

Kai Erikson noted that the survivors of Buffalo Creek seemed preoccupied with death images and constantly relived the flood:

> The survivors were still trying to come to terms with that gruesome reality. Schoolchildren drew pictures of bloated bodies in oceans of ink-black water; adults found themselves reviewing the old scenes again and again in their minds. And if their interest in the topic almost seemed to approach a macabre attraction, a perverse compulsion, it only indicates that the task of resolution is very hard.[44]

The work of Mardi Horowitz[45] is particularly enlightening regarding the crucial role of cognitive processing for understanding the repetitive, intrusive images and thoughts of trauma victims. Horowitz discusses a "completion tendency" in humans. He cites the work of George Mandler,[46] who observed that once an organized response is interrupted, there is an increased state of arousal, and the organism is motivated to complete the plan or program so as to terminate this distress. Similarly, he cites Kurt Lewin, who proposed that initiating a plan to reach a goal produces a tension system that continues until the goal is reached. People thereby have a tendency to complete what they have begun. Further, according to the Zeigarnik effect in psychology, people have a tendency to remember uncompleted tasks better than completed ones. For Horowitz, the "repetition of representation" seen in trauma victims represents this completion tendency:

> One key assumption in the following model is that there is a type of memory with motivational properties in that this memory tends to investigate a "next step" in cognitive processing. Because of this intrinsic property it will be labeled as active memory. The assertion is that *active memory storage has an intrinsic tendency towards repetition of representation of contents until the contents held in active memory are actively terminated.* A second key assumption is that *this tendency to repetition of representation is part of a general tendency towards completion of cognitive processing, and hence that completion of cognitive processing is what actively terminates a given content in active memory storage.*[47]

Consistent with the present perspective, Horowitz maintains that "completion" occurs when "differences between new information and enduring schemata" have been resolved.[48] At that time, nonstressful events will be easily assimilated into one's cognitive schemas, and information in active memory will quickly be terminated. Information related to extremely stressful events, however, is not apt to be easily assimilated, and thus the "completion tendency" will maintain relevant codings of this information in active memory. These "actively stored contents" will be represented repeatedly, allowing for a progressive integration of the new information and old schemas. Recurrent, intrusive thoughts and images terminate when cognitive processing is completed—that is, when the old and new mesh and schemas are "up to date."

In the case of overwhelming life events, the victim's coping task is an extraordinarily difficult one, for it is the survivor's most fundamental assumptions that are at stake. There is a need for a trememdous amount of cognitive processing—for progressive attempts at integrating the data. Yet the images and recollections associated with the traumatic experience are intensely painful and threatening. Denial and emotional numbing generally protect the victim from such overwhelming emotions. Even when these involuntary avoidance processes are operative, victims also experience involuntary approach processes, intrusive experiences that force them to confront their traumatic life event. Survivors report having distressing, unbidden recollections, typically involving very vivid images and powerful memories, during both waking and sleeping hours.[49]

As the distressing emotions associated with these intrusive recollections increase, avoidance processes once again take over. As Horowitz notes, as unpleasant emotions increase "beyond the limits of toleration," controls are activated and the cognitive processing ceases. As the extreme fear and anxiety are reduced, the motivation for control operations is also reduced, and active memory is then able to reassert itself. Not surprisingly, then, among trauma victims, recurrent, intrusive thoughts and images typically alternate with periods of denial and emotional numbing.

The Need to Talk and
the Cognitive Benefits of Disclosure

Over time, as the trauma is increasingly processed and the victim is progressively less threatened by trauma-related material, repetitive re-experiencing is often transformed into an ostensibly more voluntary behavior, that of talking about the traumatic event. For some survivors, there is a seemingly insatiable need to talk about what happened, to tell people about their experience.[50] It is as if they feel coerced into talking. There is still a sense of having the traumatic event forced into consciousness, and this persistent need to talk, like intrusive recollections, is a sign of "incomplete processing" of the event.[51]

Intrusions in daily thoughts are typically visual memories and images of the traumatic event; now the survivor uses language to more completely process and ultimately transform the experience and its fundamental assumptions. This need to talk is yet another manifestation of the mind's motivation to confront, reconsider, and integrate the traumatic experience. Talking and language no doubt "unload" some of the emotion and arousal associated with the trauma, but again, a more fundamental role of this need to talk is probably best understood in terms of assimilating the traumatic experience and accommodating one's basic schemas. Now words rather than images provide the mental medium for processing the powerful data.

In speaking about an event, survivors can revise it in ways that make it more tolerable; they can impose some order on the experience, which may be far more reassuring than the disjointed images often forced upon them. Further, as Martha Wolfenstein has written:

> Speaking about the disaster, in contrast to being haunted by memories that come against one's will, provides the possibility of turning passivity into activity. In retelling an experience, we volun-

108

tarily reevoke it. Narration is thus like play in that one can assume control over the repetition of an event which in its occurrence ran counter to one's wishes. While, alone at night, one may dread the vivid revival of the experience, when telling it to others one wants to evoke it as vividly a possible. Here is again the turning of passivity into activity: from being the helpless victim one becomes the effective storyteller, and it is the others, the audience, who are made to undergo the experience.[52]

Talking about one's traumatic experience plays an adaptive role in coping. This derives in part from the social support that might be forthcoming as a result of sharing one's experience.[53] However, it is important to recognize that there are benefits to talking that are independent of others' responses, and these are the benefits derived from processing the powerful victimization. Recent work by psychologist James Pennebaker provides support for this cognitive reworking view. In a series of studies, Pennebaker and his colleagues[54] have demonstrated that disclosing a traumatic life event is associated with better health outcomes over time, despite increased arousal and negative mood immediately following the disclosure. What is particularly interesting about these studies, however, is that this health-related benefit of disclosure was found even in the absence of another person or audience (i.e., was unrelated to social support). In other words, writing about the traumatic event or talking into a tape recorder about one's experience was associated with these positive health effects as well. Talking or writing about the event was adaptive in the absence of any response or reaction from other people.

According to Pennebaker, the advantages of disclosure can be understood physiologically and cognitively. Physiologically, disclosure reduces the work of active inhibition, and inhibition is associated with short-term autonomic activity and long-term stress-related disease. Cognitively, he argues that by confronting the trauma, individuals are able to reframe and assimilate their experience. The translation into language may make a traumatic experience more understandable and circumscribed. Pennebaker notes that when we think about an event, we are likely to relive the same scenes over and over again in our mind. However, when we talk about the event, it is unusual and difficult to say the same thing to the same person again and again.

Intrusive thoughts and images, and even the victim's acute need to talk, signal trauma. They are evidence that an individual's inner world is in turmoil; the old and the new do not fit. Yet they also serve an adaptive function, that of providing a means for confronting and working on the new data. The cognitive processes initiated by the intrusive, repetitive representations may lead the victim to make revisions in the new data or the old schemas.

Over time, successful recovery should involve fewer and fewer episodes of intrusive thoughts and images. Once the traumatic event is integrated into one's assumptive world, repetitive reexperiencing of the event essentially ceases. This does not mean the victim will not think about the event, but that automatic, intrusive representations and an essentially forced need to talk about the event should not occur; rather, relatively nonthreatening recollections, images, and thoughts should occur naturally, in response to situations that are associated with the event.[55]

Intrusive Recollections, Problem-Solving, and Consciousness

The intrusive memories and images of survivors, as well as their acute need to talk, all entail repetitive reexperiencing of the trauma in consciousness. The individual who has just experienced a major negative event is confronted with an extremely difficult problem: that of constructing new schemas or basic assumptions that can account for prior experience and the new victimization. Why are images, thoughts, and memories forced into consciousness? Might consciousness play some special role in finding a solution to the victim's dilemma? Perhaps an answer to these questions, as well as a better appreciation of reexperiencing phenomena, can be provided from the broader perspective of human problem-solving.

Try to remember the last very difficult problem you tried to solve. Perhaps it was an interpersonal dilemma involving a friend or family member. Perhaps someone gave you a brain teaser that you believe tested your intellectual abilities. Perhaps you were writing something of importance and could not decide how to put your thoughts on paper. No matter what the problem, it is likely that you found yourself thinking about it a great deal. Much of the time, you may have chosen to think about the problem. Yet you probably found the problem popping into your head, even at the most inopportune times, when you were trying to go to sleep, when you were trying to concentrate on some other task you had to accomplish. You may have found yourself awakened in the middle of the night, thinking about the problem.

Consciousness is a powerful tool of the human mind. Although the bulk of our mental processing might be described as automatic and nonconscious,[56] there are clearly times when consciousness and the related process of attention are invoked. Thus, for example, consciousness is often called upon in the learning process, even though particular actions or thoughts may subsequently become unconscious and automatic once well learned, as in the case of driving a car. Consciousness also appears to play a role in storage and retrieval mechanisms of memory. Yet one of the most important functions of consciousness seems to involve problem-solving.

Consider the simple case of driving a car or playing an instrument (i.e., engaging in an automatic behavior). When an animal suddenly races across the road, or we strike a discordant musical note, we immediately become conscious of our actions. We are very aware of the unexpected event. We are confronted with a problem and must choose a remedial course of action. Consciousness plays a sort of "troubleshooting" function,[57] helping us arrive at solutions to our dilemmas, whether these involve correcting a misplayed musical note, making a decision when confronting a difficult choice, or repairing fundamental schemas that are no longer viable. In consciousness we can explore alternatives, see old constructs in a new light, try out possible solutions, put together seemingly disparate ideas, consider various ways of interpreting phenomena.

Certainly, there are times when we choose to attend to particular cognitions. In fact, we typically consider consciousness a mental state that is under our control, both in terms of when and what we think about. After all, we can say to ourselves, "Okay, now I would like to think about places in the world I would love to visit," and, lo and behold, visions of exotic countries and foreign cities begin to fill your mind. In an important sense, however, we do not choose consciousness when we are driving and see the animal in the road, nor do we choose it when trying to sleep and our problem engages us instead. It is certainly the case that the contents of consciousness are not always the product of will or intent,[58] and the intrusive recollections experienced by victims are an extreme case of unintended conscious thoughts. Yet whether intended or not, the work of consciousness makes an important contribution in the search for problem solutions.

The final solutions for difficult problems, or choices in the case of trying dilemmas, are not necessarily made in consciousness. The inputs from consciousness, however, are potent and important, and serve to guide subsequent work and solutions in nonconscious processing. In this vein, it is interesting to consider the work of scientists who, in many ways like trauma survivors, are faced with the problem of creating a comprehensive theory that describes reality. Generally, this demanding task is discussed in terms of a creative process that often involves some type of sudden illumination, as if consciousness plays little or no role. These are the "Aha" or "Eureka" experiences we hear and read about. Yet such experiences are typically the end result of a lengthy, complex process involving both conscious and nonconscious processing.

Thus, renowned mathematician Jules-Henri Poincaré notes that the role of the unconscious is uncontestable in mathematical creation and invention, but this unconscious work

> is possible, and of a certainty it is only fruitful, if it is on the one hand preceded and on the other hand followed by a period of conscious work. These sudden inspirations . . . never happen except after some days of voluntary effort which has appeared absolutely fruitless. . . . These efforts then have not been as sterile as one thinks; they have set again the unconscious machine and without them it would not have moved and would have produced nothing.[59]

Similarly, R. G. Gerard maintains that unconscious work proceeds on those problems important to the conscious mind, those problems about which we worry and care passionately. He, too, argues that work from the unconscious "hopper" is fed from and feeds back to conscious awareness. And Mary Boole uses the rumination of a cow as a metaphor for the alternate conscious and unconscious digestion of a problem. Scientific and mathematical creation do not wholly occur outside of consciousness; rather, consciousness is an important partner and powerful mental tool in the creative process.

The role of consciousness in problem-solving is also evident in the role played by dreams. Dreams have been regarded as a form of consciousness by some and unconscious processing by others, the difficulty arising from the recognition that we are often conscious of the content of our dreams, although the typical, "rational" processing of wakeful consciousness clearly does not characterize dreams. Regardless of how dreams are labeled, it is nevertheless the case that dreams may play a role in problem-solving and, as in the case of scientific creation and invention, the contents of wakeful consciousness play an important role in providing material for our dreams. The remnants of the thoughts and schemas that are activated during our waking hours are likely to become the material for our dreams. When reactivated in our dreams, the absence of real world constraints enables the mind to freely play and process the material, putting together disconnected images and sequences and providing, potentially, important new ways of seeing and considering the contents of consciousness.

Perhaps the most famous example of a dream providing the basis for a solution to a scientific problem is that of Friedrich August von Kekule. He had been struggling in his attempt to discover the chemical structure of benzene. Following days and days of thinking about the problem, von Kekule dozed and had a dream, which involved structures twisting in a snakelike motion, with one snake seizing its own tail and whirling around. He awoke and knew his problem was solved—his dream provided him with a visual analogy for the ring structure of benzene.[60]

Yet, again, Kekule had been preoccupied with finding a solution during his waking hours. Consciousness represents one response to problems and, in turn, is likely to serve to direct the efforts and energies of the mind, including particularly dreams and nonconscious processes, to aid in the search for a solution. Typically, the products of our mental activities, and not the actual activities themselves, are the contents of consciousness. The troubleshooting and directorial functions of consciousness work hand in hand with our nonconscious processes. And the transforming possibilities of dreams and nonconscious processing are again, in the end, subject to the critical eye of consciousness, where a critical eye can select final solutions and finished creations.

Somehow consciousness responds to stimuli—both internal and external—that signal change or disruption and are suggestive of a problem. Trauma victims need to reconstruct a believable, relatively non-threatening assumptive world. Negative emotions may signal the need to confront threatening material. Victims are also in a state of hyperarousal, for their external world now appears frightening and their internal world is in a state of disintegration. It is conceivable that this increased autonomic arousal serves as an internal trigger that forces victimization-associated cognitions into conscious awareness, far more often than might appear desirable. Such an arousal-consciousness link could largely be understood from an evolutionary perspective; arousal is a signal to an organism that some external event requires immediate attention. There is clearly an evolutionary advantage to attending to something we perceive as dangerous.

113

The generally high state of autonomic activity in victims may thereby force the traumatic event into consciousness—from intrusive images to virtually forced verbalizations. Here new ways of perceiving the traumatic experience can be considered, and further, the energies of nonconscious processing can be directed towards the material as well. The trauma representations will be worked on—at all levels of consciousness—such that ultimately, the restoration and reconstruction of survivors' basic beliefs about the world and themselves can be accomplished.

In comparing the process of coping with traumatic life events with the process of problem-solving, particularly scientific problem-solving, we should not lose sight of fundamentally important differences. Trauma involves powerful, negative emotions. Although scientists may experience frustration and anxiety in their attempt to find solutions, the order of magnitude of distress is wholly different. The trauma survivor is constantly confronting intensely emotionally laden material. As discussed above, one important protection in the problem-solving process for victims involves the operation of denial. Denial processes enable victims to "shut down the system" and confront the problem in small, manageable doses. The highly distressing nature of the material considered by victims distinguishes it in a very real way from that considered by scientists and innovative thinkers. Nevertheless, the problem-solving analogy for victims should not be lost, for it emphasizes the creative efforts that are involved in the fundamental task of survivors, rebuilding a viable assumptive world. The problem is intensely difficult, and the solution involves innovation and transformation in the basic schemas of victims. What is involved is no less than a creative process, though a particularly difficult and painful one. The ability to transform the experience, to reinterpret the powerful data, is ultimately related to survivors' success in resolving their intense crisis.

6

Rebuilding Assumptions
Interpreting the
Traumatic Experience

W e are all familiar with the metaphor of the half-full versus the
half-empty glass. The very same stimulus—a glass with water
up to its midpoint—can be interpreted positively or negatively, in
terms of what is present or what is absent. Examples of such optimistic
versus pessimistic differences in judgments are plentiful in our culture,
suggesting our implicit recognition of the important role played by
our interpretations of objects and events in our lives.

The central role of people's evaluations and interpretations runs like
a thread through the psychological literature on coping with stress. In
his pioneering work, Richard Lazarus has emphasized the fundamental importance of people's interpretations, or *appraisals,* in determining
their stress reactions.[1] Lazarus draws a distinction between two types
of appraisals, one involving judgments about whether the individual is
in jeopardy (i.e., primary appraisal), the other involving judgments
about the options and resources available for managing potential harm
(i.e., secondary appraisal). In the first instance, we make an appraisal
of whether a particular situation is stressful, benign, or irrelevant to
our well-being; we consider the question, "Am I in trouble?" No
psychological stress occurs, according to Lazarus, unless we perceive
the situation as being one of harm, threat, or challenge. In the latter
case, we recognize that there is a potential for harm, but we also
recognize the potential for mastery and gain in the situation.

The second type of appraisal concerns the question of what we can do about the situation we have just deemed harmful, threatening, or challenging. We consider our past experiences, our personal resources, and the resources that might be provided by others. According to Lazarus, we experience stress when there is a negative balance between the demands of the situation and the resources we have available.

The significance of Lazarus's contribution lies in its emphasis on the cognitive mediation of stress and coping outcomes. In other words, what we think, our interpretations, makes a great deal of difference in how we react to and ultimately adapt to stressful situations. The very same situation will have different meanings for different people. The pop quiz will be interpreted as threatening by some college students, as a challenge or an opportunity for positive results by others.[2] A loud noise while walking alone in the woods would be frightening to some, irrelevant to others. A sharp pain in one's arm might be interpreted as an indication of serious threat or irrelevant to one's well-being.

Interestingly, the situations or events that trigger a traumatic stress response are those that are least likely to be subject to alternative interpretations regarding the presence of threat.[3] These events, which cause such tremendous cognitive and emotional upheaval, are those that "would be markedly distressing to most people."[4] Yet in addition to primary and secondary appraisals that result in the experience of extreme stress (i.e., extreme threat and/or harm and inadequate resources), a third type of appraisal process becomes very evident in the case of traumatic events. These are not the appraisals that occur during the initial confrontation with the traumatic situation, but rather interpretations and redefinitions[5] of the event that occur over the course of coping and adjustment. Essentially, these are cognitive strategies that ultimately contribute to the difficult process of rebuilding the victim's inner world.

Finding Benevolence, Meaning, and Self-Worth

Much of what we call evil is due entirely to the way men take the phenomenon. It can so often be converted into a bracing and tonic good by a simple change of the sufferer's inner attitude from one of fear to one of fight; its sting so often departs and turns into a relish when, after vainly seeking to shun it, we agree to face about and bear it cheerfully, that a man is simply bound in honor, with reference to many of the facts that seem at first to disconcert his peace, to adopt this way of escape.

—*William James*[6]

Although James is not specifically referring to traumatic victimizations here, his belief that people can alter the sting of events by a change of inner attitude is nevertheless quite appropriate in this context. Survivors of traumatic events seek to arrive at a new, nonthreatening assumptive world, one that acknowledges and integrates their negative experience and prior illusions. Cognitive strategies represent one extremely important means by which survivors facilitate this demanding reconstruction process. These are motivated cognitive strategies, not in the sense of conscious manipulation, but rather in the sense that their effect is strategic; they facilitate the coping process by better enabling victims to reformulate a view of reality that can account for the victimization and yet not be wholly threatening.[7]

These strategies are not consciously "willed"; survivors do not say to themselves, "I have to rebuild my assumptions; perhaps a change in this belief or a new interpretation of that event would help." Rather, as in the case of intrusions and denial, these are natural products of a system, the human organism, that is seeking to reestablish equilibrium following a crisis. They are reflections of an essentially healthy system striving to recover from a dramatic blow.

How do these motivated cognitive strategies facilitate the rebuilding process? They entail reevaluations and appraisals of the traumatic event that maximize the possibility of perceiving benevolence in the world, meaning, and self-worth—the very assumptions that were so seriously challenged by the victimization. Within the context of the victimization itself, survivors create and discover evidence of a benevolent world, a world in which events are meaningful and make sense, and in which they can view themselves with pride and feelings of self-worth.

Rebuilding shattered assumptions involves somehow integrating the old and the new, and this process is far easier when the distance between the two can be bridged. Most fundamentally, these motivated cognitive strategies function so as to minimize the differences between prior positive assumptions and the negative assumptions implied by the traumatic event. These appraisals may look odd or unexpected from an outsider's perspective. Yet they are creative reformulations representing the unique perspective of the survivor, a perspective that is not shared by the outside observer. These cognitive strategies reflect the basic motivation of a system to reestablish cognitive stability and emotional health.

There are three major strategies used by survivors. One involves appraisals based on comparisons with others; more specifically, survivors compare their experiences with the real or imagined outcomes of others, particularly other victims. A second strategy entails interpretations of one's own role in the victimization and involves instances of self-blame. A third process focuses on reevaluations of the traumatic experience in terms of benefits and purpose, reflecting attempts at "meaning-making" by survivors. By engaging in one or more of these reappraisal processes, survivors ultimately facilitate the assimilation of their victimization. Survivors' reappraisals locate and create evidence of benevolence, meaning, and self-worth in the very events that first challenged and shattered these illusions.

Comparison Processes

We can all think of instances in which we felt very good or bad about ourselves because of our relative standing when comparing our performance to that of others—friends, classmates, co-workers. When considered in isolation our performance may seem fine, but once we are aware of how others have done, we may find our self-perceived success extremely short-lived. The B on an exam may be good or bad, depending upon how others in the class performed, or, more particularly, on how relevant others (e.g., one's friends, or "the smart kids") did on the same test. People in our society may differ in terms of what they value, but we generally determine our "success" by comparing ourselves with others along this valued dimension. Although comparisons in terms of the accumulation of material goods too often seem the basis for comparison in Western society, it is nevertheless the case that we compare ourselves with other people across a variety of dimensions.

Such comparison processes are an important means of determining our "success" or "failure." Intellectuals may compare in terms of how much one knows or how many books one has read; artists may compare in terms of exhibits—where and how many; athletes may compare in terms of important stats or records. In all cases, comparison of outcomes is more likely to be the norm than the exception in people's lives.

The notion that people evaluate their outcomes by comparing them with that of others has been a major tenet of social psychological theory and research since Leon Festinger's discussion of "social comparison theory" in 1954.[8] Work on social comparison has been based largely on Festinger's prediction that people evaluate their situation or performance by comparing themselves with similar others. Festinger argued that we are motivated by a desire for accurate self-evaluations of our attitudes and abilities. He also discussed our drive to compare "upwards," with those who have performed somewhat better than we in particular domains.

Recent work in social psychology has distinguished between self-evaluation and self-improvement as motivations for comparison processes.[9] In self-evaluation, we compare ourselves with similar others to obtain diagnostic information, primarily about our abilities. We also engage in comparison processes for purposes of self-improvement, as a way to obtain information about how to perform better. In such cases, we tend to look towards those who perform better than we do, reflecting Festinger's "unidirectional drive upward" in comparisons. In this way, we can potentially obtain information about how to improve our outcomes.

Unfortunately, most work on social comparison would lead us to conclude that people always seek comparisons with similar or "better" others, and feel good about such comparisons. It is as if we are solely information processors who seek diagnostic information and data as to how to improve our performance on tasks. Until recently, little attention was given to the more emotional side of the comparison experience. Clearly, there are times when it does not feel good to compare ourselves with others, particularly similar or more successful others, and we struggle to avoid social comparisons.[10]

Further, there are times when we are motivated by a different need—self-enhancement—in comparing ourselves to others. These are times when we want to feel better about ourselves, when we want to do something that is emotionally palliative.[11] Thus, as psychologist Thomas Wills has argued, when we are experiencing negative emotions or find ourselves threatened, we engage in "downward comparisons."[12] We enhance our sense of well-being by comparing ourselves with people whose outcomes are not as good as our own. Benjamin Franklin seemed well aware of this strategy when, in 1757, he wrote in *Poor Richard's Almanac:* "To be content, look backward on those who possess less than yourself, not forward on those who possess more."

By comparing ourselves with less fortunate others, we manage to feel better about our own situation. It is not that people like to see others suffer; rather, people prefer this when they themselves are suffering.[13] Not only does misery love company; misery loves more miserable company.

An interesting aspect of social comparison processes is the apparent freedom we have in choosing relevant comparisons. Although downward comparisons can occur on a passive basis, in which people take advantage of opportunities that naturally present themselves, such comparisons can also be made actively.[14] In other words, when threatened, we may seek comparisons with others who are worse off than we are. Certainly, we may not be aware of why we are making such comparisons; in other words, we may not feel as if we are intentionally choosing others to make ourselves feel better (although we may know we could do so).[15] Yet choose others we do, and who or what we choose makes a difference.

In the end, our comparisons are not limited by our knowledge or awareness of real people in worse circumstances, but by our ability to imagine such people and circumstances. Following traumatic life events, involving extremely negative outcomes, survivors demonstrate the pervasiveness of downward comparisons. Victims compare their own experience with that of real or hypothetical others as one means of feeling better about themselves and their world.[16]

"It Could Have Been Worse"

Survivors of extreme negative events often compare their lot with that of others who have experienced the same type of victimization. Yet in making these comparisons, they seem to focus on less fortunate others. Thus, rape victims frequently compare themselves with those who have endured greater physical injury or degradation, or were killed.[17] Victims of natural catastrophes often look to others to minimize their self-perception of loss; these survivors focus on those who have lost more. For example, survivors of tornadoes, floods, and earthquakes who have lost physical possessions compare themselves to those who have lost loved ones; and those who have lost a loved one turn to those who have lost entire families. Young adults who were paralyzed from the waist down (i.e., paraplegics) in freak accidents compare themselves to others who were completely paralyzed (i.e., quadraplegics) from similar accidents.[18]

Surely some downward comparisons are easier to make than others; some outcomes, on their face, do not appear as awful as others. It is thus no doubt easier for some people to compare with less fortunate victims than it is for others. Nevertheless, there is an additional factor that should be considered when we compare ourselves with others, which is that we are also free to choose the dimension along which we compare ourselves. Shelley Taylor has written about this strategy of focusing on attributes that make a person seem advantaged. In other words, it is not a particular person but a particular dimension, or attribute of a person, that is compared. Thus, in her own study of women with breast cancer, Taylor found that a woman who was treated with a lumpectomy compared herself to women who had mastectomies; a woman who had a mastectomy compared herself to women who had greater lymph node involvement; an older woman compared herself to younger women, claiming that "To lose a breast when you're so young must be awful"; and a married woman compared herself to single women who must deal with dating. The women who were the worst off in Taylor's study compared themselves to those who appeared to be dying and/or were in considerable pain, and even some who were dying focused on their success in achieving spiritual peace, which others might never reach.[19] As long as we pick the right attribute or dimension, we may be able to perceive ourselves as better off than someone else.

At this point, it may be apparent that the comparison other may not be an actual person. In other words, survivors may not have a particular individual in mind when making their comparisons, but may instead use instances they have read or heard about or simply believe exist. When we make social comparisons we are not limited by our actual knowledge of specific others but rather by our willingness and ability to create comparisons in our mind that enable us to view our own outcomes in a more positive light. The married breast cancer patient may not have a specific single woman in mind when making comparisons about outcomes; she may simply believe that such women exist. The rape victim who compares herself to a survivor who has suffered greater physical injury or degradation may not have a specific other in mind, but she knows that such women exist or are likely to exist.

Comparisons with these hypothetical others suggests another, related strategy survivors use for purposes of social comparisons, and this involves simply imagining worst outcomes. In this case, the victim compares his or her misfortune to what *could* have happened. In other words, the comparison is with a worse scenario that is conjured up in one's mind; compared to what could have happened, the victim feels somewhat reassured.

This creation of hypothetical worse worlds[20] is reflected in the common reaction of many victims, "I was lucky. It could have been a lot worse." We have had rape victims, cancer patients, and paralyzed victims of freak accidents tell us how lucky they were that their situation was not worse. Each had imagined worse outcomes than they had experienced. This feeling of luck is a recurrent theme of many disaster victims. They regard their situation in a way that demonstrates the relative benevolence of it having happened as it did.

The comparison processes engaged in by trauma victims often look somewhat surprising or odd to nonvictim observers. Nonvictims, however, are comparing the survivors' outcomes with no victimization—with benign outcomes—and thus the lot of victims falls far short of these expectations. Yet, for survivors who have experienced extremely negative outcomes, the recognition that something worse could have happened becomes a relevant basis for comparison.

"I'm Coping Well"

In our studies with survivors of extreme negative events, we have been struck by the number of people who have indicated that they feel they are coping very well. They tell us that, given the circumstances, they are doing well. And they go on to tell us of others who are having a more difficult time coping with their rape, accident, or disease. Often these "others" are, again, not actual people but hypothetical individuals, reflecting the survivors' beliefs about coping norms. Victims are interested in knowing how others react, yet norms about how others are doing are simply not available and survivors therefore create their own normative standards of adjustment for purposes of comparison. Victims want to believe they are coping well, and thus "the manufactured normative standards of adjustment may be defined in such a way that one's own adjustment appears exceptional."[21]

Processes involving comparisons—with actual or hypothetical people, outcomes, or norms—are important means of minimizing the threat and malevolence of one's own victimization. By choosing the bases for their comparisons, survivors create the possibility for reevaluating their situation and themselves in a more benign fashion. Their world does not seem quite so hostile after these appraisals of the traumatic event. And it is very self-enhancing to perceive oneself as strong and capable enough to deal with an extreme situation, an evaluation often derived from comparisons with hypothetical norms of adjustment. These strategically constructed social comparisons are an important means of coping with traumatic victimization, and reflect not simply the needs of an organism striving to adjust, but the remarkable creativity and flexibility inherent in the coping process.

Self-Blame

Survivors use comparison processes in evaluating their situation and their coping success. They ask, "How bad was this event? and "How am I doing?" These are questions that largely address concerns about benevolence and self-worth. Survivors also ask questions more directly related to meaning. "Why did this event happen?" "Why did it happen to me?" In asking and answering these attributional questions, victims are confronting the trauma-related material and trying to make sense of it.

One common response to these questions involves self-blame. I would like to suggest that survivors' self-blaming strategies, too, reflect adaptive motivations by survivors, for they actually entail perceptions of the traumatic event that strive to minimize threat to the survivor's conceptual system.

The suggestion that self-blaming strategies follow from a positive, adaptive impulse by victims—that of rebuilding a valid, comfortable assumptive world—immediately raises people's hackles. Such a claim seems to imply a prescription, that victims therefore should blame themselves. At the outset, then, let me clarify my position. By positing that self-blame may reflect positive impulses, I in no way believe that victims are to blame for their victimization. As will be discussed in the next chapter, victim-blaming is all too common and is extremely unwarranted. In this chapter we are considering appraisals and interpretations, and in the case of self-blame, I believe that the victim's response often reflects a need to minimize the threatening, meaningless nature of the event.

Survivors are motivated by recovery, not accuracy in attributions. Victims do not alter the events themselves, but rather their interpretations of the events. Reasonable people can always disagree about interpretations. Post-trauma, however, the interpretations of victims are apt to be motivated, to a considerable extent, by the need to assimilate and integrate the traumatic experience.

The reactions of observers do not reflect this same motivation for recovery. If survivors blame themselves, this in no way gives others the right to also blame them. It is important to differentiate between survivors' reactions and observers' reactions, for their motivations and implications are very different.[22] Thus, if I belittle myself, this does not give another person the right to belittle me. Consider the different implications of an individual's own statement, "I can't believe how stupid I am!" and the reaction of another person, "I can't believe how stupid you are!" The self-statement might reflect a desire to motivate onself to do better; the other-statement is likely to be an outright condemnation. Most assuredly, the meaning of the two is unlikely to be the same. What we say about ourselves means something very different from what it would when said by another.

In order to make the case for the adaptive motivation behind survivors' self-blame, let me provide a mini-history of my own interest in this area. In the mid-seventies, Camille Wortman and I conducted a study on reactions of paralyzed survivors of accidents.[23] I interviewed, at length, each of these men and women, and they also completed a number of psychological scales. One of the findings from this study was, somewhat surprisingly, that self-blame was associated with coping success, as rated by a social worker and nurse familiar with each individual. Further, the amount of self-blame reported in the study was far greater than any "objective" measure of blameworthiness would suggest. Most of these men and women were involved in freak accidents. Many had been passengers in automobiles that were in serious accidents, several were engaged in "benign" activities they had often done previously, such as diving into a familar pool or playing a sport on a high school team. There were freak industrial accidents and a random gunshot on a city street. This was not a blameworthy group by anyone's standards, and yet fully 63 percent of the sample blamed themselves at least in part for their accident.

It was not long after this that I became involved in a number of projects related to women's victimizations, and particularly research and work with rape victims. Again, as I spoke at length with these women, self-blaming statements were all too frequent. The psychological literature on rape acknowledged self-blame by rape victims as a pervasive phenomenon,[24] but it was apparent that these self-attributions were not accurate appraisals of the woman's causal role in the assaults. Even the National Commission on the Causes and Prevention of Violence concluded that only 4.4 percent of all rapes are precipitated by the victim.[25] Yet I was very concerned about the interpretations provided for this self-blame, for the primary explanation involved some form of female masochism; masochism was presented as a female trait, albeit one that is socialized by our culture,[26] and, for many, seemed to provide a complete explanation for rape victim's self-blame. Unfortunately, such a perspective may unwittingly perpetuate a view of women too consistent with the role of victim. Further, this perspective also overlooks the fact that self-blame is a common response of both men and women to many types of victimization. Thus, self-blame is often expressed by survivors of all sorts of crimes, accidents, and diseases.[27]

Why is there so much self-blame? Post-trauma, the survivor's efforts are largely aimed at rebuilding a viable assumptive world, and it is from this perspective, I believe, that self-blame can best be understood. Self-blame reflects the struggle of survivors to make sense of their victimization, to understand "Why me?" and minimize the possibility of randomness in their world. Our Western conceptions, and the survivors' earlier assumptions about the world, suggest answers related to justice and control: The victim deserved it because of who he or she is, or because of what he or she did or failed to do.

Given the basic assumptions about the benevolence of the world, the meaningfulness of the world, and self-worth, self-blame is most directly tied to the need to maintain or reestablish meaningfulness. Yet it may appear odd that victims would engage in these self-attributions, for while satisfying the survivor's need for meaning, they seem to further disrupt beliefs about self-worth. After all, the popular conception of self-blame is consistent with work on depression, in which self-blame is associated with low evaluations of one's worth and harsh self-criticism.[28] Why rebuild one assumption only to leave another shattered? One could argue that rebuilding one is better than none; in other words, if a victim's assumptions about meaning and self-worth are ruptured, rebuilding a meaningful world is an important step on the road to recovery.[29] No doubt this is the case for some survivors. Yet it does not describe the experience of many other survivors who, I believe, engage in a type of self-blame that facilitates the reestablishment of a meaningful world, while at the same time not negatively affecting their perceived self-worth.

Two Types of Self-Blame

There are, in other words, at least two types of self-blame, one that I have labeled "characterological self-blame," the other "behavioral self-blame."[30] Characterological self-blame is esteem-related and corresponds to the more popular notions of self-blame associated with depression. In this case, the blame is focused on the individual's character or enduring qualities. Behavioral self-blame, on the other hand, is control-related. Blame is focused on one's own behavior, the acts or omissions a person believes causally contributed to an outcome.

The distinction between these two self-attributional strategies is represented in the differences between the following two statements by rape victims: "I should not have gone back to his apartment" (behavioral self-blame) and "I am a very bad judge of character" (characterological self-blame).[31] Although both involve person-outcome contingencies (i.e., nonrandomness), behavioral self-blame also invokes beliefs about control. There is something one could have done differently to have altered the outcome.

Behavioral self-blame reflects the reestablishment of meaning primarily through control-related attributions for the victimization. Further, the behavior is not generalized to the whole person—that is, it is as if the person made a mistake, or did a stupid thing, but is not a bad or stupid person.[32] In fact, survivors who engage in behavioral self-blame generally say, "I should have done . . ." or "I should not have done . . ." using the past tense in their presentation. Characterological self-blamers, on the other hand, generally use the present tense, "I am . . ." or "I am not. . . ."[33] The former are relatively narrow, specific assessments that do not describe oneself in the present, whereas the latter reflect a present self-definition, a more general, global assessment of the self.

It is important to note that it is not simply behavioral self-blame that may reflect adaptive motivations for reestablishing meaning through control beliefs but rather behavioral self-blame in the absence of characterological self-blame. People can believe they have done careless things without believing they are careless people. The opposite, however, is unlikely. People who believe they are careless are likely to believe they have done careless things. Thus, people who engage in characterological self-blame almost necessarily also engage in behavioral self-blame. It is behavioral self-blamers who do not also engage in characterological self-blame who are likely to be engaging in the most adaptive attributional strategy.[34]

The adaptive impulse behind behavioral self-blame is evident in survivors' control-related appraisals of their own role in the victimization. As Andra Medea and Kathleen Thompson write in the case of rape: "If the woman can believe that somehow she got herself into the situation, if she can make herself responsible for it, then she's established some sort of control over rape. It wasn't someone arbitrarily smashing into her life and wreaking havoc."[35] Or, as Carolyn Hursch writes, referring to self-blame: "If you have been raped and are still alive, you will forever ask yourself why you didn't fight harder, why you didn't think of some trick to break away, or why you didn't engage in some other act—obvious to you now—which would have prevented rape."[36]

Based on their work with victims of crime, Morton Bard and Dawn Sangrey suggest that victims often seem very eager to take responsibility and point to behaviors (leaving a window open, walking in a dangerous neighborhood, forgetting money for a taxi) for which they now fault themselves. Even when these crime victims see the crime as some form of punishment, it is generally regarded as a punishment for some prior behavior (e.g., having had a fight with one's spouse).

In a study of parents of children with leukemia, psychologists found that parents often blame themselves for their child's illness. They seem eager to try to prove that something they did or failed to do might have been responsible for their child's illness. In blaming themselves, they thereby defend against "the intolerable conclusion that no one is responsible, and therefore that neither expiation nor propitiation can undo a malign event which has come about impersonally and meaninglessly."[37] Similarly, victims of disease often blame themselves for behaviors they believe brought about the disease, such as not eating healthy foods or working too hard; or they see it as divine retribution for past transgressions.[38]

In reviewing the responses of the paralyzed accident victims, we found that they, too, appeared more likely to engage in behavioral than characterological self-blame. These were individuals who would not walk again, and thus the adaptive motivation behind this attribution was unlikely to be that they would change their behavior in the future and thereby prevent future recurrences of the negative outcome. Instead, the use of behavioral self-blame here requires a broader understanding of the phenomenon, one that involves a more complete picture of the survivor's coping task.

This attribution fits into the larger, richer efforts of survivors to rebuild their inner world following traumatic life events. This is only one piece of the greater picture, yet it is a reflection of the larger task— to integrate their victimization by somehow getting it to fit better with prior self- and worldviews. The survivor is striving to find benevolence, meaning, and self-worth, while having been forced to confront malevolence, meaningfulness, and helplessness. By interpreting an event so as to maximize control, meaningfulness and helplessness are minimized. Most important, the possibility of cognitive-emotional integration of the event is maximized.

By holding onto earlier beliefs about control, survivors are on the road to reestablishing a viable assumptive world. The world is perceived as one in which they can positively affect outcomes and the course of events. The world reflected in these beliefs is no longer extremely threatening, for a person can, from this perspective, engage in precautionary behaviors and thereby prevent negative outcomes in the future; people, in other words, continue to control their outcomes.

Victims can maintain a belief in a controllable world, one in which behaviors cause outcomes. As a result, they may engage in new behaviors to protect against misfortune and ensure safety. As Bard and Sangrey write:

> Believing that they know the cause and that the cause is in themselves, these victims can plan for their experience to be a lesson that will not be repeated. Such planning can be useful in reordering the fragmented self because it allows the victim to feel that he or she has regained control.
>
> A person who has been victimized may become obsessed with preventive measures after the crime. Some burglary victims invest in elaborate new locks or alarm systems. Many people who have been assaulted on the street change their patterns of travel; they may walk several blocks out of their way to avoid the street where the crime occurred. Some people buy guns or sign up for self-defense courses. . . .[39]

The cancer patient who blames past eating behavior will change these, and the rape victim who tells herself she should not have hitchhiked will avoid doing so in the future. Although these behavior changes may reduce the future probability of cancer or rape somewhat, they will not reduce the probability to zero.[40] Nevertheless, to believe one can make a difference is very comforting. This is the belief structure of nonvictims who assume they are relatively invulnerable. By engaging in behavioral self-blame, victims are reestablishing some sense of invulnerability, a belief in person-outcome contingency.[41] The importance of understanding self-blaming strategies within the larger framework of the survivor's cognitive-emotional task following a traumatic event raises questions about empirical research on self-blame. Over the past decade there have been numerous studies that have attempted to test the adaptiveness of behavioral self-blame. Researchers have found that behavioral self-blame is associated with positive coping outcomes, although not consistently.[42] In these same studies, results have consistently shown that characterological self-blame is associated with poor coping outcomes.[43]

In these studies,[44] researchers typically measure people's attributions (including, particularly, behavioral self-blame) as well as psychological distress, depression, or symptomatology. Surely survivors' psychological distress is associated with far more than their attributional strategies. More important, however, it is essential to recognize that those who are most distressed may be those who most need to engage in behavioral self-blame.[45] Those whose conceptual world has been most ruptured may be those with the greatest need to rebuild using a number of cognitive strategies, including self-blame.

From this perspective, it is naive to assume that behavioral self-blame would be associated with decreased distress or fewer psychological symptoms measured at the same point in time. This would be the case when the self-blame and other strategies are beginning to assist the victim's task of integrating the new data. The benefits of behavioral self-blame, however, may be apparent at some later time. Similarly, James Pennebaker's work has shown that self-disclosure is associated with immediate increases in distress but better long-term outcomes.[46]

The benefits of self-blame would be evident at the point, arrived at over time, when the survivor's assumptive world is reestablished and integrated. Although this process may be facilitated by behavioral self-blame, this would only be a small piece of the picture and would be apparent only in longitudinal studies that tapped attributional strategies within the far richer context of the victim's coping task and coping efforts. Behavioral self-blaming strategies should be used less over time, as the traumatic event is integrated into the survivor's inner world.

It is probably apparent that it may be easier to invoke behaviors as a contributing cause for some victimizations as compared with others, and thus the strategic use of behavioral self-blame may be easier under some circumstances than others, just as strategic social comparisons may become more difficult the more extreme and severe one's own victimization. Whereas the woman who has been raped while hitchhiking may find it relatively easy to focus on her behavior, the woman who is raped while sleeping in her bed in her locked home will have a far more difficult time doing so. Similarly, the disease victim who has never paid attention to health-related behaviors may focus on past acts or omissions (e.g., smoking, poor diet, lack of exercise), but this would be far more difficult for the individual who has attended to all the obvious health behaviors and yet has been diagnosed with a life-threatening illness.

There is empirical evidence that victims who have engaged in the safest, most cautious behaviors are often those who have the most difficult time coping. In a study of rape victims, for example, women who experienced the most extreme psychological distress were those who had followed their personal "rules of safety" for avoiding rape and who were, therefore, in an apparently safe situation at the time of the attack.[47] For some survivors, behavioral self-blame is less available as a means for understanding their misfortune. Nevertheless, to the extent that victims use this strategy, the perceived randomness of the negative outcome is minimized.

Behavioral self-blame is not essential for coping with victimization. Clearly, many survivors do fine without it. I would certainly not recommend that survivors who do not engage in behavioral self-blame be taught to do so. These are individuals who are tackling the coping task with other, conceivably more personally compatible, strategies and processes. The only clinical prescription that one might derive from this discussion of self-blame would be that of helping survivors who are already manifesting characterological self-blame to transform this attribution to behavioral self-blame. This would counter the overgeneralization and self-abasement of characterological self-blaming strategies and still provide a means for addressing the meaning-related concerns of survivors. Self-blame attributions are not the only way that survivors can seek to reestablish meaning following their victimization. Before discussing these other paths, however, let's briefly explore a phenomenon known as "survival guilt," a response related to self-blame.

Survivor Guilt

Traumatic events such as the concentration camp experience, bombings and atomic disasters, natural and technological disasters, and life-threatening disease epidemics strike a group of people. Although the question "Why us?" may be asked, the disturbing question "Why me?" is frequently posed by the individual who has experienced victimization with others but has survived while others have lost their lives. "Why have I lived while others have not?" The answer to the "Why me" query for this population is similar to that for victims who have been singled out for victimization: self-blame, which in this instance has been labeled "survivor guilt."[48]

Following the Coconut Grove disaster, in which nearly two hundred people died when the Boston nightclub burned to the ground, survivors often blamed themselves for prior behaviors that they felt could have affected the outcomes of the fire for a loved one. Typical was the survival guilt of a young woman who had quarreled with her husband, who subsequently left and died in the fire; or that of a young man who was preoccupied with having fainted too soon to have saved his wife. As Erich Lindemann, who studied grief reactions after the fire, wrote: "The bereaved searches the time before the death for evidence of failure to do right by the lost one. He accuses himself of negligence and exaggerates minor omissions."[49]

These reactions suggest similarities between survivors of group disasters and the reactions of victims of individual victimizations. Both scan behaviors for acts or omissions that could have altered the outcome. Instances of survivor guilt appear in contemporary newspapers and magazines in discussions of reactions of air crash survivors. As the words of a survivor of the crash of Flight 232 in July 1989 indicated, the guilt often reflects a need to understand, and the belief that one did not do enough for those who perished:

> I feel guilt for surviving because I didn't help more. [She led her nephew Tom from the plane.] I've had a great life so far, and some of the children who died had only had ten years or less. Some of my belongings were recovered from the crash site, but I don't want them back. I don't want anything to remind me of the crash. . . . I wonder why I got so lucky. Why me?[50]

The pained words of a survivor of Hiroshima describe the degree of self-blame and self-reproach that can follow traumatic life events and one's personal survival:

> Those who survived the atomic bomb were people who ignored their friends crying out *in extremis;* or who shook off wounded neighbors who clung to them, pleading to be saved. . . . Those who survived the bomb were, if not merely lucky, in a greater or lesser degree selfish, self-centered, guided by instinct more than by civilization . . . and we know it, we who have survived. Knowing it is a dull ache without surcease.[51]

Here is a person who believes he could have done otherwise; he believes he could have saved some who were lost. The bombing of Hiroshima resulted in a great deal of survival guilt, involving what Robert J. Lifton has discussed as guilt over "survival priority." Lifton reports that many survivors felt guilty about the deaths of specific family members whom they were unable to help; others were guilty about the death of the "anonymous" dead. Survivors related how they would walk through the city and feel the eyes of the dead looking up at them for help.[52]

Those who survived the Nazi concentration camps often experienced intense survivor guilt as well. In many cases these survivors felt they had done something to save their own life at increased risk to others. The concentration camp experience was particularly conducive to these self-accusations, for competition for survival was essentially built into the experience. The epitome of such competition was the "selections," in which prisoners were brought before an official to have their fate decided by the point of a finger.

These survivors suffered so much. How, then, can we understand their guilt? Again, these are people crying out for some understanding of their world. The belief in our own ability to affect outcomes, to make a difference runs very deep. To a considerable extent the guilt experienced was a reflection of the survivor's need to believe that ultimately events are not completely random, that in the face of devastation and destruction people can still make a difference. As Yael Danieli has suggested in her work with concentration camp survivors, guilt is essentially an unconscious attempt to undo the utter helplessness of the victim's situation.[53] It is the survivor's form of behavioral self-blame: "If I had only done . . ." It is an attempt to survey what one could have done so that one can maximize any possibility of believing in a world that is not completely out of whack. Survival guilt represents the intense longings of the human psyche to understand the world, to search for meaning in the wake of suffering.

Transforming the Victimization: Benefits for Self and Others

Survivors' self-blame is an early response to victimization, virtually a knee-jerk reaction of an organism that has believed so fundamentally in personal control over outcomes, enveloped in a culture that has powerfully reinforced such a belief. In the face of the traumatic experience, the victim reviews his or her prior behaviors to see what could have prevented the victimization. Again, this is not to suggest that the victim is to blame but rather that the victim is trying to hold onto beliefs about control and a nonrandom world.

Over time, the survivor's motivation to reestablish fundamental beliefs in a meaningful world are also reflected in another particularly powerful cognitive strategy, one that also fosters beliefs about benevolence and self-worth. This is the survivor's process of accepting and ultimately transforming the traumatic experience by perceiving positive elements in the victimization. By engaging in interpretations and evaluations that focus on benefits and lessons learned, survivors emphasize benevolence over malevolence, meaningfulness over randomness, and self-worth over self-abasement. Such interpretations are extremely important components in the successful rebuilding of nonthreatening assumptions, and contribute significantly to the resolution of the survivor's existential dilemma.

It may seem remarkable, yet it is not unusual for survivors, over time, to wholly reevaluate their traumatic experience by altering the positive value and meaningfulness of the event itself. The victimization certainly would not have been chosen, but it is ultimately seen by many as a powerful, even to some extent worthwhile, teacher of life's most important lessons.

Suffering for a Purpose

According to Aristotle, to know an object is to understand the "why" of it, an undertaking that can be satisfied by four distinct "explanatory factors." These factors are generally known as Aristotle's four "causes" and refer, specifically, to the material from which the object is made (material cause), the form or pattern that it takes (formal cause), the agent by which the object was wrought (efficient cause), and the end or purpose for which it was produced (final cause). Typically, our everyday use of the term *cause* corresponds to Aristotle's efficient cause, that by which a change or state of being is wrought. It is this category of response to "Why" that is generally invoked when we want to explain why something happened.

In our daily actions and interactions, we typically understand events and outcomes in terms of efficient causality and generally perceive people as potent causal agents. Thus, we believe we control what happens to us, and the behavioral self-blame of victims reflects this orientation. One route to believing in a meaningful world—one in which events make sense—involves this type of efficient causality. Perceived control is maximized and perceived randomness is minimized.

A second route to belief in a meaningful world involves explanatory factors that are closer to Aristotle's final cause. Just as we see ourselves as the efficient cause of our own actions, we also typically see ourselves as engaging in behaviors for some end. In the case of victimization, although one's character may be regarded as an efficient cause of outcomes, our conceptions of justice also involve the notion that people get what they deserve. They may not have brought about the outcome directly, but something happened "for the purpose" of punishment or reward. The world is not random and outcomes make sense (i.e., are meaningful) because there is a meaningful link, established via the concept of purpose, between people and what happens to them.

Following traumatic life events, as victims are trying to reestablish a viable assumptive world, final causes often play a special role in people's construals of events. Meaning is often discovered or imposed through the concept of purpose.[54] It can be invoked whether or not a survivor engages in other strategies, including behavioral self-blame. For some, behaviors may not be "big" enough causes of such extreme negative events. In understanding why certain events happen, we often rely upon a resemblance criterion, which involves equating the relative sizes of causes and effects.[55] Thus, great events are believed to have great causes; the assassination of a powerful leader, for example, is regarded as the work of a conspiracy, not a single individual. Similarly, traumatic life events, with their huge impact, ought to have large causes. For many survivors, an understanding of their victimization in terms of some end or purpose provides this larger cause. Most important, it provides a way to reestablish meaning, as well as benevolence and self-worth, even in the direst of circumstances.

For what purpose? What types of interpretations do survivors make that facilitate rebuilding fundamental assumptions? Certainly, perceiving the victimization as a punishment, perhaps some divine punishment, might provide meaning, but it precludes seeing oneself and the world in a positive way. Thus a perception of the victimization as punishment is similar to characterological self-blame; both may satisfy questions of meaning but negatively affect assumptions about benevolence and self-worth. In answering the question "For what end?," survivors more frequently provide responses that have a positive impact on all three assumptions. These are responses that involve positive reevaluations of their victimization, or some aspect of their victimization. These are responses that involve the transformation of unavoidable suffering into suffering that is meaningful and significant.

Victor Frankl, a concentration camp survivor and founder of logotherapy, or meaning therapy, writes that meaning can be found through people's own attitudes, through the choices they make in facing tragedy:

> Even though conditions such as lack of sleep, insufficient food and various mental stresses may suggest that the inmates were bound to react in certain ways, in the final analysis it becomes clear that the sort of person the prisoner became was the result of an inner decision, and not the result of camp influences alone. Fundamentally, therefore, any man can, even under such circumstances, decide what shall become of him—mentally and spiritually. He may retain his human dignity even in a concentration camp. Dostoevski said once, "There is only one thing that I dread: not to be worthy of my sufferings." . . . It is this spiritual freedom—which cannot be taken away—that makes life meaningful and purposeful.
>
> . . . The way in which a man accepts his fate and all the suffering it entails, the way in which he takes up his cross, gives ample opportunity—even under the most difficult circumstances—to add a deeper meaning to his life.[56]

It is this ability to "add a deeper meaning to life" that is often reported by survivors. By choosing to positively construe aspects of their experience, they are able to find meaning in their suffering.

Although there may be numerous possibilities for positive interpretations of traumatic events, two types of interpretations are particularly common. The first involves evaluations of the victimization in terms of important lessons learned. Such interpretations entail perceiving the victimization in terms of benefits for oneself. The second entails understanding the traumatic experience in terms of its long-term benefits for others. This involves turning the victimization into a personally altruistic act.[57] Both categories of interpretation provide a response to the question "For what end?" and thereby enable some survivors, ultimately, to make sense of their powerful, painful experience. It didn't happen for nothing; it served some purpose.

Benefits to the Self: Lessons Learned

In the face of their tremendous psychological pain and suffering, many survivors, over time, are able to consider the "redeeming" value of their suffering in terms of lessons learned. Most often, these lessons involve either a newfound appreciation of life or a newfound appreciation of oneself.

Lessons About Life. The experience of victimization often leads survivors to a reconsideration of life and what is important. The confrontation with physical and psychological annihilation essentially strips life to its essentials, and for many survivors becomes a turning point from the superficial to the profound. Life takes on new meaning and one's own life is often reprioritized. Survivors, in essence, possess a new kind of wisdom, achieved at great cost, providing a sense of "enlightenment" about what is truly worthwhile in this world.

In our own work with survivors of life-threatening diseases, crimes, and accidents, men and women frequently reported that only now can they truly enjoy life because they no longer take it for granted, as they had done before. For many, this translated into a tendency to take life one day at a time and reordering their priorities so they spend far less time on insignificant tasks, such as household chores, and far more time on really important ones, such as spending time with their loved ones. Phrases such as the following were voiced again and again: only now do I really appreciate life; I no longer care if the kitchen is dirty or the beds aren't made; little things that seemed important to me don't seem important anymore.[58]

This feeling of reprioritizing is apparent in the words of an air crash survivor: "I think I recognize trivial things as trivial now. My point of reference has shifted dramatically since this. I'm not nearly so much in a hurry to get anywhere as I used to be. To me it reinforced the importance of doing the right thing, not the expedient or politically smart thing, but the right thing."[59]

A newfound ability to cherish and appreciate life is apparent in the words of individuals who have tested positive for the AIDS virus:

This forces you to investigate what you really want your life to be.

I can't say I'm glad I have it. But it has had its unknown and unseen gifts that have made my life better.

I was just existing; now my life is much fuller.

There is an immediate shift in your priorities. You don't realize how driven you are by the fear of death.

One becomes better about some of the planks, even platforms, on which life is built.[60]

Survivors often report that they now realize how precious life is. They often speak of their new appreciation for loved ones, the beauty of nature, for "what really matters." Many note how sad it is that it takes so devastating an experience to make people realize what is really important. From this perspective, the victimization rescues people from the perceived superficiality and emptiness of their prior existence. In the face of death, life is cherished and each day counts.

Lessons About Oneself. Another benefit often reported by survivors of traumatic events involves newfound knowledge and appreciation of themselves. Many trauma victims report changes in themselves as a direct result of their experience; they are now more compassionate, caring, patient human beings. They are better people now, as difficult as their path has been. A cancer patient explained how she is now much more aware of other people's problems; she is more sensitive and caring. A paralyzed accident victim told me that he was now aware of how wonderful it was to have a good mind; he had been so involved in sports and physical pursuits that he was unaware of how precious books and learning could be.

Survivors also frequently report that they are far stronger people now. This coincides with a "character building" aspect of suffering; what doesn't kill you will make you stronger. Individuals who have been victimized at the hands of others (e.g., rape victims, incest victims, victims of physical assault) often find it more difficult to reinterpret their experience in terms of a newfound appreciation for life; yet these survivors frequently report learning important lessons about their own personal strengths. In the words of two rape victims:

I feel much stronger now, even though I feel vulnerable to being raped in this culture. Part of that rape was to dominate and humiliate me and he didn't succeed at that. I came through with my integrity—I got through those months of hell.

The world is more dangerous to me now, but I am less vulnerable. I am stronger, able to handle anything . . . I have a certain pride in my own invulnerability; internally, I feel much stronger. I hold myself in higher esteem, and I'm also more sensitive to the feelings of others.

Despite the common recognition that the world is far more dangerous, there is a newfound awareness of one's own strengths and possibilities. One can endure "months of hell" and come through it stronger, more able to handle life's future difficulties.

The personal insights that are gained from one's traumatic experience have important parallels in religious teachings. Common religious themes emphasize the redemptive and strengthening role of suffering. Thus, the Koran suggests that suffering forms character and helps create a faithful disposition. Suffering also serves to expose character, in that it discriminates the sincere from the insincere.[61] In Christianity, the redemptive role of suffering is made extremely evident in the form of Christ. Christian teachings suggest that identification with Christ involves both suffering and consolation.

Further, according to John Bowker,[62] the supreme contribution of Judaism, represented in the Old Testament, is that suffering can be made redemptive; it can become the foundation for better things, collectively if not individually. This view of suffering cannot and should not be imposed on others; rather, it can be accepted for oneself. The collective benefits to be derived from suffering represent another means by which survivors of traumatic life events engage in meaning-making. From this perspective, purpose is understood in terms of sacrifice, an experience that will somehow benefit others.

Benefits to Others: Suffering as Altruism

Over the years I have remained particularly touched by a sensitive young man who had been paralyzed in a serious car accident. In the course of our conversation, he told me that he believed his misfortune happened because God probably needed his legs for someone else. Here was an individual trying to understand what happened to him, and his response involved an altruistic interpretation of his experience. The extent to which his belief "makes sense" to someone else is essentially irrelevant. Meaning-making is a very personal endeavor and a very powerful coping process after victimization.

Victor Frankl relates the transformative effects of an altruistic interpretation of misfortune when he discusses the case of an elderly doctor who remained intensely depressed two years after the death of his wife, whom he had loved above all else. Frankl asked the doctor what would have happened if he had died before his wife, and the doctor replied that this would have been terrible because his wife would have suffered. Frankl went on to point out that her suffering had been spared by her husband, who now had to pay by surviving and mourning her loss. The doctor shook Frankl's hand and calmly left his office. As Frankl writes, suffering in some way is no longer suffering when it finds a meaning such as sacrifice.[63]

Whether or not survivors can derive any benefits from the victimization for themselves, they can nevertheless choose to derive benefits for others. They can turn their traumatic experience into an altruistic outcome, either through interpretation or behavior. Thus the parents of children who died from leukemia may make sense of their loss by maintaining that their child's treatment contributed to medical knowledge that may help other children.[64] Concentration camp survivors sometimes interpreted their suffering in terms of "bearing witness," with the ultimate aim of protecting against future evils. Transmitting the horror of the camps to an unknowing world created purpose in their lives.[65]

Through changes in their own lives, survivors often transform the trauma into altruistic acts that provide some basis for meaning and value in their lives. Rape victims may work at rape crisis centers, and AIDS victims may work helping others diagnosed with the disease. Their tragic experiences have led some Vietnam veterans to help other vets through various outreach projects and to inform the public, particularly high school students, about the evils of war through veteran education projects.

Numerous scholarships have been established by parents in response to the loss of their children; Stanford University, for example, was originally a memorial from a grieving parent. Perhaps the best-known example of this active altruism is that of Norma Phillips, whose sixteen-year-old daughter was killed by a drunk driver. Ms. Phillips founded the organization Mothers Against Drunk Driving (MADD), which aims to prevent similar tragedies through alcohol education and the imposition of tougher penalties for drunk driving. Similarly, the mother of seventeen-year-old Lionel Harris, who was shot in a parking lot on the way home from a shopping jaunt, devoted herself to her Stop the Madness campaign. Ms. Harris has said that she didn't want her son to die in vain; she preferred to make the world safer than only to mourn.[66] By interpreting or acting on events in a way that benefits others, trauma survivors are able to establish some meaning and benevolence even in the midst of meaninglessness and malevolence.

Not a Chosen Fate, But Some Choice in Coping

The survivor's ability to focus on the positive, make sense of the victimization, and derive new personal strengths and insights about life should not blind us to the reality of the victim's suffering and distress. Traumatic victimization is painful and unwanted. These are not events that would be chosen, even in retrospect with the awareness of spiritual growth. As Harold Kushner wrote concerning his son's rare disease (involving rapid aging) and death in his popular book *When Bad Things Happen to Good People,*

> I am a more sensitive person, a more effective pastor, a more sympathetic counselor because of Aaron's life and death than I would have been without it. And I would give up all those gains in a second if I could have my son back. If I could choose, I would forego all the spiritual growth and depth which has come my way because of our experience, and be what I was fifteen years ago, an average rabbi, an indifferent counselor, helping some people and unable to help others, and the father of a bright, happy boy. But I cannot choose.[67]

Nevertheless, the fact that survivors are able to confront their experience and reestablish some of their prior assumptions in the face of their tragic experience suggests the awesome capacity of humans to survive and cope with extreme adversity.

Adaptive cognitive strategies such as downward social comparison, self-blame, and finding benefits for self or others are not used or used equally by all survivors. Thus, work by psychologist Roxane Silver has shown that some incest victims were still struggling to make sense of their victimization as much as fifty years after their experience. These women were unable to find meaning or see any good in their experience, and psychologically they remained distressed even years later.[68]

There are some events that are more difficult to reinterpret as positive, meaningful, or reflective of self-worth than others, and no doubt there are some people who are more capable of reappraising events in a positive, meaning-making way. Those who are able to use these strategies over time are better off for them. Their assumptions will ultimately be closer to their earlier illusions; their views of themselves and their world will become less threatening, more positive, and more supportive of personal optimism in one's ongoing interactions in the world.

Traumatic victimizations are unwanted and unchosen. Yet the cognitive strategies used by trauma survivors attest to the possibility for some human choice even in the face of uncontrollable, unavoidable negative outcomes. These choices reside in the interpretations and reinterpretations, appraisals and reappraisals, evaluations and reevaluations made of the traumatic experience and one's pain and suffering.

In the well-known poem "Invictus," William Ernest Henley wrote of his "unconquerable soul,"

It matters not how strait the gate,
   How charged with punishments the scroll,
I am the master of my fate:
   I am the captain of my soul.

I much prefer a line written by psychologist Philip Brickman, which better captures the reality of victimization: "Though not the master of one's fate, one may still be captain of one's soul."[69]

7

The External World
The Crucial Role of Other People

Although rebuilding one's assumptive world necessarily entails arduous, often inventive, internal processes, the important role of the external world should not be underestimated. The interactions of survivors with others provide crucial inputs into a system that is attempting to construct a valid, believable representation of reality. On an ongoing basis, victims are receiving information about the efficacy of their own behaviors and the reactions of other people. This feedback is entered into a cognitive-emotional equation that provides the basis for a new assumptive world.

The Importance of Action, No Matter How Minor

The behaviors and activities of survivors in the aftermath of trauma have the potential to provide some evidence of a world in which outcomes are not always unrelated to actions, a world in which the victim can sometimes, at least, make a difference. It is by taking action, rather than giving up, that survivors can get constructive feedback about the possibilities of a benevolent, meaningful world and a worthy, effective self.

An interesting analog to the need for action in the face of the helplessness experienced by many victims is the animal learning paradigm used by psychologist Martin Seligman and his colleagues in their studies of "learned helplessness."[1] Although much recent work has focused on people's attributions (i.e., their beliefs about the causes of their behavior) as a way of understanding helplessness in humans, the earliest studies were conducted with dogs. Seligman and his colleagues trained dogs to jump from one side of a shuttle avoidance box to the other to avoid electric shocks. Researchers then raised a barrier so that the dogs could no longer jump and avoid the shocks. Eventually, the animals stopped trying. When the researchers lowered the barrier, thereby again enabling the dogs to escape the shock, most continued to fail to try. They had learned to be helpless and lay in the box, passively taking the shocks. Only by physically dragging the dogs across the lowered barrier was the passivity and helplessness of most of these animals dissipated.

To the extent that survivors begin to have an impact on their environment, they perceive some small measure of self-efficacy[2] and control in a world that is not wholly random. Survivors have learned through painful personal experience that their fundamental assumptions were illusions. What remains for them to decide, ultimately, is the extent to which they were illusions. Is the world wholly malevolent and meaningless, for example, or were the earlier assumptions overgeneralizations, as we discussed in Chapter 1, which now need to be modified but not eliminated?

Through actions, even minor ones, survivors are able to see that at least some parts of their world may not be meaningless and malevolent, and that weakness and worthlessness need not be general characterizations of the self. By making appointments, doing work on the job, buying needed items, signing up for a class, writing a list, calling a phone number for some information, and driving one's car to a desired destination survivors are in essence getting new data. Their actions are producing results. Surely, these data are far, far less powerful than that of their traumatic life event, but though relatively weak, over time they provide an increasing amount of evidence that, at least within certain domains, the world is not wholly threatening.

The Crucial Role of Social Support

Following traumatic life events, victims receive feedback about the world and themselves not only from the impact of their own behaviors but also from the responses of other people. The restorative efforts of survivors to rebuild a valid and comfortable assumptive world are always embedded within the larger context of social relationships.

Certainly, we are not only biological and psychological beings but social ones as well. Our fundamentally social nature is evident in the aftermath of victimization, for the reactions of others are extremely important in understanding victims' post-traumatic adjustment.

Within psychology, there is an enormous literature on the importance of social support, and, perhaps not surprisingly, the bottom line of all of this work is that social support is strongly associated with psychological well-being. In a recent comprehensive review of empirical studies, Sheldon Cohen and Thomas Wills concluded that interpersonal support protects people from the potentially adverse effects of stressful events (referred to as the "buffering model of social support"), and integration in a social network has beneficial effects on people even in the absence of stressful events ("main-effect model").[3]

The benefits of social support are well-documented. The results of numerous prospective studies have shown that such support, typically measured in terms of reported social ties and help received, is positively related to mental health and negatively related to physical illness and mortality from all causes.[4] In studies of various crises, social support has consistently been associated with better adjustment, including decreased distress following job loss, increased rehabilitation success among the physically disabled, recovery from illness, and emotional adjustment among the bereaved.[5]

The positive impact of social support is also very evident in studies of trauma victims. For example, Ann Burgess and Lynda Holmstrom found that it was strongly associated with recovery from rape trauma. Rape victims lacking support were still symptomatic several months after their assault, whereas 45 percent of those who were supported had already recovered. Four to six years postrape, 80 percent of those with social support had recovered, whereas 53 percent of those who lacked support were still symptomatic.[6]

Similarly, John Wilson and Gustave Krauss found that post-traumatic stress was strongly associated with the extent to which Vietnam veterans felt psychologically isolated during the first six months of homecoming.[7] In fact, the presence of a rejecting environment at homecoming has been a consistent theme in literature on stress reactions among Vietnam veterans. The absence of support has generally been regarded as a serious obstacle to recovery for these veterans.[8]

There is considerable empirical evidence of the positive role of social support among victims of life-threatening diseases. Studies of cancer patients, for example, suggest that the amount of social support at time of diagnosis is positively associated with psychological well-being up to two years later, and even with patients' length of life.[9] In the case of large-scale natural or technological disasters, high levels of long-term psychological impairment have often been attributed to the destruction of one's psychological community that would otherwise have been available for support. Thus, in the Buffalo Creek disaster, Kai Erikson maintains that the total devastation of a "recovery environment" was related to the considerable psychological difficulties and distress still apparent two years after the flood.[10]

What is it about social support that is so beneficial? Psychologists have attempted to distinguish among various functions of social support, although most theorists recognize that these functions are not entirely independent of each other. Cohen and Wills discuss four different types of support resources: esteem support, instrumental support, informational support, and social companionship. In the case of esteem support, other people provide information that an individual is accepted, valued, and esteemed. Instrumental support involves the ability of others to provide financial assistance, material resources, and needed services. Informational support entails providing information that helps a person understand or cope better with a problematic event. This may include information or advice about the problem itself or about available resources. Social companionship is defined as having other people as companions for pleasurable, informal leisure activities, such as parties, travel, sporting events, or visiting.

Similarly, Roxane Silver and Camille Wortman have talked about different components of support: the expression of positive affect (e.g., information that one is cared for, loved, and respected); the acknowledgment of the appropriateness of a person's beliefs, feelings, or interpretations; the encouragement of open expression of these feelings and beliefs; the provision of material aid; and the provision of information that the person is part of a social network or support system.[11]

In the aftermath of traumatic life events, all of these resources—whether emotional, material, instrumental, informational—are apt to contribute positively to the survivor's psychological adjustment. Yet simply concluding that all are helpful does not provide any understanding of the special role of social support after victimization, for the responses of other people, particularly close family members and friends, plays a vital role in survivors' efforts to reconstruct their inner world.

The victim's coping task involves rebuilding a sense of self and world that are positive and nonthreatening. In Chapter 1, the significant role of other people—primary caregivers—was discussed in terms of the "data" provided in the initial process of building fundamental assumptions about the self and the world. "Good enough" caregivers provide infants with the preverbal recognition of benevolence, meaningfulness, and self-worth. The very origins of these assumptions are interpersonal in nature, having been derived directly from interpersonal experiences with another.

Following overwhelming life events, we are again involved in a process involving conceptual building, although now survivors are engaged in efforts to reconstruct rather than construct. Again, other people play a crucial and powerful role in the process. The survivor's social world is no doubt far larger than that of the infant, yet the importance of data derived from interpersonal interactions is similarly compelling. We are social animals, and interpersonal experiences have a major impact throughout the life span on the initial development, maintenance, and, when necessary, rebuilding of our world- and self-views.

Through their ongoing interactions with others, survivors learn directly about their world postvictimization. In a figure-ground sense, people are the moving figures that provide victims with the richest and most available information about their world. Through their interactions with other people, survivors simultaneously learn about themselves and their perceived self-worth in the eyes of others. Throughout development, people provide us with important information about who we are and what we are like; as captured in sociologist Charles Cooley's phrase "the looking-glass self,"[12] people are mirrors that enable us to view and understand ourselves. The reflections provided may be particularly important postvictimization, when questions about self-worth are powerful and pervasive.

Those close to the victim provide the most potent data available about the nature of the world and the worth of the individual victim, at a time when the victim is particularly sensitive to such information. If people fail to be supportive—if they turn away—what greater evidence is there that the world is truly malevolent and the victim is not a worthy individual? On the other hand, a warm, supportive environment provides strong, emotionally laden evidence that people are good, the world is not evil and meaningless, and the victim is worthy.

Positive, supportive reactions by others provide direct evidence—important data—to be entered into the victim's conceptual equation. Further, such social support provides the victim with a holding environment within which to do the necessary cognitive-emotional work without suffering further assaults or forcing further questioning. At a time when survivors are struggling to understand and reconstruct their basic beliefs about themselves and the world, the reactions of others, as in infancy, are fundamentally important.

Unfortunately, the responses of other people are unlikely to be unequivocally positive. Although social support may be forthcoming in certain close relationships, there is a dark side to the reactions of others. This dark side should not be surprising to us once we recognize other people's investment in maintaining their own fundamental assumptions about benevolence, meaning, and self-worth. A confrontation with victimization and misfortune is very threatening to other people. An unfortunate result of this threat is a negative, rejecting reaction to victims at a time when they are supremely sensitive to the responses of others. Martin Symonds has labeled this rejection by others the "second injury" to victims.[13] Following their traumatic experience, the survivors are "re-injured" through the failure to receive expected support from social agencies, communities, society in general, and even from family and friends.

Responses of Others: Discomfort and Blame

Understanding the difficulties survivors often experience in receiving social support involves recognizing general responses by others towards victims. These responses, which typically involve some measure of discomfort and blame, do not define the reactions of all people but rather represent generalized tendencies towards others who have experienced misfortune. Following a discussion of these global propensities, we will consider the unique responses and difficulties of those who are closest to the victim, particularly close family members. Let us turn, then, to people's unfortunate yet common inclinations in responding to victims of traumatic life events.

Corresponding to the perspective of survivors prior to their victimization, nonvictims take for granted their fundamental assumptions about the world. Nonvictims believe in a benevolent, meaningful universe in which they are worthy, competent individuals who can control what happens to them, and these core beliefs provide them with a sense of relative invulnerability. These are positively biased assumptions—illusions—that make daily life feel relatively safe and secure, even in the midst of ontological chaos. Yet just as trauma can be understood in terms of threats to, and ultimately the shattering of, the assumptive

147

world, likewise I believe the reactions of other people to victims can also be understood in terms of threats posed to nonvictims' fundamental assumptions. People's discomfort with and around victims speaks to this threat.

To the extent that other people are relatively distant from the event, they are readily able to minimize or eliminate the threat posed to their own inner world. Nonvictims often simply ignore victims. When they do not wholly ignore victims, but instead pay some attention to them, nonvictims experience considerable discomfort, which is often accompanied by victim-blaming.

Discomfort: Victimization as Stigma

Victims are threatening to nonvictims, for they are manifestations of a malevolent universe rather than a benevolent one. They are regarded as "deviants" because they have been marked by misfortune. In the overwhelming majority of cases involving traumatic life events, survivors do not physically appear different from before. Yet all too often their victim status sets them apart; it is information rather than appearance or behavior that typically marks them as different. Victims carry with them a social stigma, for they are now viewed as somehow flawed or blemished. Victims are stigmatized because they violate the expectations established by people's illusions.

Survivors of extreme events are threatening, not because they pose any direct physical threat but because of the more subtle, yet potent threat they pose to our most fundamental assumptions, core beliefs that enable us to feel safe, secure, and confident.[14] Survivors of extreme events are powerful reminders of human frailty and the fact that the world can be malevolent, callous, and cruel.

People do not want to acknowledge that life can be tragic. We spend our lives preserving positive illusions about ourselves and the world. These same illusions, which are shattered in victims by the experience of traumatic life events, are threatened in others by the acknowledgment of such victimization. In the presence of victims, as in the presence of all stigmatized groups, people feel uncomfortable, ill at ease. For some, this discomfort results in outright, even hostile, rejection of victims. For others it results in avoidance of the victim. In the case of large-scale, massive victimizations, it accounts for the community's desire to forget, to draw a veil of oblivion over the horrifying events.[15]

For those people who place a high value on the norms of caring, altruism, and sympathy, the discomfort elicited by victims results in considerable ambivalence. They know they should express care and concern, yet they are extremely uncomfortable in their interactions. In studies of people's reactions to stigmatized individuals, respondents often express positive feelings verbally and on evaluations forms, but negative feelings and discomfort are evident in less conscious behavioral measures, such as nonverbal expressions and movements.[16] Respondents often maintain greater interpersonal distance, smile less, engage in more rigid motor activity, and leave these interactions sooner than they do when interacting with nonmarked individuals. These are people who may want to react appropriately and in a caring manner, yet their personal discomfort is often belied by more subtle responses. Ultimately, their extreme ambivalence only serves to exacerbate nonvictims' discomfort around victims and often leads to a widespread tendency to avoid such interactions. At a time when social support would be particularly helpful, it may be particularly difficult to come by.

Blaming the Victim

The symbolic threat posed by trauma victims is apparent not only in the discomfort and ambivalence of nonvictims but in their attributional strategies as well. A great deal of victim-blaming follows extreme, negative life events. The mere existence of victims provides compelling evidence of tragedy and malevolence, and this results in considerable discomfort for nonvictims. Nevertheless, nonvictims can continue to believe in their own safety and security if they can convince themselves that they are protected because of who they are. In other words, if the victim can be blamed for what happened, then the world is not a random, malevolent, meaningless place. Rather, it is a place in which outcomes are contingent upon who you are and what you do.

Motivational Bases of Victim-Blaming. Just as some self-blaming strategies enable the victim to hold on to old assumptions, victim-blaming also reflects people's efforts to maintain their fundamental assumptions, to minimize the threat posed by the acknowledgment of misfortune. Motivated cognitive strategies not only play an important role in reconstructing shattered assumptions for the victim, but in maintaining prior assumptions for the nonvictim as well. By blaming victims, people minimize the personal threat posed by extreme life events. This self-protective perspective is presented in the work of

Melvin Lerner on people's need to believe in a "just world." In a series of experiments, Lerner and his colleagues demonstrated that innocent victims—individuals who have been randomly selected to receive aversive outcomes—are derogated and blamed by study respondents.[17] Lerner argues that if we believe others suffer because they deserve it, we can feel protected from similar misfortune. In other words, we can tell ourselves that something about the victim brought about the misfortune, maintain that we are different from the victim, and conclude that we are protected and secure.

By blaming victims, people not only maintain their own illusion of invulnerability, but also minimize their sense of responsibility for helping. Psychological research has shown that people are less likely to help when those in need are regarded as blameworthy.[18] If nonvictims engage in victim-blaming, they can eliminate any felt need to help. Instead, they can simply not get involved and can wash their hands of any responsibility for improving the victim's lot. Thus, William Ryan refers to the dilemma facing most charitable, progressive people in response to poverty and racism. They don't want to attack the system that has been so good to them, but they also want to help the victims of injustice. Their brilliant solution is to turn their attention to the victims in their postvictimized state, to explain what's wrong in terms of past social experiences that have left wounds and disabilities. He says that this is the Blaming the Victim solution. People "are, most crucially, rejecting the possibility of blaming, not the victims, but themselves. They are all unconsciously passing judgments on themselves and bringing in a unanimous verdict of Not Guilty."[19]

Nonvictims are motivated to blame victims so that they may continue to maintain their core assumptions about the nature of the world and themselves, and a secondary benefit of such blame is the minimization of responsibility and any need they have to help. Yet, unfortunately, victim-blaming seems overdetermined, for, in addition to these motivational factors, there are cognitive factors that also contribute to such attributions. Most specifically, a "hindsight bias" seems to operate to the detriment of victims.

Cognitive Bases of Victim-Blaming. Psychologist Baruch Fischhoff suggested the existence of this bias, which he described as "creeping determinism."[20] In a series of studies, he found that once people knew the outcome of events, such as who won a war following a series of battles and historical events, they overestimated the prior likelihood of that outcome—that is, they believed that in the absence of information about who won, they would still have estimated the actual outcome as most likely. Once people know what actually happens, they assume that it virtually had to have happened given the events that led up to it. People typically fail to imagine alternative outcomes and instead strengthen the causal links between prior occurrences and the known outcome. This is essentially what we commonly refer to as Monday morning quarterbacking. With the benefit of hindsight, we are wonderful at predicting what the quarterback should have done, what plays should have been called. After all, the game's outcome seems so obvious after the fact.

When applied to victims, the hindsight bias is particularly insidious. With hindsight, we blame victims for behaviors that they engaged in with only the benefit of foresight. Once we know what happened, we blame victims for what we believe they, too, should have known. Thus, in a series of studies, my students and I found that a woman who is raped is blamed for prior behaviors, whereas these same behaviors are not regarded as problematic or blameworthy when they are followed by neutral or positive outcomes.[21] Yet the rape victim engaged in these behaviors without knowing that she would be raped. Thus, it is not particularly uncommon for a man to come back to a woman's apartment following a date. If the woman is raped, however, she is apt to be blamed for allowing him to come back to her apartment. Common behaviors can suddenly look very different in hindsight, particularly when it includes awareness of a victimization.[22]

The reactions to German Jews during World War II also, at least in part, reflects this hindsight bias. People have questioned why Jews were so compliant and docile in responding to German orders that ultimately took them to the concentration camps. In hindsight, with knowledge of Nazi atrocities and the extermination of 6 million Jews, people are shocked by the relative absence of Jewish resistance. Implicit in people's questions about why Jews did not fight back is an element of blame, an attempt to place some responsibility on the victims themselves. Yet again the judgment is made with the benefit of hindsight. Operating without such benefit, it is apparent that Jews did not believe that they were being herded into cattle cars to be exterminated. How could any decent human being believe this was a real possibility? It could only be the stuff of nightmares. The fact that it was reality does not warrant our overestimating the likelihood that it was foreseeable to the victims. Hindsight leads to such overestimation. Hindsight also leads to unwarranted victim-blaming.

Victimizations That Intensify Victim-Blaming. People's victim-blaming propensities are deeply rooted, stemming from self-protective needs and further supported by biases in information-processing. There are, nevertheless, particular types of events that are most apt to elicit these generalized tendencies. Victimizations that involve a perpetrator, an intentional act by another human being, typically result in greater victim-blaming.

Recall that in discussing differences between human-induced and "natural" victimizations in Chapter 4 we noted that people tend to see human behavior as rational and largely dependent upon cues from others in the context of social interactions. When a person behaves in a particular way towards another person, we assume that these actions are in part responses to the verbal or nonverbal behaviors of this other individual. In fact, the smooth functioning of our social exchanges are largely attributable to this mutual regulation of behaviors. In the case of victimizations involving the malicious intent of another individual, this premise of social interaction results in increased victim-blaming.

Nonvictims believe that the victim must have done something to bring about his or her victimization; the victim must have behaved in a way that somehow caused the perpetrator to act in such a terrible, harmful way. Other people fail to take sufficiently into account the extent to which perpetrators do not respond to another's cues or wholly misread any verbal or nonverbal behaviors of the victim. As a consequence, innocent victims are blamed for playing a contributory role in their own victimization.

In general, then, victims of crime are apt to be blamed more than victims of natural disasters or life-threatening diseases, and this victim-blaming often seems to be evident in responses of the criminal justice system and social agencies that work with crime victims. The nagging question—by agency personnel and within the courtroom—too often seems to be "What did the victim do to bring about this crime?"[23] The second injury to the victim is particularly marked in the case of human-induced victimizations.

Within the population of survivors who have been victimized by another person, there is one group that is particularly blamed by other people: female victims of sexual violence. Women who have been raped, molested, or sexually assaulted are deemed particularly blame-worthy, for the cultural myth of "woman as seductress" is virtually universal. As Carol Tavris and Carole Wade note, "Woman as a treacherous, seductive manipulator of sexual wiles appears in the earliest recorded literature." Thus, even in an age-old Babylonian classic known as the Gilgamesh epic, Enkidu is seduced by a woman sent by the enemy to distract him. Woman has been viewed as a seductress throughout history and across cultures. "Every great religion and almost all regional ones warn men about women's seductiveness."[24] These myths

> are as old as communication and as persistent as the sex drive itself. On one level, they are stories, simple or epic, about man rendered powerless. . . . On another level, they represent his projections upon her of his own worst fears about himself, of that dark part of his nature with which he constantly struggles. . . . Thus for the statement "Against my better judgment I did something that was very bad," he substitutes, "She bewitched me, and caused me to do something which I would otherwise never have done."[25]

The rape myths that pervade our culture—that women really want to be raped, that they could successfully resist any rape if they really want to—are simply a variant of these myths of the seductive woman. Viewed in the light of these sexist, demeaning societal beliefs, it is small wonder that women who have been raped, molested, or sexually assaulted are deemed particularly blameworthy. However, the gross injustice and inaccuracy of such victim-blaming must be recognized. The horrifying power of these myths is all too apparent in those cases of incest or child sexual abuse in which very young girls are blamed for being seductive.

Women and girls who have been raped or sexually abused have experienced the psychological pain of incredible violation. Unfortunately, they are subjected to even further violation in the form of social isolation and rejection, stemming not simply from the discomfort people feel around such victims but, most notably, from the extreme victim-blaming that surrounds such victimizations. Despite the fact that these are acts of violence and aggression, the violence and aggression are manifested through sexual acts, and the blame associated with deep-seated seductress myths is unleashed.

Although these myths are largely cross-cultural and transhistorical, they nevertheless suggest the crucial role of the larger society in understanding people's responses to victims. They may experience particular rejection in societies that themselves do not appear to recognize the possibility of victimization. Victims as a group may be more accepted in societies that recognize misfortune and thereby make cultural allowances for this role. Thus, a society's myths or cultural assumptions may serve to exacerbate or minimize people's tendencies to turn their backs on victims.

Societal Considerations

In a competitive society, which stresses winning and losing, one notes a cultural contempt for victims and losers, only mildly tempered by a humanitarian concern that demands compassion for the less fortunate.[26]

Within Western culture, the powerful role of positively biased illusions is very evident. Societies maintain cultural myths, just as individuals maintain illusions, and in Western society our primary myths emphasize justice and control, optimism, and a positive outlook. Within Western society, these myths are probably most extreme in the United States, where the ethos of individualism is coupled with the postulate that anyone can make it in this "land of opportunity." There is little or no place for losers. There is little or no place for victims of misfortune. Ours is a culture in which the benevolence and meaningfulness of the world are emphasized, and beliefs in people's own abilities to "make it" are quite astounding.

The Horatio Alger heroes demonstrate that we can overcome great odds and attain happiness and success if we only try hard enough. Contrast this with the Buddhist perspective described by anthropologist Gananath Obeyesekere, who argues that Buddhism teaches about the hopelessness of one's lot.[27] Even the happiness people experience in their daily lives is actually an expression of suffering, for it is impermanent and temporary, as is everything in the universe. Obeyesekere notes that Buddhists are socialized by parables and legends that deal with personal loss and sorrow as the nature of existence. Suffering is thereby given meaning and significance by the culture.

In Western society, and particularly in the United States, such meaning and significance is absent, and suffering is typically culturally ignored. The societal ideology emphasizes success and happiness, and deemphasizes failure and suffering. There is no "cultural role" for victims except decidedly as outsiders. Within such a cultural context, the interpersonal lot of victims is apt to be all the more difficult and devastating. The trauma victim is an invisible person, an individual who is essentially not culturally acknowledged.

Reactions of Close Family and Intimates

The cultural avoidance of tragedy and misfortune is echoed in the interpersonal avoidance of victims. People often choose not to notice, or to avoid victims they do notice. In addition to the lack of social support and validation that this rejection involves, there is also an odd juxtaposition that often becomes painfully obvious to survivors who have experienced a traumatic life event: life for others typically goes on as usual. Victims' inner and outer worlds have been shattered, and yet other people's lives continue as before.

The conjunction of the victim's total upheaval and the continued, seemingly mundane existence of others seems to take on a somewhat surreal quality. W. H. Auden captured this aspect of victimization in his poem "Musée des Beaux Arts" when he wrote that the Old Masters understood that suffering takes place "While someone else is eating or opening a window or just walking dully along. . . ." In describing Brueghel's *Icarus* in the poem, Auden notes how everything turned away from the disaster, and the sun continued to shine:

> . . . and the expensive delicate ship that must have seen
> Something amazing, a boy falling out of the sky,
> Had somewhere to get to and sailed calmly on.

Yet there are people whose lives do not "sail calmly on" following a traumatic life event. Apart from the victim, these are individuals who are very close to the survivor—in particular, close family members and intimates. By virtue of their relationship with the victim, their lives are also altered by the overwhelming life event.

Those who are very close to trauma victims are embedded within the larger society and are not wholly immune to the discomfort and blaming that so often define people's reactions to victims of misfortune. Nevertheless, their intimate association with the survivor suggests that they are not simply responding to another's misfortune, but suffer themselves. Some victimizations, such as fires and natural disasters, often directly involve other family members as victims. Yet even when the traumatic event does not directly involve close loved ones, these family members are apt to experience "vicarious" effects.[28] We are extremely distressed when catastrophe strikes someone we love; our emotional attachment leads us to feel for and with the loved one. Our own inner world is shaken as well. Overwhelming life events affect not simply individuals, but the families and intimates of these individuals as well.

Thus far the psychological literature has devoted relatively little attention to reactions of close family members and intimates postvictimization, and too often there has been a tendency to group all "others" together in assessing responses to victims. Consequently, family, friends, and strangers have often not been distinguished in discussions of social support postvictimization, and all have been regarded as uncomfortable, avoidant, and rejecting of victims.

There are certainly instances of spouses and lovers leaving their partners in the aftermath of trauma.[29] Clearly, there are also victimizations, such as incest, that arise within the family and require recognizing the dysfunctional nature of the family. Yet as psychologist Charles Figley has noted, the psychological literature "has represented the *family as a victimizing system*—far more than the empirical literature can justify."[30] We have too often assumed that the family creates problems rather than experiences problems as a result of a member's traumatic episode. Figley urges that, in general, we should assume the victim's family was functioning "acceptably well" prior to the impact of the traumatic life event, and that often interventions should occur at the level of the family system; in this way, the pain of all family members can be addressed and alleviated, and the family, in the end, will be better able to cope with future challenges and problems that may arise from the victimization.[31]

It has often been assumed that there is an absence of social support from those closest to the victim. Yet recent research suggests otherwise; a more benevolent picture of spouses'/lovers' responses has begun to be painted. In a study of rape survivors, all of those who had a significant other described these men as supportive.[32] In a study of male and female cancer patients, not a single individual reported avoidance from a spouse or close family member; interestingly, avoidance of social contact was problematic in the case of friends, not close family. In another study, over 95 percent of the cancer patients indicated that they received as much love, approval, assistance, advice, and understanding from their spouse or closest significant other as they needed.[33]

In the aftermath of victimization, close family members often blame themselves, not the victim. They engage in a lot of "if only" thinking, believing that if only they had been with the person, or had themselves done something different, the traumatic experience could have been avoided.[34] Following a traumatic event, loved ones are frequently protective, not avoidant. For example, researchers have discussed the existence of a "trauma membrane" established by those close to survivors in order to protect them from people or situations that might further threaten them. Thus, in disaster populations, researchers and mental health workers often must be deemed helpful by close family members in order to penetrate the "trauma membrane" and gain access to survivors.[35]

Although a complete picture of the nature and adequacy of social support from close family members awaits further research on a wide variety of victimizations, it nevertheless appears that reactions from intimates and loved ones may be markedly different from that of more distant others. There is increasing evidence that sincere attempts to provide social support are the rule of these relationships rather than the exception. Nevertheless, acknowledging that family members make genuine efforts to be supportive, helpful, and understanding does not deny the existence of problems, stresses, and strains in survivors' families. In spite of real caring and concern, there are particular difficulties that arise in even the best of close relationships in the aftermath of traumatic life events.

Role Strain and Ambivalence

Traumatic life events may produce considerable role strain in relationships between the survivor and close family members.[36] Victims, because of their intense psychological distress, may require considerable caretaking by a spouse in a marital relationship. If there is a physical disability as a result of the victimization, this caretaking role is likely to be intensified and, perhaps, permanent rather than temporary. The caretaking role may be new for some family members and, even if familiar and initially comfortable to others, may nevertheless feel overwhelming. A spouse who has not worked before may now need to get a job. A family member who has never done household chores may now need to do so.

Trauma victims may seem different in the aftermath of victimization. In addition to intense anxiety and depression, victims frequently experience emotional numbing, which may preclude intimate interactions between spouses or partners. Thus psychologists have reported that among Vietnam veterans there is sometimes a purposeful distancing, a sort of self-protective shield that enables the individual to maintain tight control over social interactions. Intimacy is specifically avoided because of its potential for painful outcomes; if one doesn't get too close, one won't get too hurt if things don't work out.[37] Further, survivors such as rape victims, who have experienced violent physical violation and degradation often have a particularly difficult time reestablishing intimacy, both emotional and physical, in the aftermath of their traumatic experience.[38] Unable to reestablish intimacy, close family members may feel helpless and inadequate, unable to make any emotional connection and confused about how best to help.

Coincident with the role shifts or stresses is ambivalence. The new relationship is not what one bargained for or expected, and the new strains raise uncomfortable questions and feelings. Spouses may be deeply committed to their partners, yet nevertheless experience negative thoughts and emotions in response to the new situation. In addition to feeling compassionate, loving, and concerned, they may feel trapped, cheated, resentful, frustrated, and worried. They may feel that their own needs are now too often unnoticed and unmet. Things are not what they were, and even the most patient, understanding family members are apt to direct occasional negative outbursts at the victim.[39]

Communication Difficulties

What gets communicated, and by whom, is obviously very important in any close relationship. Not surprisingly, studies of victims suggest that particularly helpful responses by spouses and close family members include expressions of concern, empathy, affection, and a willingness to listen.[40] Such reactions provide personal validation of self-worth and benevolence, of a caring, loving environment. They also provide an atmosphere that maximally allows the victim to cognitively work on the powerful, threatening new data; specific inputs from the spouse or close family member may help the survivor rework the experience. Further, expressions of caring, affection, and a willingness to listen also help establish an environment that feels sufficiently safe and protective to allow the victim to confront and consider the traumatic experience, rather than avoid it.

The responses of spouses and loved ones are certainly not universally positive and supportive, and negative messages also get communicated. Particularly unhelpful responses include criticisms of the victim (e.g., of his or her mental attitude or behavior) and the expression of too much worry and pessimism. Also problematic are attempts by family members to minimize the impact of the victimization.[41] It is upsetting to hear that the crime, or accident, or disease is really not so formidable and distressing as the victim seems to think, or that the victim really should not be so preoccupied with what happened and should get over it. Implicit in these minimization responses is a failure to understand the shattered state of the victim's inner world and the overwhelming nature of the rebuilding process.

Sometimes, the attempts by others to minimize the traumatic experience may reflect people's beliefs that it is best to be optimistic and cheerful in interactions with the victim, to inhibit expressions of anxiety and worry.[42] This is the "Everything's okay . . . You'll be over it soon . . . It's not as big a deal as you might think" variety of reaction. These comments are probably intended to be helpful and supportive, to somehow engender some optimism and positive response in the victim. Unfortunately, they typically do not correspond to the survivor's experience.

Nevertheless, trauma victims, who are supremely sensitive to reactions of others, often realize all too well that other people often respond more positively towards them when they appear cheerful and optimistic. This includes not only friends and distant acquaintances but close family members and intimates, too. An unfortunate dilemma is created for survivors, not simply in their interactions with friends and more distant others but in their sustained close contact with family members and intimates. Should they express what they really feel, or should they present a more positive facade? Psychologists Camille Wortman and Christine Dunkel-Schetter label this the victim's catch-22: they can express their feelings, be themselves, and incur negative responses, or they can enact a charade and pretend everything is fine and incur more positive responses. Neither is satisfactory, and the victim may therefore vacillate between expressing pain and putting on a good face, thereby often making it even more difficult for close family members to know how to react.[43]

In addition to a positive self-presentation, survivors may choose to avoid trauma-related discussions in the family. This avoidance may be minimal, involving the occasional inhibition of unpleasant thoughts and feelings. The avoidance may also be extreme, involving a sort of "conspiracy of silence."[44] Survivors sometimes choose to avoid openly discussing their experience because it is simply too painful. Often, however, this avoidance stems from well-meaning intentions to protect and respect loved ones. Survivors of crime, disease, accidents, or disasters may feel that others don't want to hear about their suffering and may want to protect loved ones from their pain. Thus, in a recent study of cancer patients, 87 percent of the sample reported that they sometimes tried to cope by keeping their thoughts and feelings to themselves, and of these, the majority reported they did so because they were concerned about the reactions of others, particularly about bothering or upsetting loved ones.[45]

The unfortunate irony, however, is that some loved ones may also want to talk and listen; spouses and intimates may want to know what the victim is experiencing so as to be able to be more helpful and supportive. Yet they may similarly avoid opening the discussion for fear that it might be too painful for the victim. Thus, even in those instances when both the victim and close family members want to talk openly, communication may nevertheless be avoided because of misunderstandings rather than bad intentions.

Communication difficulties within families of survivors are very common. That survivors typically feel supported by loved ones following traumatic life events is not belied by these communication difficulties; in most instances there is genuine caring and concern within the family. In fact, communication problems may often stem from this concern for one another rather than from a lack of same. The trauma victim and family members often try to protect one another and are unsure about how best to address the survivor's experience in the aftermath of the event. Certainly, criticisms and attempts to minimize the overwhelming nature of the survivor's experience are detrimental, for they indicate not simply a lack of support but a lack of understanding. In this light, it is noteworthy that in a recent review of empirical studies conducted with community samples of aging Holocaust victims, the researchers found a remarkable degree of psychological well-being and resilience; and two of the variables that best predicted good psychological functioning were self-disclosure and having a survivor spouse.[46] Those who were married to a survivor were likely to be those who knew they were understood, whose experience was validated and acknowledged, who could share their experience without having their thoughts and feelings criticized or minimized.

The understanding and appreciation by others of what the victim has gone through—and may still be going through—enables the survivor to reestablish and maintain positive self-perceptions in the midst of his or her psychological distress. Given both the difficulties close family members may have in truly understanding the survivor's experience, and the survivor's inhibition of thoughts and feelings within the family, the attraction of self-help or support groups becomes evident. The experience of the rape victim is understood—at a fundamental experiential level—by other rape victims. The cancer patient can speak openly of his or her fears and concerns, without upsetting a loved one or risking having the traumatic experience minimized. The Vietnam veteran knows that others in the group also remember the horrors of war and can feel the same pain.

Within the group, survivors can learn from one another; they can see, firsthand, that their reactions are not abnormal and overblown.

Group members can openly process their thoughts, can vent their anxieties, and can approach their experience with and through the acknowledgment of others. Within the group, the survivor is unlikely to hear, "What you went through is over, it's really not such a big deal."

The Therapist's Role

Research suggests that among people experiencing significant psychological distress, approximately 25 percent will seek help from professionals (i.e., psychologists, psychiatrists, or other formal helping agencies).[47] This being the case, it is likely that the majority of trauma victims rely upon informal sources of support such as family and friends. Nevertheless, therapists can play an extremely important role in the healing process.

The therapeutic effects of good clinical interventions for survivors derive from two types of learning and processing that occur simultaneously in therapy. In the first, the therapist serves as a caring other who provides the client with the experience of acceptance and caring in the face of open acknowledgment of the survivor's experience. In the other, the therapist functions as a sort of teacher who provides the client with ways of minimizing the trauma's affective overload and maximizing the reworking and reappraisal of the experience.

Ultimately, successful coping with victimization involves integrating the traumatic experience and arriving at a reconstructed set of assumptions that acknowledge benevolence, meaning, and self-worth in the world and oneself, though not absolutely. Shattered assumptions need to be rebuilt, and this involves parallel tasks of processing new, powerful victimization-data, while at the same time getting new information from one's real interactions in the world. The therapist can provide inputs that not only directly affect the processing of the traumatic event but also involve firsthand knowledge of a powerful new relationship, that of the client and therapist.

Therapist as "Caring Other"

As therapists assess their clients and choose appropriate treatments, they are interacting with people who are very sensitive to the responses of others. Trauma survivors are likely to question the extent to which they can trust others, particularly strangers, and the therapist falls into this category. An essential part of the therapeutic process with trauma victims is the building of a relationship that can serve as firsthand evidence that others can be good, that the client is worthy despite the traumatic experience, and that trust rather than mistrust may often be appropriate in one's approach to the world.

In their excellent book on therapy with trauma survivors, psychologists Lisa McCann and Laurie Pearlman note the importance of involvement rather than distance:

> Our therapeutic approach is to be as involved and engaged with trauma victims as is possible without violating therapist-client boundaries. A classical analytic neutrality may be appropriate for treating neurotic disorder and during some phrases of work with traumatized persons. However, most people who are traumatized want and need to experience a relationship with a real, warm, concerned human being who is actively involved with them in an empathetic, responsive way.[48]

This does not mean that the therapist loses all neutrality, but rather that she or he shows an emotionally warm interest in the client's problems and progress. Certainly, this is easier in the case of some clients than others; thus, just as borderline patients may engage in the constant testing of therapists, such testing may define the interactions of some trauma survivors. There may be both a desire to get close and a fear of getting close, a desire to trust and an awareness of the pain that can be associated with trusting.

The development of a caring therapist-client relationship enables the trauma survivor to explore trauma-related thoughts and feelings in the context of a safe environment. Such a relationship also enables the therapist to function as a "container" for the survivor's painful, overwhelming affects.[49] Perhaps most important, it provides the survivor with the actual experience of being valued, of being understood and cared for in the aftermath of the traumatic event. The Kohutian notion of "positive mirroring"[50] is a useful metaphor to describe the value of the therapist's empathy, respect, and responsiveness; through a mirroring process, clients learn directly about themselves. Interestingly, the therapist's soothing, empathic stance serves as a mirror not only reflecting the self but also reflecting, from the other side of the mirror, a more positive, benevolent world than the one powerfully experienced through victimization.

Therapist as "Teacher"

In the role of teacher, the therapist provides the client with strategies and appraisals that ultimately facilitate the integration of the traumatic event within the victim's inner world. The automatic processes that occur postvictimization—denial and numbing versus intrusions and reexperience of the event—alert the therapist to the victim's need to both approach and avoid the trauma.[51] Cognitively, the survivor needs to approach the traumatic experience—to confront, reappraise, and rework it. Emotionally, the experience can be too painful; survivors need to avoid it, to protect themselves from the overwhelming negative affects.

As discussed in Chapter 5, trauma survivors use denial and numbing to moderate the impact and intensity of the trauma. These processes enable the survivor to confront the experience gradually, in manageable doses. Periods of denial and intrusion alternate, keeping the cognitive-emotional system in balance. Optimally, avoidance strategies decrease over time, and the threatening material is increasingly confronted. For some victims, however, the process is not so successful, and they appear to get stuck in one phase or another—completely numb and not confronting the experience, or extraordinarily anxious and feeling as if the event is constantly intruding. Much of the therapist's work involves helping the client reach some equilibrium in these processes, so that the material can be confronted, gradually, with a minimum of emotional distress.

For clients who remain anxious and plagued by intrusive thoughts, the therapist teaches skills or strategies that provide some distance and emotional numbing (i.e., avoidance). For clients who remain numb and unable to feel or confront the traumatic experience, the therapist helps the survivor gain access to and reappraise trauma-related thoughts and feelings (i.e., approach). Psychologists Ellen Dye and Susan Roth superbly capture this "approach-avoidance" conception of therapeutic interventions:

> Regardless of the therapeutic strategies they employ, all psychotherapists presented with patients who have been unable to successfully resolve a traumatic experience on their own are faced with decisions about how to encourage approach and/or avoidance of traumatic material. Psychotherapy techniques which help individuals to resolve psychological trauma by consciously focusing on the trauma event through talking about the trauma, think-

ing about the trauma, and exploring its meaning for the individual can be usefully thought of as "approach" techniques. In contrast, psychotherapy techniques which advocate focusing the individual's attention away from the trauma experience and onto other aspects of her/his life can be considered "avoidance" techniques. Most psychotherapies combine both approach and avoidance techniques but vary in their emphasis.[52]

Behavioral and cognitive-behavioral therapies typically involve stress management techniques, including such strategies as systematic desensitization, progressive relaxation, thought-stopping, and cognitive restructuring. These are generally used to eliminate intrusive thoughts, reduce anxiety, and, in general, to control distressing symptoms. The primary focus is on the avoidance, or minimization, of threatening stimuli. Pharmacological treatments that are intended to reduce the affective arousal associated with post-traumatic stress are consistent with these avoidance approaches as well. Insight therapies, psychodynamic therapies that focus on interpretations and meanings, art therapies, and hypnosis are techniques that focus more directly on the traumatic experience and as such represent attempts to approach the threatening material.[53]

Although therapists often have their preferred therapies, it is nevertheless the case that the particular client—where she or he is "stuck"—should determine the optimal therapeutic approach. Work with trauma survivors may call for particularly eclectic therapists. Traumatic experiences are difficult to assimilate and an immense amount of work is typically required to enable the client, over time, to work with the thoughts, feelings, and images associated with the traumatic event and, ultimately, rebuild self- and worldviews. A combination of therapies may be required; in many cases, techniques that minimize anxiety may first be necessary, and more "approach" modalities (e.g., insight therapies) may be effective only after these "avoidance" techniques are successful.

In comparing therapists to teachers, the intent is to focus both on the transmission of particular strategies and skills, as well as the process of providing new interpretations and meanings to material. Excellent teachers recognize our special strengths and weaknesses and pace the learning task to coincide with our distinct needs and abilities. They provide us with methods for solving certain problems and engage us to consider not only new information but also old material in new and different ways. Excellent therapists provide trauma survivors with methods for minimizing distressing symptoms, and engage them in an exploration that involves considering trauma-related material in new, diverse ways. Over time, these new appraisals and interpretations facilitate the integration of trauma-related thoughts, feelings, and images. The survivor's reconstructed assumptive world acknowledges the traumatic experience but is no longer wholly immersed in it.

PART FOUR

Conclusion

8

Recovery
Some Final Thoughts

Traumatic life events shatter our fundamental assumptions about ourselves and our world. In the aftermath of these extreme experiences, coping involves the arduous task of reconstructing an assumptive world, a task that requires a delicate balance between confronting and avoiding trauma-related thoughts, feelings, and images. Over time, with the help of personally meaningful cognitive reappraisals and genuine support from close, caring others, most trauma victims manage to rebuild their inner world. They can move on with their lives, which no longer seem to be wholly defined by their victimization. Victims become survivors.[1] They have "recovered."

Trauma Survivors' Recovery

The term *recovery,* however, is somewhat problematic when applied to trauma survivors. In one sense, it is quite appropriate, for recovery connotes health. In another sense, however, it is inappropriate, for it suggests a return to one's previous condition, to where one began. Trauma survivors return to a state of health; they do not, however, go back to where they began.

On the basis of his studies of bereavement, Robert Weiss questions the usefulness of the term *recovery* for those who have suffered a severe loss. He claims that "adaptation," "accommodation," or even "degree of damage" might be more appropriate. Yet, he argues, there is one area in which "recovery" is an indispensable term, and that is in the extent to which people return to some degree of effective functioning.

What is effective functioning? Weiss presents a list of "reasonable expectations" that might be considered criteria for ordinary levels of effective functioning:

1. Ability to give energy to everyday life.
2. Psychological comfort, as demonstrated by freedom from pain and distress.
3. Ability to experience gratification—to feel pleasure when desirable, hoped-for, or enriching events occur.
4. Hopefulness regarding the future, being able to plan and care about plans.
5. Ability to function with reasonable adequacy in social roles as spouse, parent, and member of the community.[2]

Based on these criteria, the trauma survivor who has recovered is invested in the present and hopeful about the future, capable of feeling pleasure, free of particularly disturbing thoughts and feelings, and able to maintain close, emotionally significant relationships. This is clearly a formula for psychological well-being for all of us, regardless of whether we have experienced a traumatic life event. Extreme levels of energy, comfort, hope, optimism, and social engagement are not the criteria; simply "good enough" levels.

It is this sense of recovery—evidence of healthy functioning—that is appropriate for trauma survivors. In fact, victims probably fare better than has generally been assumed. Most of what we presently know about survivors of traumatic life events is based on clinical samples. These are victims who have sought professional help in the aftermath of their victimization, and those having the greater difficulties are apt to be overrepresented in this population. It is likely that trauma victims who have had the fewest problems are those who have been studied least. Not surprisingly, clinical studies have tended to emphasize survivors' long-term psychological difficulties.

There is great variation in adaptation following trauma, and there are clearly some victims who continue to struggle for years. Yet research with community samples has begun to paint a more positive picture, one that highlights the psychological adjustment and well-being of survivors. As has been noted with regard to children in extreme situations, the evidence for resilience is "far more ubiquitous a phenomenon than mental health personnel ever realized, largely because of their long-term attention to behavior pathology."[3]

In my own studies with nonclinical samples, most survivors appear to have coped successfully over time; they are functioning well in terms of the criteria presented above. And recent community-based studies of Holocaust victims in the United States, Canada, and Israel have found that large percentages of these survivors have adjusted very well; they are not suffering from chronic forms of psychopathology, as suggested by earlier clinical reports.[4]

It appears that trauma victims may return to effective levels of functioning, even after the most extreme experiences. They rarely, however, return to where they began psychologically. It is this sense of "recovery" that is inappropriate for survivors. Typically, when we think of recovery, we think of physical illness. We "get over" an illness, and recovery is largely defined by the similarity between one's condition pre- and postillness. We do not pay much attention to the fact that diseases are often "encoded" biologically, and thus there remains a physiological memory of the illness, as in the case of antibodies. Diseases primarily attack the biological being and make long-term, even permanent changes. Traumatic life events primarily attack the psychological being, and analogously, make long-term, even permanent changes—in the psychological world of the survivor.

Trauma survivors do not simply get over their experience. It is permanently encoded in their assumptive world; the legacy of traumatic life events is some degree of disillusionment. From the perspective of their inner worlds, victims recover not when they return to their prior assumptive world but when they reestablish an integrated, comfortable assumptive world that incorporates their traumatic experience.

Factors that Facilitate Recovery

Most victims complete this reconstruction process; for some it takes weeks, others years. There are also victims who are unable to complete this formidable task.[5] What factors are most apt to facilitate or impede recovery?

Any traumatic reaction reflects both the individual victim and the particular victimizing event. This may appear to be a simplistic point, but it is an important one, for there is considerable evidence that we typically underestimate the power of situations and overestimate the power of the individual in understanding any given behavior.[6] We must therefore attend particularly to situational demands and influences. We need to recognize that some traumatic events are more difficult to integrate than others. That victims generally do recover from experiences such as violent rapes and concentration camps speaks to the remarkable capacities of the human spirit and psyche. We should remind ourselves just how threatening and terrifying traumatic events are as we consider the factors that contribute to recovery.

Successfully resolving the survivor's intense cognitive-emotional dilemma involves, as we have seen, confronting the unpleasant thoughts, feelings, and images associated with the traumatic event, and modulating these confrontations, when necessary, through avoidance processes such as denial and numbing. Three factors are likely to be of particular significance in the recovery process: (1) the victim's ability to tolerate arousal and distressing emotions; (2) the victim's ability to creatively rework and reappraise the powerful new "data"; and (3) the support of close, caring others.

The more tolerance for arousal and distressing emotions, the greater the likelihood the survivor will directly confront the threatening material relatively early and often, and thus the greater the opportunity afforded for reworking and reappraising the victimization. The more the survivor can bear the distress associated with trauma-related thoughts, feelings, and images, the less likely he or she will get "stuck" in avoidance and fail to work with the traumatic material, a necessary precondition for the ultimate integration of the experience. Denial and numbing are useful temporary protections against overwhelming distress. If overused, they preclude the possibility of rebuilding an inner world that incorporates the traumatic experience. These processes are apt to be overused by survivors who are least able to tolerate strong emotions and arousal.

There are biological and psychological bases of this tolerance. Thus, people differ in physiological reactivity, both in terms of their threshold for responding and the strength of their response. Research has shown that infants vary considerably in their responsivity, with some reacting to slight movements and noise, and others requiring stronger stimulation. They also differ in the intensity of their reactions, both physiologically (i.e., arousal level) and behaviorally (e.g., howling versus whimpering).[7] People who are most reactive will need to tolerate higher levels of arousal.

In addition to reactivity, affect tolerance also depends on the person's ability to self-regulate arousal and emotions. Thus, we differ in our self-soothing abilities. This is very apparent when observing some infants who are readily able to calm themselves by thumb-sucking. Psychologists have maintained that we first learn affect tolerance through empathic caregiving. From this perspective, the mother or primary caregiver allows the child to bear increasingly intense feelings, but intercedes before they become overwhelming.

> Actually it is more accurate to say that competent parents assist their children in practicing affect tolerance, in much the same way they help their children to regulate their excitements and motoric functions in learning to walk or swim. Basically, the affectively motivated disturbances are not allowed to exceed for too long the child's ability to maintain his equilibrium.[8]

Throughout our lifetimes, we practice handling our emotions and soothing our hurt feelings. Our successful efforts are apt to contribute to the development of a greater capacity to tolerate distressing feelings and high levels of arousal. For trauma victims, the greater the tolerance, the more likely they will be able to confront and, ultimately integrate, their terrifying experience.

This integration involves reappraisals and new interpretations and requires creativity in the way one approaches the traumatic material and renders it somehow less threatening. Motivated cognitive strategies involving social comparisons, self-attributions, and the imposition of purpose represent some of the impressive ways in which survivors reconsider and rework the data. People who can think flexibly and creatively, who can view and reshape from multiple perspectives, are apt to have an advantage in the aftermath of traumatic life events.

The support of close, caring others is also of crucial significance during the survivor's recovery. It provides direct evidence that the world is not necessarily malevolent and meaningless, and that the survivor is worthy of support. Other people can acknowledge and validate the enormity of the victim's coping task. They can also provide a safe, protected environment within which to openly explore the traumatic experience. Talking, discussing, venting, and sharing trauma-related thoughts and feelings provide rich opportunities for survivors to approach, reappraise, and work through their experience.

To the extent that victims are able to tolerate distressing emotions, are cognitively creative and flexible, and have the support of close, caring others, recovery is facilitated. These survivors are most successful at rebuilding their assumptive worlds; still, these worlds are not the same as they were.

The New Psychological World of the Survivor

The inner worlds of victims who have "recovered" now reflect an acknowledgment of misfortune, an awareness of vulnerability. These survivors know that their prior assumptions were naive, that tragedy can strike and that no one is invulnerable. Their new assumptive worlds, however, are typically not completely negative; malevolence, meaningfulness, and self-abasement do not characterize their core schemas. Rather, these survivors recognize the possibility of tragedy, but do not allow it to pervade their self- and worldviews. In the words of one rape victim: "I think about what happened and I know how terrible things can be. But I can also see the good things in my life now—and there's an awful lot that's good."

Survivors can remember the traumatic event, but not constantly. Over time, they manage to minimize the extent to which the traumatic experience defines their fundamental assumptions. Rather than over-generalize from the trauma to all aspects of the world and the self, over the course of successful coping, survivors reestablish positive, yet less absolutely positive, core assumptions.

They balance what they know can happen with more benign views of themselves and the world. They know they are not entirely safe and protected, yet they don't see the entire world as dangerous. Long after the rape, assault, serious accident, diagnosis of life-threatening disease, or disaster, the victim's assumptions remain somewhat more negative than that of their nonvictim counterparts. The world is benevolent, but not absolutely; events that happen make sense, but not always; the self can be counted on to be decent and competent, but helplessness is at times a reality. Survivors are often guardedly optimistic, but the rosy absolutism of earlier days is gone.[9]

Hope and Wisdom

Pain can make a whole winter bright,
Like fever, force us to live deep and hard,
Betrayal focus in a peculiar light
All we have ever dreamed or known or heard,
And from great shocks we do recover.[10]

—May Sarton

In the aftermath of traumatic life events, survivors are often forced to live "deep and hard." They have come face to face with reality. There is disillusionment, yet it is generally not the disillusionment of despair. Rather, it is disillusionment tempered by hope. Trauma survivors can now acknowledge their experience rather than disavow it. The work of denial is completed, and hope can take its place.[11] As a cancer survivor told me: "I do what I can to take care of myself; I eat well, I exercise. . . . Still, I know it could come back. In the end, what I really do is hope."

To be "crazy-human with hope"[12] is not a naive wish. It involves an acknowledgment of real possibilities, both bad and good—of disaster in spite of human efforts, of triumph in spite of human limitations.

For the survivor, the traumatic experience serves as an unexpected source of strength rather than weakness. There is a feeling of personal triumph, of mastery in spite of the extraordinary difficulties and demands of the experience. There is also the sense of possessing a new, special sort of wisdom, which derives from the most potent type of education—personal experience. Schooled in anxiety and disillusionment, victims are "educated by dread."[13] Once you know that catastrophe dwells next door and can strike anyone at any time, you interpret reality differently.

Trauma survivors no longer move through life unmindful of existence; they can more readily relish the good, for they all too well know the bad. They have made their peace with the inevitable shortcomings of our existence and have a new appreciation of life and a realization of what is really important. The wisdom of maturity, which acknowledges the possibility that catastrophe will disrupt ordinary routine, replaces the ignorance of naivete. And the trauma survivor emerges somewhat sadder, but considerably wiser.

Notes

Chapter 1
Our Fundamental Assumptions

1. James, 1907, p. 4.
2. Parkes, 1975, p. 132. See also Parkes, 1971. Parkes credited Hadley Cantril for the phrase "assumptive world," which Cantril initially used in his work on perception.
3. Bowlby, 1969, 1973.
4. It could be argued that this interest in fundamental assumptions represents an orientation largely reflected in the work of George Kelley (1955). Kelley's work on personal constructs is based on a system of dichotomizing the world in terms of similarities and contrasts and does not capture the nature of the generalized beliefs systems discussed here. Nevertheless, his emphasis on the importance of understanding people's own formulations and the lenses through which they perceive the world is consistent with the present approach.
5. Epstein, 1984, p. 65. See also Epstein, 1973, 1979, 1980, 1984.
6. See the important contributions of Epstein (1980), on the hierarchical nature of our theories of reality. See also Bem's (1970) discussion of a hierarchical model of cognitive structures and Rogers's (1981) analysis of the self as represented in memory as a hierarchical category structure.
7. For earlier discussions of these assumptions, see Janoff-Bulman & Frieze, 1983, and Janoff-Bulman, 1985b, 1989a.
8. See, for example, Janoff-Bulman, 1989a.
9. Weller, 1973.
10. For a review, see Taylor, 1990. See also Tiger, 1979.

11. Watts & Free, 1978. See also Cantril, 1965.

12. Watts & Free, 1978.

13. Matlin & Stang, 1978.

14. For more discussion of meaning, to be further examined in Chapter 6, see Frankl, 1963; Lifton, 1967; Silver, Boon, & Stones, 1983; and Silver & Wortman, 1980.

15. Wilder, 1927, p. 19.

16. Gluckman, 1944.

17. Science is often very good at providing an understanding of an independent causal chain, how each event in a chain leads to the next. Yet it is often very inadequate at providing an understanding of the intersection of two otherwise independent causal chains. In the Azande case, for example, the path of the boy's boat and the path of the hippopotamus were essentially independent causal chains. It is the intersection of these paths that remains unanswered by science.

18. This is clearly a much more simplistic notion of justice than that which is the focus of attention for philosophers such as Rawls (1971).

19. See, for example, Lerner & Matthews, 1967, and Lerner & Simmons, 1966. See also Lerner, 1970, 1980.

20. Wilder, 1927, p. 219.

21. According to Lerner, we look to people's behaviors first. Also see this behavior-character distinction in Janoff-Bulman, 1979, 1982.

22. See Rotter, 1966. See also Seligman, 1975, and Abramson, Seligman, & Teasdale, 1978, for a discussion of learned helplessness.

23. Langer, 1975. See also Wortman, 1975.

24. Henslin, 1967. See also Goffman, 1967.

25. See Antonovsky's (1979) discussion of an emphasis on a "sense of control" as a superfluous cultural bias.

26. Antonovsky, 1979, p. 128.

27. This is what is meant by Bandura's (1982) notion of "self-efficacy."

28. See, for example, Brown, 1986; Campbell, 1986; Matlin & Stang, 1978; and Rosenberg, 1979. For reviews, see Greenwald, 1980; Taylor, 1990; and Taylor & Brown, 1988.

29. See for example, Harvey, Harris, & Barnes, 1975; Miller & Ross, 1975; Rosenzweig, 1943; Snyder, Higgins, & Stucky, 1983; and Tesser & Campbell, 1983.

30. In the area of social cognition, refer to Fiske & Pavelchak (1986) for a discussion of "affective tags" for category labels and attributes of a category.

31. Spock, 1976, pp. 1–2.

32. E. Erikson, 1968, p. 96.

33. In Erikson's work, the mother is regarded as the child's caregiver. Yet caregiving need not rest solely with mothers; responsive caregiving can be provided by another adult or adults.

34. See Greenberg & Mitchell, 1983, for an excellent review of the major theorists. The object relations theorists have generally stressed the importance of the mother-child relationship only; again, the present perspective views responsive caretaking as something that need not describe only mothers or even a single caregiver.

35. Fairbairn, 1952.

36. Winnecott, 1965.

37. Kohut, 1971, 1977. See also Ulman & Brothers, 1988.

38. Bowlby, 1969, 1973.

39. Stern, 1985, p. 67.

40. Stern, 1985, p. 95.

41. Stern, 1985, p. 96. Stern discusses what happens when a deviation from the generalized episode occurs (i.e., the baby is hungry, placed at the breast, and is unable to successfully get any milk). The baby now has a new specific episode and one of three things can happen: (1) the new event never recurs and simply exists as a specific episodic memory; it becomes part of cued-recall memory; (2) The new experience may recur again and again and therefore becomes generalized to form a new generalized episode; or (3) the infant may never again experience a specific instance of the original "breast milk" episode (e.g., the mother switches to bottle-feeding), in which case the "breast milk" generalized episode after a time is no longer an expected part of daily living; it may therefore no longer be an active, or even retrievable, memory structure.

42. In particular, he cites the work of Strauss (1979) on the reactions of ten-month-olds to schematic face drawings.

43. Harry Harlow's (1971) work with monkeys has demonstrated the extreme importance of contact comfort for the young. Unfortunately, he concludes that it is physical contact with the mother that is necessary, although it necessarily follows from his research that any contact comfort—not only the mother's—is essential for normal social development.

44. The role of culture and society will be more fully addressed in Chapter 7.

45. Bowlby, 1973.

46. See, for example, the work of Kagan and his colleagues (Kagan, Kearsley, & Zelazo, 1978) on the plasticity of psychological structures throughout childhood. After reviewing relevant studies, Kagan notes that if early structures are not supported by the child's current environment, one is likely to see dramatic changes. Kagan is particularly struck by the ability

of experientially deprived children to "rebound" in supportive environments. See also Garmezy, 1983, on resilience in children.

47. Wolfenstein, 1957, p. 3.

48. Antonovsky, 1979, p. 123.

49. Tiger, 1979.

50. Becker, 1973, p. 23.

51. Janoff-Bulman, Madden, & Timko, 1983, and Janoff-Bulman & Frieze, 1983. For reviews, see Perloff, 1983, and Taylor, 1990.

52. Weinstein, 1980, 1982, and Weinstein & Lachendro, 1982.

53. See, for example, Irwin, 1944; Perloff & Fetzer, 1986; Robertson, 1977; and Weinstein, 1987.

54. See Taylor, 1990.

55. These two types of "knowing" are distinguished and discussed at length in Chapter 4.

56. Wolfenstein, 1957, p. 5.

57. Freud, 1927.

58. Langer, 1975.

59. Wortman, 1975.

60. See Janoff-Bulman, 1989b. This perspective may help inform intriguing recent findings regarding optimistic biases and errors of nondepressives in the laboratory, as compared to the more accurate yet pessimistic judgments made by depressives (e.g., Alloy & Abramson, 1979, 1982, and Alloy & Tabachnik, 1984). Depressives in real life may confront failure and misfortune more than nondepressives, and these real experiences may, in fact, account for their increased depression (Coyne & Gotlib, 1983). The noncontingencies established in the laboratory may more accurately reflect the outside-lab experiences of depressives more than nondepressives. Both groups, in other words, are making contingency estimates based on their extra-lab experiences, but these experiences are more similar to the lab experience for the depressives.

61. See, for example, Allport, 1943; Haan, 1977; Jahoda, 1958; Jourard & Landsman, 1980; and Menninger, 1930.

62. Taylor, 1990. See also Taylor & Brown, 1988.

63. Janoff-Bulman & Brickman, 1982, p. 212.

64. Ainsworth, 1979; Ainsworth, Blehar, Waters, & Wall, 1978; and Ainsworth & Wittig, 1969.

65. James, 1962, pp. 96–97.

66. See, for example, Janoff-Bulman & Brickman, 1982, and McFarlin, 1985. When people were informed that not all of the problems confronting them would be soluble (unlike most lab situations, but corresponding more to the real world), people with the highest self-esteem and

expectancies were best at discriminating between soluble and insoluble tasks. They could then devote their energies to the soluble problems. Further, people with high versus low expectancies are more likely to seek unambiguous information about their performance (Trope, 1975). They may also be better able to externalize failure (Abramson, Seligman, & Teasdale, 1978), thereby minimizing the likelihood that they will be emotionally affected in a negative way by failure. Those with high self-esteem are also likely to have a greater number of alternative tasks from which to derive success experiences. All of this suggests that it may be easier rather than harder for them to know when to quit and feel comfortable quitting. It is interesting that in work on self-handicapping strategies, it is not people with the most positively biased assumptions about themselves who engage in such counterproductive strategies, but people who are far more insecure about their self-worth (Jones & Berglas, 1978). These are the people who cannot afford to bump up against their limits, to confront failure.

Certainly, there must be some feedback loop between the different levels (e.g., global versus specific); if all the narrower assumptions are negative, it would no doubt be quite difficult to maintain positive generalized assumptions. Yet it should be recognized that positive assumptions about the self, other people, and the world can be based on the domain of evidence one chooses. Thus, a person may see him or herself as incompetent in certain areas, and yet maintain very high self-esteem by devaluing these domains and overvaluing those in which he or she excels.

67. Interestingly, this notion echoes ideas put forth in the 1960s regarding one's views of the United States. It was argued that one could feel very positive, in general, about one's country yet still be critical of specific national behaviors, such as those related to the Vietnam War.

Chapter 2
Cognitive Conservatism and Resistance to Change

1. Lecky, 1945, p. 84.

2. See, for example, Epstein, 1973, 1980, 1984; Sarbin, 1981; Snyder, 1989; and Snyder & Higgins, 1988.

3. In the field of social psychology, the 1960s, in particular, witnessed an explosion in research on cognitive consistency theories, including cognitive dissonance theory (Festinger, 1957), balance theory (Heider, 1958), and interpersonal-congruity theory (Secord & Backman, 1965). In particular, work on cognitive dissonance theory, which dominated the field for more than a decade, demonstrated people's powerful motivation to maintain congruency in their attitudes and behaviors, especially in those most related to their self-concept; see Aronson, 1968, for a review of cognitive dissonance theory and research.

4. Popper, 1963, pp. 46–47. Popper does not believe in inborn ideas; he favors inborn reactions or responses, among which are particular expectations. He believes one of the most important of these expectations is that of finding regularities. Popper claims that "we expect regularities everywhere and attempt to find them even when there are none" (p. 49). This propensity to look for regularities is, he maintains, the basis for our imposition of laws upon nature.

5. Kuhn, 1962.

6. Fiske & Taylor, 1991. Bartlett (1932) used the term *schema* to describe the central cognitive structure in perception. See also Piaget, 1952, 1954, and Neisser, 1976—other noteworthy users of the term.

7. Goleman, 1985, p. 75.

8. See the work on categorization by Rosch, 1978.

9. Our schemas for categories include a conception of the prototype, the typical or ideal instance of the category. Category membership is generally determined using judgments of similarity to the prototype, based on a Wittgenstein-like "family resemblance" criterion; no single set of features defines category membership, but any of several features contribute to the judgment that the object in question resembles the prototype. See Fiske & Taylor, 1991. See also Wittgenstein, 1953.

10. Abelson, 1981.

11. The similarity to Daniel Stern's conceptions has probably not escaped the reader. Stern's "generalized episodes" largely parallel our narrowest schemas; RIGs—representations of interactions that have been generalized—largely parallel mid-level schemas; and "working models or theories" parallel our most global, abstract schemas.

12. Rumelhart, 1978, quoted in Goleman, 1985, p. 77.

13. Piaget, 1952.

14. See, for example, Alba & Hasher, 1983; Hastie, 1981; Judd & Kulik, 1980; and Markus, 1977. It should be noted that research has shown there are particular instances when people do not prefer schema-consistent information. When people are developing schemas, or have weak, tentative schemas, they are likely to attend to inconsistent information (see Fiske & Taylor, 1991). Our fundamental assumptions represent strong, well-developed schemas and are thus subject to powerful consistency biases.

15. Rothbart, Evans, & Fulero, 1979.

16. See, for example, Alba & Hasher, 1983; Cantor & Mischel, 1979; Judd & Kulik, 1980; and Swann & Read, 1981a, 1981b.

17. For example, Cantor & Mischel, 1979, and Schlenker, 1980.

18. Cohen, 1981.

19. Tesser, 1978; Tesser & Conlee, 1975; and Tesser & Leone, 1977. See also Srull & Wyer, 1989.

20. Duncan, 1976, and Sagar & Schofield, 1980.

21. Josefowitz, 1980, p. 14.

22. Beck, 1967.

23. Beck, 1967, p. 287.

24. There is also research evidence that in our interactions with others, our methods of data-gathering confirms our schemas, for we typically ask questions in ways that support what we already believe. For research on confirmatory hypothesis-testing, see Snyder & Swann, 1978, and Snyder & Gangestad, 1981.

25. See Rosenthal, 1974, for a review. See also Jones & Panitch, 1971; Snyder & Swann, 1978; and Zanna & Pack, 1975.

26. Ross, Lepper, & Hubbard, 1975. See also Anderson, Lepper, & Ross, 1980.

27. Nisbett & Ross, 1980.

28. See Fiske & Taylor, 1991.

29. Tajfel & Wilkes, 1963; Park & Rothbart, 1982; and Linville & Jones, 1980.

30. Rothbart & John, 1985.

31. Rothbart & Park, 1986.

32. In such instances we combine information in a "piecemeal" rather than "category-based" fashion; see Fiske & Neuberg, 1990.

33. Rothbart & John, 1985, p. 93.

34. Rothbart & John, 1985.

35. See Jones & Goethals, 1972, and Nisbett & Ross, 1980. Although recency effects (in which the most recent material is most influential) are sometimes found, they are, as Nisbett and Ross write, "rare and appear to depend on the existence of one or more potently manipulated factors" (p. 172).

36. Asch, 1946.

37. Work by Anderson (see, for example, Anderson, 1974) challenges this change-of-meaning interpretation. He argues instead for a mathematical formula that involves differential weighting of adjectives based on position. His view, however, does not actually challenge the primacy effect, for later information is "discounted," given a lower weight, if it is inconsistent with earlier information.

38. Jones, Rock, Shaver, Goethals, & Ward, 1968.

39. See Janoff-Bulman & Schwartzberg, 1991, for a lengthier discussion of these issues. See also Frank, 1963, who wrote about therapeutic change in terms of people's assumptive worlds, but equated assumptive worlds

183

with attitudes and thereby emphasized the importance of the therapist's power and similarity to client.

40. Freud, 1921, p. 248.

41. Janoff-Bulman & Schwartzberg, 1991.

42. Fairbairn, 1952.

43. Nisbett & Ross, 1980.

44. Popper, 1963.

45. Marris, 1975, pp. 19–20.

46. See Epstein, 1973, 1980, 1984, and Sarbin, 1981.

47. Epstein, 1980.

48. Kuhn, 1962.

49. Watzalawick, Weakland, & Fisch, 1974.

50. Rothbart, 1981.

51. Crocker, 1962.

52. After reviewing research and theory, for example, Wylie (1979) concluded that therapy has little lasting impact on people's self-concepts, despite the fact that this is frequently a goal of therapy. Nevertheless, reviews and extensive meta-analyses have shown formal psychological therapies to be effective for a broad range of psychological problems (see, for example, Miller & Berman, 1983; Shapiro & Shapiro, 1982; and Smith, Glass, & Miller, 1980). Certainly, adjustment problems may often be alleviated without any fundamental change in core assumptions; the substantial improvement generally found in control (i.e., untreated) groups supports this perspective.

Chapter 3
Trauma and the Terror of Our Own Fragility

1. van der Kolk uses the phrase "overwhelming life experiences" to describe trauma; see van der Kolk, 1987.

2. American Psychiatric Association, DSM-III, 1980.

3. American Psychiatric Association, DSM-III-R, 1987; these revisions primarily reflected a desire to stress denial and not simply reexperiencing symptoms.

4. American Psychiatric Association, DSM-III-R, 1987, p. 247.

5. American Psychiatric Association, DSM-III-R, 1987, p. 249.

6. See, for example, Keane, Litz, & Blake's (1990) review of research on estimates of the prevalence of PTSD in specific populations.

   The National Vietnam Veterans Readjustment Study (Kulka, Schlenger, Fairbank, Hough, Jordan, Marmar, & Weiss, 1988) is clearly the most comprehensive evaluation of PTSD in Vietnam veterans. Based on a nationwide probability sample and using multiple measures to diagnose PTSD, these researchers found that 30.9 percent of the men and 26.9 percent of the women who served in Vietnam developed PTSD. Compared to these lifetime estimates, 15 percent of the men and 8.5 percent of the women are currently still troubled by PTSD. Male veterans who were injured or exposed to intensive combat stresses were roughly four times as likely to have developed PTSD in their lifetime; women exposed to high levels of war zone stress, such as exposure to dead soldiers, were seven times as likely to develop PTSD sometime during their lifetime.

Kilpatrick, Saunders, Veronen, Best, & Von (1987) studied the incidence of PTSD in a community sample of women using DIS-based interviews. For all crimes, they found a 27.8 percent overall lifetime prevalence rate of PTSD, and a current prevalence rate of 7.5 percent. The lifetime prevalence rates for different crimes were 57.1 percent for completed rape, 15.7 percent for attempted rape, 33.3 percent for completed molestation, 36.8 percent for aggravated assault, 18.2 percent for robbery, and 28.2 percent for burglary.

Frederick (1986) studied three hundred adults, aged twenty to sixty-seven, all of whom were victims of different violent acts—POWs, physical assault, natural disasters, hostages, and sexual abuse. Frederick used the Reaction Index, a scale measuring the presence and degree of severity of PTSD, and found that between 89 and 96 percent of the victim groups showed some symptoms of PTSD (i.e., were positive on the index). Frederick found that 50 percent of the POWs had scores indicating "very severe" or "severe" PTSD symptoms, and 42 percent had scores indicating "moderate" or "mild" PTSD symptoms. Of the physical assault victims, 36 percent showed very severe/severe PTSD, and 54 percent indicated moderate/mild symptoms; among the disaster victims, 28 percent scored in the very severe/severe range, 61 percent in the moderate/mild range; 66 percent of the hostage victims indicated very severe/severe PTSD and 30 percent moderate/mild PTSD; and 54 percent of the rape victims scored in the very severe/severe range, 40 percent in the moderate/mild range. Frederick notes that in previous studies, 75 percent of victims have typically shown some symptoms of PTSD, 25 percent showing severe symptoms and 50 percent mild to moderate symptoms. The remaining 25 percent have typically fallen into a doubtful category. In his own study, the population groups clearly exceeded the expected numbers.

7. For a discussion of comorbidity in PTSD, see Keane & Wolfe, 1990. Data clearly support the conclusion that PTSD is associated with high rates of other psychological disorders, including major depression, personality disorders, and substance abuse.

8. McCann & Pearlman, 1990, p. 39.

9. PTSD is a piece of the trauma picture, the piece that is most useful for

diagnostic purposes. As H. Krystal (1968) has noted, it is perhaps not surprising that traumatized individuals show many symptoms and many kinds of disturbances. From his work with massively traumatized concentration camp survivors, for example, he concluded that "disturbances of a neurotic depressive, psychosomatic, psychotic-like nature occur at the same time and disturbances of cognition, memory and affectivity of 'atypical' kinds overlie all of these" (1968, p. 27). The present focus is on commonalities in the psychological experience of trauma. The emphasis is not on diagnostic issues, but on better understanding what the victim goes through in the aftermath of overwhelming life events.

10. Laplanche & Pontalis, 1973.

11. See Lifton, 1967. See also Janoff-Bulman, 1985b, and Perloff, 1983.

12. Kuhn, 1962.

13. See Janoff-Bulman, 1985b, 1989a, and Janoff-Bulman & Frieze, 1983. See also Horowitz, 1976, 1980, 1982, on the importance of assimilating new trauma-based material into one's schemas. There are several recent related conceptualizations of trauma. Epstein (1991) writes of the breakdown of people's basic theories of reality, a view that he developed out of his cognitive-experiential self-theory. McCann & Pearlman (1990) also conceptualize trauma in terms of the disruption of psychological needs and schemas in their Constructivist Self-Development Theory, and Roth (Dye & Roth, 1991; Roth & Lebowitz, 1988) emphasizes the importance of disrupted schemas. A related view that is informed by psychoanalytic theory is that of Ulman & Brothers (1988), whose self-psychological theory of trauma stresses the shattering of the self, which is an individual's central organizing fantasy.

14. From "Her Becoming," a poem by Theodore Roethke.

15. Lazarus (1966, and Lazarus & Folkman, 1984) wrote of primary appraisal, which involves the interpretation of a threat. See Chapter 6 in this volume, which discusses the important role of appraisal in coping.

16. DSM-III-R, 1987, p. 250.

17. See also McCann & Pearlman, 1990.

18. American Psychiatric Association, 1987, p. 247.

19. See Janoff-Bulman & Schwartzberg, 1991, for a more complete discussion of this issue.

20. See Ornstein, 1972.

21. Brickman, 1978.

22. Epstein, 1980, 1985.

23. According to Epstein (1980, 1985), these minds are generally integrated but may, at times, be a source of conflict, as represented most simply by the individual who rationally "knows" it is extremely safe to fly but is still

frightened and unwilling to fly. Both, he argues, provide valid information to the individual.

Recent work on the two sides of the brain provides an intriguing metaphor for thinking about these two different ways of knowing. The left side of the brain is associated with reason and intellectual knowledge, and thereby parallels Epstein's rational mind and Brickman's inferential validity. The right side of the brain is associated with feelings and emotions, and as such parallels Epstein's experiential mind and Brickman's phenomenological validity. Usually, the two are not in conflict and communicate with one another in order to provide an individual with effective guides to understanding and behavior. The corpus callosum may be regarded as an anatomical analog for this communication.

24. Nash, 1976, p. 129.
25. In a related vein, it is interesting to note the recent work by Weinstein (1989) on the very important role of personal experience for understanding people's self-protective behaviors.
26. McCann & Pearlman, 1990.
27. Lifton, 1980, p. 117.
28. For a review, see Oei, Lim, & Hennessy, 1990. See also Kaylor, King, & King, 1987.
29. Foy, Resnick, Sipprelle, & Carroll, 1987.
30. Lifton, 1967, p. 480.
31. Lifton, 1967, p. 481.
32. Gleser, Green, & Winget, 1981, and Green, Grace, & Gleser, 1985.
33. The words of a thirty-eight-year-old crash victim; *Life magazine,* September 1989, vol. 12, no. 10, p. 38.
34. Kushner, 1975, p. 223.
35. Kushner, 1975, p. 221.
36. Neiderbach, 1986, pp. 113–14.
37. Barkas, 1978, p. 150.
38. Bard & Sangrey, 1979, p. 15. See also Barkas, 1978.
39. Terr, 1979, 1983.
40. From Shakespeare's *King Lear.*
41. Kierkegaard, 1944.
42. Becker, 1973, p. 26.
43. See also Lifton, 1967, 1980, 1988, on the importance of human symbolic systems for understanding trauma.
44. See Becker, 1973, Chapter 4.
45. The words of a rape victim reported in the *Daily Hampshire Gazette,* April 10, 1991, p. 1.

46. Wolfenstein, 1957, p. 159.

47. In (Janoff-)Bulman & Wortman, 1977, all of the accident victims reported having asked this question. Rose Kushner aptly titled her book about her experience with breast cancer, *Why Me?* For a review, see Janoff-Bulman & Lang-Gunn, 1989.

48. Taylor, 1983.

49. Wortman & Dunkel-Schetter, 1979, p. 125.

50. Lifton & Olson, 1976. See also the work off Titchener, Kapp, & Winget, 1976, also on the Buffalo Creek disaster.

51. Burgess & Holmstrom, 1974.

52. McCullers, 1951.

53. McCullers, 1951, p. 111.

54. Irving, 1978.

55. Fear and anxiety are common reactions among survivors of crimes, diseases, accidents, and disasters. See, for example, Bard & Sangrey, 1986; Burgess, Hartman, McCausland, & Powers, 1984; Calhoun, Atkeson, & Resick, 1982; Ellis, Atkeson, & Calhoun, 1981; K. T. Erikson, 1976; Frederick, 1980; Hilberman & Munson, 1977–78; Maguire, 1980; Terr, 1981; and Wilkinson, 1983.

56. The physiological representation of the traumatic response is discussed later in this chapter.

57. Calhoun, Atkeson, & Resick, 1982.

58. Keane, Fairbank, Caddell, Zimmerling, & Bender, 1985, and Keane, Zimering, & Caddell, 1985. Work with rape victims (Kilpatrick, Veronen, & Resick, 1982) and Vietnam veterans (Keane, Zimering, & Caddell, 1985) suggests that by avoiding these anxiety-provoking stimuli, victims reduce their anxiety, and thus the fear and anxiety are not given a chance to extinguish.

59. See *People* magazine, November 14, 1989, on actress Kelly McGillis's terrifying experiences as a rape victim.

60. Arieti, 1970, p. 138.

61. *New York Times,* October 23, 1989, p. B11.

62. See *Newsweek,* January 8, 1990, p. 54.

63. Horney, 1937.

64. Averill, 1976.

65. See Litz, Penk, Gerardi & Keane, in press.

66. Blanchard, Kolb, Gerardi, Ryan, & Pallmeyer, 1986.

67. For example, Anisman, Ritch, & Sklar, 1981; Redmond & Krystal, 1984; and van der Kolk, Greenberg, Boyd, & Krystal, 1985.

68. Ciaranello, 1983.

69. See, for example, van der Kolk & Greenberg, 1987, and van der Kolk, Greenberg, Boyd, & Krystal, 1985. See also Anisman, Ritch, & Sklar, 1981.

70. Mason, Thomas, Kosten, Southwick, & Giller, 1990. These researchers also found extremely high levels of throxine and testosterone in their sample of Vietnam veterans with PTSD. Research by Mason and his colleagues with monkeys have found norepinephrine elevations in conditions involving threat or anticipation of aversive stimulation and epinephrine elevations in situations involving uncertainty, ambiguity, and possibly uncontrollability (Mason, Mangan, Brady, Conrad, & Rioch, 1961, and Mason, Brady, & Tolson, 1966).

71. For example, Bourne, Rose, & Mason, 1967, 1968; Pallmeyer, Blanchard, & Kolb, 1986; and Rose, Bourne, Poe, Mougey, Collins, & Mason, 1979; cf. Hoffman, Burges-Watson, Wilson, & Montgomery, 1989.

72. Mason, Kosten, Southwick, & Giller, 1990. This argument is also consistent with Levine's (1983) emphasis on the biological utility of the organism's capacity to reduce endocrine responses to persistently aversive stimuli. Because heightened corticoids have numerous deleterious biological effects (e.g., suppress the immune mechanisms, interfere with the action of insulin, cause calcium loss), the reduction of hypersecretions of the neuroendocrine system should thus be a major consequence of coping mechanisms.

73. See ver Ellen & van Kammen, 1990. These researchers suggest that some type of dissociation may characterize other biological substrates of trauma, including cerebral lateralization and receptor-enzyme system changes.

74. J. H. Krystal, 1990.

75. DeSouza, 1988; Owens & Meniroff, 1988; and Stone, 1988.

76. Burges-Watson, Hoffman, & Wilson, 1988, and ver Ellen & van Kammen, 1990.

77. ver Ellen & van Kammen, 1990.

78. American Psychiatric Association, 1987.

79. Neiderbach, 1986, p. 167.

80. Burgess & Holmstrom, 1974, pp. 45–46.

81. K. T. Erikson, 1976, p. 143.

Chapter 4
Disillusionment and Change in the Assumptive World

1. From Henrik Ibsen's *The Wild Duck*.

2. O'Neill, 1946.

3. According to the American Psychiatric Association, DSM-III-R, regarding symptoms of PTSD: "Symptoms of depression and anxiety are com-

mon, and in some instances may be sufficiently severe to be diagnosed as an Anxiety or Depressive Disorder" (p. 249).

Depression has been commonly found among victims of rape, other crimes, childhood sexual abuse, disasters, disease, and combat; see, for example, Atkeson, Calhoun, Resick, & Ellis, 1982; K. T. Erikson, 1976; Helzer, Robins, Wish, & Hesselbrock, 1979; Jones, 1985; Walker, 1979; and Weisman, 1979.

4. Arieti & Bemporad, 1978.

5. For a review, see Taylor, 1990. See also the work of Abramson and Alloy (e.g., Abramson & Alloy, 1981; Alloy & Abramson, 1979, 1982; Alloy & Ahrens, 1987; and Alloy & Tabachnik, 1984).

6. See, for example, Abramson, Alloy, & Rossoff, 1981; Beck, 1967; Gotlib, 1983; and Taylor, 1990.

7. In a parallel fashion, there is considerable psychological research on grieving that suggests that the sudden, unexpected death of loved ones is psychologically far more difficult than anticipated losses; see, for example, Glick, Weiss, & Parkes, 1974; Parkes & Weiss, 1983; and Stroebe & Stroebe, 1987.

8. Viorst, 1986.

9. Gould, 1978.

10. In numerous research studies that have included the World Assumptions Scale, alpha reliability coefficients for each of the three subscales—benevolence of the world, meaningfulness of the world, and self-worth—have been between .81 and .87; see Janoff-Bulman, 1989b, for more on scale development.

11. The correlations between items mentioning the world and those mentioning people is very high, typically around .80.

12. Across all of our studies we have rarely found gender differences in victims' assumptions. One gender main effect is consistently found: females (victims and nonvictims) have higher scores on the benevolence of the world scale than males; this difference is small but statistically significant. Given that the benevolence of the world scale largely taps respondents' views of people, it is likely that women's higher scores reflect their more relational perspective (see Chodorow, 1978, and Gilligan, 1982).

13. To our surprise initially, men represented approximately one-third of the rape and incest victims in these studies. More recent studies have suggested that the number of male incest and rape victims is far higher than had been assumed. For a review and discussion of gender and victimization, particularly incest, rape, and sexual abuse, see Janoff-Bulman & Frieze, 1987.

14. In some instances, one or two of the three assumptions have been more negative. In these studies, there has been less representation of particular

types of victimizations, as will become clearer in the discussion on differences between particular types of overwhelming life events.

15. This was a mail survey with a 31 percent return rate, higher than is typical
in studies of this sort.

16. See, for example, Baum, O'Keefe, & Davidson's (1990) distinction between acute and chronic events based on duration of the stressor. They
argue that the duration of a stressful episode can be considered in terms
of the duration of the physical stressor, the duration of threat perception
or demand, and the persistence of response. They suggest that traumatic
events are often very brief but give rise to chronic threat and stubborn
response patterns.

Acute and chronic victimizations may also be associated with different
types of coping, as distinguished by Lazarus and his colleagues (Lazarus,
1966, and Folkman & Lazarus, 1984). Whereas emotion-focused coping
(involving palliative efforts to reduce one's emotional distress) is no
doubt called for in both instances, problem-focused coping, involving
direct interventions on the environment (i.e., attempts to alter the
stressor) might appear to be called for more in the case of chronic events.

17. An important aspect of self-help groups is a minimization of these negative self-perceptions. "It didn't just happen to me." See, for example,
Coates & Winston, 1983, on deviance and self-help groups.

18. Lifton, 1988. See also K. T. Erikson, 1976, and Lifton & Olson, 1976.

19. This will become particularly apparent in the discussions of self-blame in
Chapter 6.

20. Bard & Sangrey, 1979, pp. 14–15.

21. Fischer, 1984.

22. See, for example, Bard & Sangrey, 1979. See also Hilberman, 1980;
Kilpatrick, Resick, & Veronen, 1979, 1982; and Roth & Lebowitz,
1988, on rape victims.

23. A discussion of blaming the victim is presented in Chapter 7.

24. Perloff's (1983) distinction between "universal vulnerability" and
"unique vulnerability" is relevant here. In the former instance, a person
sees all people as vulnerable to misfortune, whereas in the latter case an
individual sees him/herself as particularly vulnerable to misfortune.

25. Janoff-Bulman, 1985a.

26. Fischer, 1984, p. 168.

27. Wilson, 1988a, 1988b.

28. Hayman, Sommers-Flanagan, & Parsons, 1987.

29. See, for example, Frederick, 1980. The reactions of others to victims will
be addressed in Chapter 7.

30. Sontag, 1978.

31. Collins, Taylor, & Skokan, 1990.

32. Schwartzberg & Janoff-Bulman, in press.

33. Schwartzberg & Janoff-Bulman, in press.

34. See, for example, the work of Robert Pynoos (e.g., Pynoos & Eth, 1985).

35. See, for example, Finkelhor (1984, and Finkelhor & Browne, 1985); Pynoos & Eth, 1985; and Terr, 1979, 1983.

36. See *New York Times,* January 7, 1990, p. 41.

37. The question of long-term effects based on specific age of impact during childhood is a separate yet interesting question. An interest in long-term effects has led us to explore the impact of age at time of victimization on psychological indices of well-being. In our numerous studies of college students, we have asked about age at time of victimization and have not found differences due to specific childhood age. This has even been the case in two recent studies we conducted on parental divorce, which has often been discussed in terms of age of child at the time of divorce. One was a large questionnaire study of 568 university students from divorced versus intact homes, the other a smaller, more intensive study involving fifty-seven college students whose parents had been divorced and fifty-seven matched respondents whose parents were still married (see Franklin, Janoff-Bulman, & Roberts, 1990). We looked closely at age at time of parents' divorce and found no effect—that is, by the time these students were young adults, there did not appear to be differences that could be accounted for by age. Certainly, this does not preclude the possibility of differences immediately after the divorce; there are many researchers who have written about the differential impact of parental divorce based on child's age. Nevertheless, over time it seems possible that specific age-related differences dissipate. Certainly, these samples do not include individuals who are most psychologically disturbed by these events. More specific data on age-related effects following traumatic life events awaits further research. Nevertheless, it is interesting to consider that it may be most important to distinguish between an event that happens in childhood versus adulthood, rather than specifically when in childhood.

38. For a review, see Janoff-Bulman & Frieze, 1987.

39. Relevant here is an excellent review by Garmezy (1983) on resilience in children under stress. He discusses a "steeling" effect that enables some children to be invulnerable to the negative impact of extreme stressors. He found that a particular triad—personality dispositions (e.g., autonomous, active, socially responsive) in infancy and childhood, family milieu (e.g., supportive parents, family closeness), and the presence of external support (from e.g., peers and teachers)—differentiated this group of resilient children.

40. Carey-Trefzer, 1949.

41. This was the conclusion reached by Garmezy (1983) after reviewing studies of children in war.

42. Gleser, Green, & Winget, 1981. These similarities are likely to be due, at least in part, to the less threatening interpretations and appraisals provided by less troubled parents. Of course, the similarities are also likely to be attributable to the greater support that could be afforded by parents who suffered less themselves. In separate analyses, these authors found that the supportiveness of the child's household was also related to psychological health.

43. Kinzie, 1986.

44. Westen, Ludolph, Misle, Ruffins, & Block, 1990.

45. Herman & van der Kolk, 1987. These researchers also suggest that this may help explain the considerably greater incidence of borderline personality disorder in women than is found in men. Data on childhood abuse indicate that although boys and girls are at approximately equal risk for physical abuse, girls are two to three times more likely to be the victims of sexual abuse, which, typically, is more prevalent and more prolonged than physical abuse. See also Herman, 1986.

46. Adler, 1985.

47. See, for example, Adler, 1985; Gunderson, 1984; Herman & van der Kolk, 1987; Kernberg, 1975; and Rinsley, 1982.

48. See, for example, Putnam, Post, Guroff, et al., 1986; and Sachs, Goodwin, & Braun, 1986.

49. See also Horevitz & Braun, 1984.

50. Herman & van der Kolk, 1987.

51. For a review, see Fish-Murray, Koby, & van der Kolk, 1987.

52. Burgess & Holmstrom, 1979. See also Atkeson, Calhoun, Resick, & Ellis, 1982, and Frank, Turner, Stewart, Jacob, & West, 1981.

53. Work on "priming" in the area of social cognition suggests that frequently or recently activated ideas come to mind more easily than those that have not been activated; in turn, new information is interpreted in light of the primed construct (see, e.g., Higgins & King, 1981, and Srull & Wyer, 1977). The notion of severe threat is likely to be frequently activated and therefore considerably more accessible for victims whose self- and worldviews are dominated by their victimization. In the face of an overwhelming life event, these individuals are subject to an intense reactivation of stress.

54. These would be instances characterized as acute PTSD; chronic PTSD would apply to those who continue to have problems over time.

55. See Perloff, 1983. See also Wortman (1976) regarding the dangers of

high expectations of control in the face of uncontrollable outcomes. I am reminded of a study we conducted a number of years ago at a nursing home; elderly patients who had been most active and psychologically expected to control outcomes in their lives had the most difficulty adjusting to nursing homes (see Janoff-Bulman & Marshall, 1982).

56. There is some research that suggests the best predictor of long-term outcomes is the victim's initial response to an extreme life event. These findings might appear to preclude the possibility that one could do very poorly in the short run and very well in the long run. Thus, work on rape victims' reactions by Dean Kilpatrick, Lois Veronen, and Connie Best (1985) has suggested no significant differences between rape victims' scores on anxiety, fear, self-esteem, general symptomatology, and mood state at three months and four years postrape.

It is important to note that at three months, the scores of most rape victims in their sample showed significant improvement over measures at six to twenty-one days. Further, although the latter scores were predictive of three-month scores on a distress index, a closer look at their findings shows correlations ranging from .21 to .38 (and −.21 to −.34), numbers suggesting considerable variability.

It is possible, in part, to account for their conclusion that early responses are predictive of later ones by pointing to the responses of the least-distressed victims. Those who showed the least distress at time 1 also showed the least distress at subsequent data points.

Kilpatrick and his colleagues suggest this by pointing out that there is little evidence for a period of low distress followed by an exacerbation of symptoms, and observed low distress should be taken at face value. If a victim manifests little distress and few symptoms in the immediate aftermath of victimization, he or she is likely to manifest few long-term reactions. Thus, survivors whose assumptions are least shattered are not likely to manifest marked short- or long-term reactions. This does not preclude the possibility that extremely high initial distress will be associated with decreased long-term distress for some victims; this is a pattern that may be most likely to describe responses of particular survivors, those with very positive preexisting assumptions. Certainly there are others with high initial distress who will remain very distressed over time; this is a group with chronic post-traumatic stress disorder.

57. McGuire, 1964.

58. Burgess & Holmstrom, 1978.

59. Ruch, Chandler, & Harter, 1980.

60. See Gleser, & Winget, 1981, and Huerta & Horton, 1978.

61. Solomon, 1990.

62. van der Kolk, 1985; he also notes that these veterans stated they had learned not to trust anyone in childhood. He concludes that they there-

fore did not form any close attachments to their comrades and thus were not vulnerable to object losses from combat. Their lack of trust, however, also suggests more negative fundamental assumptions, and thus a decreased likelihood of a shattered inner world.

Studies by John Wilson and his colleagues (Wilson, 1989, and Wilson & Krauss, 1985) have shown that premorbid personality measures are generally not associated with the development of PTSD among Vietnam veterans.

63. See also Thompson & Janigian, 1988, on "threat-resistant" life schemes.

Chapter 5
Processing the Powerful New Data

1. In general, I find the recent debates about the primacy of cognitions or emotions a matter of semantics. Depending upon what one considers "cognitive processing," cognitions do or do not always precede emotions. Thus, one needs to recognize danger (i.e., cognitively process the stimulus in some fashion) for a primary emotion such as fear to occur. Yet fear has an "immediacy" that may preclude the label "cognitive processing" for what precedes it. These systems interact, and each can precede—and affect—the other. Thus, most simply, our interpretations of events can clearly affect our emotional experience of that event; and our affective experience can clearly motivate how and when we process information. Adjustment post-trauma, I believe, illustrates both of these directions.

2. See Roth & Cohen, 1976, regarding the importance of both approach and avoidance orientations to acute stress. In his work on the psychological aspects of physical illness and disability, Shontz (1965) also emphasizes this continual alternation between encounter and retreat. See also Horowitz, 1976, 1980, 1982.

3. American Psychiatric Association, 1987.

4. Kushner, 1975.

5. Goldberger, 1983, p. 85.

6. Lazarus, 1983.

7. See Janoff-Bulman & Timko, 1987.

8. Freud, 1924.

9. For example, Eitinger, 1983, and Hackett & Cassem, 1974.

10. Freud, 1936.

11. See Goldberger, 1983, for more discussion of these issues.

12. See Epstein, 1967; Horowitz 1967, 1980, 1982; and Lazarus, 1983, for other discussions of the adaptive value of denial.

13. Epstein, 1967, p. 52.

14. From Emily Dickinson's poem 341.

15. See American Psychiatric Association, 1987, p. 248.

16. See Horowitz, 1975, 1976, 1980, 1982.

17. Lifton, 1967, p. 31.

18. Lifton, 1967, p. 33.

19. See, for example, Dimsdale, 1980; H. Krystal, 1968; and Meerloo, 1963.

20. See Lifton, 1967, 1980, 1988, on psychic closing-off as a symbolic form of death.

21. See, for example, Bard & Sangrey, 1979; Cassem & Hackett, 1971; Chodoff, Friedman, & Hamburg, 1964; Druss & Kornfeld, 1967; Dudley, Verney, Masuda, Martin, & Holmes, 1969; Hackett & Weisman, 1969; Hinton, 1984; Lindemann, 1944; Sutherland & Scherl, 1970; and Weisman, 1972. For a general review, see Janoff-Bulman & Timko, 1987.

22. Sutherland and Scherl (1970) have reported that this is common in the case of rape victims.

23. According to Bard and Sangrey (1979), this is a "hyperactive" form of denial.

24. Hilgard, 1977. Recently, van der Kolk and his colleagues have more specifically discussed Janet's work on dissociation in the face of overwhelming threat. According to Janet, the trauma response is biologically based and results in the fragmentation of mental cohesion (see van der Kolk, Brown, & van der Hart, 1989, and van der Kolk & van der Hart, 1989).

25. Hilgard, 1977, p. 5.

26. van der Kolk & Kadish, 1987. See also Bliss, 1980; Fisher, 1945; and Jaffe, 1968.

27. See, for example, Bliss, 1980; Herman & van der Kolk, 1987; and Kluft, 1985. See also previous discussion on childhood victimization, Chapter 4.

28. Lifton (1986) has written about a type of dissociation he calls doubling, which involves the formation of a part self that ultimately becomes autonomous. He argues that this doubling characterized the Nazi doctors, for the development of this second self enabled the ordinary person to commit incredible evil. He maintains that for this group doubling was also a response to extreme stress.

29. These dissociative reactions appear in marked contrast to the phenomenon of "embracing the trauma" (Epstein, 1991). Epstein argues that some victims change their personalities and actively seek to reexperience the trauma, as if changing their personalities to fit the extreme event. By redefining it as desirable, the event becomes unthreatening.

30. van der Kolk & Kadish, 1987. See also Greenberg & van der Kolk, 1987, and Lindemann, 1944.

31. van der Kolk, 1987, p. 7.

32. Epstein, 1967, and Horowitz, 1976, 1980, 1982.

33. Burgess & Holmstrom, 1974, p. 40.

34. K. T. Erikson, 1976, pp. 143–44.

35. Goodwin, 1980.

36. It is interesting to speculate that one major difference between traumas resulting from a diagnosis of life-threatening illness and events such as disasters and crimes may lie in the nature of the intrusive experiences. Disasters and crime victims may be more likely to be plagued with vivid visual memories of the event, whereas disease victims may be more apt to experience intrusive thoughts.

37. Freud, [1928] 1959, p. 46.

38. Freud, [1928] 1959, p. 60.

39. A psychoanalytic conceptualization of the repetition compulsion suggests an ego and id component. The "id-aspect" is regarded as responsible for the reexperience of the painful situation, and the "ego-aspect" as responsible for attempts at mastery of the event.

40. Becker, 1976, p. 99.

41. Wolfenstein, 1957, p. 136. See also Rachman, 1979, on emotional processing.

42. Sokolov, 1963.

43. See, for example, Horowitz, 1975, 1980, 1982; Janoff-Bulman & Thomas, 1989; Martin & Tesser, 1989; Silver, Boon, & Stones, 1983; and Tait & Silver, 1989.

44. K. T. Erikson, 1976, p. 167.

45. See Horowitz, 1976, 1980, 1982.

46. Mandler, 1964.

47. Horowitz, 1976, p. 93.

48. Horowitz, 1976, p. 95.

49. It is intriguing to consider that the need to process the data—to complete one's conceptual task—is so fundamental that reexperiencing phenomena occur even in cases of amnesic dissociation, primarily through nightmares that are typically not recalled (see van der Kolk, 1987) and flashbacks, in which victims report not being themselves.

50. See, for example, Coates & Wortman, 1980; Dunkel-Schetter & Wortman, 1982; and Wortman & Dunkel-Schetter, 1979.

51. Rachman, 1979.

52. Wolfenstein, 1957, p. 139.

53. Social support will be discussed in Chapter 7.

54. Pennebaker, 1990; Pennebaker & Beall, 1986; Pennebaker, Hughes, & O'Heeron, 1987; and Pennebaker, Kiecolt-Glaser, & Glaser, 1988.

55. See Horowitz, 1976, 1980, 1982. See also Janoff-Bulman & Thomas, 1989.

56. It is interesting to note that nonconscious processes were largely ignored by social psychologists until recently. Langer's (1978) paper on mindlessness and Nisbett and Wilson's (1977) article on "knowing more than we can tell" both served to open the field to the possibility and operation of automatic, nonconscious processes.

57. See Mandler, 1984.

58. See, for example, Uleman & Bargh's (1989) edited volume on "unintended thought" and Wegner (1989) on "unwanted thoughts." See also Fiske, 1989, on the concept of "intent."

59. Ghiselin, 1952, p. 38.

60. Rothenberg, 1979.

Chapter 6
Rebuilding Assumptions: Interpreting the Traumatic Experience

1. Lazarus, 1966, and Folkman & Lazarus, 1984.

2. See the work on "hardiness" by Kobasa (1979; Kobasa, Maddi, & Kahn, 1982; and Kobasa & Pucetti, 1983). People characterized as hardy tend to reinterpret threats as challenges, focusing on what they can gain rather than lose.

3. Of course, there is still room for individual differences, with some people not regarding seemingly very threatening situations as such, and others regarding situations that would not bother most people as extremely threatening.

4. American Psychiatric Association, 1987, p. 250.

5. Moos & Schaefer, 1986.

6. James, 1985, p. 79.

7. Pearlin and Schooler (1978) discuss people's attempts to reduce stress by cognitively neutralizing the threats through control over the meaning of a problem. See also Hobfoll, 1989, on people's motivation to reappraise stressors so as to conserve resources.

8. Festinger, 1954. See also Miller & Suls, 1977.

9. Wood, 1989.

10. See Brickman & (Janoff)-Bulman, 1977.

11. Richard Lazarus's (1966, and Lazarus & Folkman, 1984) important distinction between problem-focused and emotion-focused coping is relevant here. In response to stressful situations, people can engage in two

types of coping efforts: those involving concrete actions to deal directly with the crisis; the other involving efforts to regulate one's emotional response to the crisis.

12. Wills, 1981. See also Taylor, Wood, & Lichtman, 1983, and Wood, 1989.

13. See Wills, 1981. See also early studies on fear and affiliation (e.g., Darley & Aronson, 1966; Schachter, 1959; and Zimbardo & Formica, 1963). In these studies, researchers found that threatened subjects felt better when they could compare themselves and affiliate with others who were also unfortunate, particularly others who felt even more threatened and fearful than they.

14. Wills, 1981.

15. Rather, it is more likely that the process is often a "spontaneous" one that is activated under conditions of negative affect and threat. For more on spontaneous inferences, see Uleman, 1989.

16. The contributions of Shelley Taylor (1990, and Taylor, Wood, & Lichtman, 1983) have been particularly important in understanding social comparison processes following victimization.

17. Burgess & Holmstrom, 1979.

18. (Janoff-) Bulman & Wortman, 1977.

19. Taylor, Wood, & Lichtman, 1983.

20. See Taylor, Lichtman, & Wood, 1983. See also Wolfenstein, 1957.

21. Taylor, Wood, & Lichtman, 1983, p. 34.

22. In a related vein, see work on the differences between actors and observers in accounting for a person's behaviors (Jones & Nisbett, 1972). The actor-observer difference in attributions reflects not simply differences in information processing but in motivation as well.

23. (Janoff)-Bulman & Wortman, 1977.

24. See, for example, Burgess & Holmstrom, 1974; Medea & Thompson, 1974; and Weis & Weis, 1975.

25. National Commission on the Causes and Prevention of Violence, 1969. Amir (1971) proposed a higher figure, 19 percent. He used a considerably broader definition in establishing his criteria for victim precipitation, including "risky situations marred with sexuality." Even in light of the 19 percent, however, the pervasiveness of self-blame is far higher than would be expected.

26. See Brownmiller, 1975, who suggests that women are conditioned to a female victim mentality. See also the psychologies of Deutsch (1944) and Horney (1973).

27. For a review, see Janoff-Bulman & Lang-Gunn, 1989.

28. See, for example, Beck, 1967.

29. See Wortman, 1976, regarding the importance of control, even in the face of possible self-esteem deficits.

30. See Janoff-Bulman, 1979, and Janoff-Bulman & Thomas, 1989.

31. This distinction parallels those drawn in work on the just world theory (e.g., Lerner, 1970, 1980) in which innocent victims will be blamed for some behavior in which they engaged or will be derogated (i.e., characterologically blamed). The distinctions made by Weiner and his colleagues (Weiner et al., 1972) in the domain of achievement attributions is also very relevant. In attributing failure to oneself, an individual can point to a lack of ability (i.e., characterological) or effort (i.e., behavioral). The implications for perceived control are very different, for the ability attribution is associated with beliefs that there is little one could have done, or can do in the future, to change the situation. Effort attributions, on the other hand, are associated with beliefs that if one tried harder one could have succeeded, and if one tries harder in the future one will succeed.

32. This represents a difference in both the stable and global dimensions of attributional formulations (e.g., Abramson, Seligman, & Teasdale, 1978).

33. These differences are apparent in examples provided by rape crisis counselors; see Janoff-Bulman, 1979. Frequently reported examples of behavioral self-blame included: I shouldn't have let someone I didn't know into the house, I shouldn't have been out that late, I should not have walked alone (in that neighborhood), I should not have hitchhiked, I should not have gone to his apartment, I shouldn't have left my window open, and I should have locked my car. Frequently reported examples of characterological self-blame included: I'm too trusting, I'm a weak person, I'm too naive and gullible, I'm the kind of person who attracts trouble, I'm not a very aware person, I'm not at all assertive—I can't say no, I'm immature and can't take care of myself, I'm not a good judge of character, I'm basically a bad person. It is important to note that engaging in self-blame did not preclude other-blaming. In other words, although they blamed themselves in part, the rape victims were also likely to blame the perpetrator a great deal. It is as if the victims recognized that there were a number of contributing conditions, and the absence of one of them might have prevented the rape.

    In this study of rape crisis centers across the country, counselors reported that 74 percent of the rape victims they see blame themselves at least in part for the rape. When they were presented with a description of behavioral and characterological types of self-blame, an average of 69 percent were reported as blaming themselves behaviorally, whereas an average of 19 percent were reported as blaming themselves characterologically.

34. This distinction is important and has not been adequately addressed in empirical research. For example, statistically, the effects of characterologi-

cal self-blame should be partialed out of correlations between behavioral self-blame and coping outcomes. This has not been done in research studies, and thus the adaptive value of behavioral self-blame is apt to be missed or seriously underestimated.

35. Medea & Thompson, 1974, p. 105.

36. Hursch, 1977, p. 95.

37. Chodoff, Friedman, & Hamburg, 1964.

38. See, for example, Abrams & Finesinger, 1953; Bard & Dyk, 1956; Chodoff, Friedman, & Hamburg, 1964; Davis, 1963; and Kubler-Ross, 1969.

39. Bard & Sangrey, 1979, p. 57.

40. Work by Taylor (1983) suggests that if cancer patients change behaviors and experience a recurrence of the cancer, they often simply make an attribution to a new behavior and change this new behavior.

41. It is possible for victims to believe that behavior change will prevent future misfortunes and yet not engage in self-blame for past behaviors. Such a response could follow from an analysis by Philip Brickman and his colleagues (Brickman, Rabinowitz, Karuza, Coates, Cohn, & Kidder, 1982) in which attributions for the past are distinguished from attributions for the future. A person can feel responsible for solutions without feeling responsible for the problem. Nevertheless, in our own research we have generally found that self-blame attributions are strongly associated with attributions about what one can do to prevent future instances of misfortune (see, e.g., Timko & Janoff-Bulman, 1985).

42. Studies suggesting the adaptiveness of behavioral self-blame include Affleck, Allen, Tennen, McGrade, & Ratzan, 1985; Affleck, McGrade, Allen, & McQueeney, 1985; Baum, Flemming, & Singer, 1983; Fischer, 1984; Peterson, Schwartz, & Seligman, 1981; Tennen, Affleck, Allen, McGrade, & Ratzan, 1984; Tennen, Affleck, & Gershman, 1986; and Timko & Janoff-Bulman, 1985. Studies suggesting the maladaptiveness of self-blame include Frasier, 1990; Kiecolt-Glaser & Williams, 1987; and Meyer & Taylor, 1986.

43. The consistent finding that characterological self-blame is associated with poorer coping outcomes can be understood in terms of its association with low self-esteem, which is virtually always related to measures of depression and psychological symptomatology. It should be noted that those with the lowest perceived self-worth to begin with may also be those most apt to invoke characterological self-blame. In this regard, it is instructive to read McCann & Pearlman, 1990, on the useful versus destructive impact of self-blame: "We believe that individuals who have impaired capacities for affect regulation and self-loathing are most vulnerable to a destructive impact of self-blame. Conversely, individuals with

strong resources and capacities who have high needs for independence may find behavioral self-blame strategies comforting" (p. 177).

It is also interesting to note that blaming other people has consistently been found to be associated with poor coping; see Tennen & Affleck, 1990, for a review of this literature.

44. These studies include my own early studies, which also reflected an unfortunate naivete in empirically studying self-blame.

45. This is consistent with the view that attributions are a byproduct of distress; see, for example, Downey, Silver, & Wortman, 1990. In this study of parents whose infants died of Sudden Infant Death, attributions appeared to be symptomatic of distress. Thus, those who are most distressed may be those who are most likely to engage in attributional processes, which reflect one means of cognitively confronting the trauma-related material.

46. Pennebaker, 1990. See also Pennebaker & Beall, 1986; Pennebaker, Hughes, & O'Heeron, 1987; and Pennebaker, Kiecolt-Glaser, & Glaser, 1988. This work is discussed in Chapter 5.

47. Scheppele & Bart, 1983.

48. Niederland, 1964.

49. Lindemann, 1977, p. 336.

50. The words of a twenty-one-year-old plane crash victim, reported in *Life* magazine, September 1989, p. 30.

51. Nagai, 1951; cited in Wolfenstein, 1957, pp. 217–18.

52. Lifton, 1967.

53. Danieli, 1985, p. 301.

54. The importance of finding this type of meaning in the event has been emphasized by Wortman & Silver, 1980. See also Lifton, 1967, 1980, 1988, and the importance of meaning in people's "formulations" post-trauma.

55. See Nisbett & Ross, 1980. An example of this type of thinking is the almost automatic assumption by some people that conspiracies are responsible for the assassination of national leaders; after all, how could the action of a single deranged person result in such a powerful outcome?

56. Frankl, 1963, pp. 105–107.

57. See Brickman, 1987, on these two sources of commitment in situations one cannot control.

58. See also, for example, Silver & Wortman, 1980; Taylor, 1983; Taylor, Wood, & Lichtman, 1983; Taylor, Lichtman, & Wood, 1984; Thompson, 1985; and Thompson & Janigian, 1988.

59. Reported in *Life* magazine, September 1989, p. 32. Of course, the downside of recognizing what is important in life is simultaneously recognizing how trivial and superficial some people appear to be.

60. Reported in the *New York Times,* June 17, 1990, pp. 1 and 20.
61. Bowker, 1970.
62. Bowker, 1970.
63. Frankl, 1963.
64. Chodoff, Friedman, & Hamburg, 1964.
65. See Lifton's (1980) discussion of "survivor mission."
66. See the *Washington Post,* March 27, 1988, p. A1.
67. Kushner, 1981, pp. 133–34.
68. Silver, Boon, & Stones, 1983.
69. Brickman, 1987. Philip Brickman, my teacher, mentor, and friend, was a brilliant, caring, social psychologist. He took his own life at the age of thirty-eight. His death was a tremendous loss not only to those who knew him but to the field of psychology as a whole.

Chapter 7
The External World: The Crucial Role of Other People

1. Seligman, 1975.
2. According to Albert Bandura (1982), self-efficacy involves both the confidence that one can produce a desired behavior and the belief that the behavior will have the desired effect.
3. Cohen & Wills, 1985.
4. See Cohen and Wills, 1985, for a review of these studies. See also overview by Dunkel-Schetter, 1984.
5. See, for example, Bornstein, Clayton, Halikas, Maurice, & Robins, 1973; Cobb & Kasl, 1977; Dunkel-Schetter, 1984; Smits, 1974; and Wallston, Alagna, DeVellis, & DeVellis, 1983. For an excellent review, see Silver & Wortman, 1980.
6. Burgess & Holmstrom, 1978.
7. Wilson & Krauss, 1985.
8. See, for example, Figley, 1978, and Figley & Leventman, 1980.
9. See, for example, Funch & Marshall, 1983, and Weisman & Worden, 1975. For a review, see Dunkel-Schetter & Wortman, 1984.
10. K. Erikson, 1976.
11. Wortman & Silver, 1980. See also Caplan, 1979, and Cobb, 1976.
12. Cooley, 1902.
13. Symonds, 1980.
14. For a related discussion, see Chapter 3 of Jones, Farina, Hastorf, Markus, Miller, & Scott, 1984. See also Goffman, 1963, on the danger associated with stigma.

15. See Eitinger's (1980) discussion of the "unequal dialogue" between Holocaust victims and the wider community, with its desire to forget.

16. See, for example, Farina, Holland, & Ring, 1966; Farina, Thaw, Felner, & Hust, 1976; Kleck, 1968; and Kleck, Ono, & Hastorf, 1966. Typically, the stigma is physically apparent in these studies.

17. See, for example, Lerner, 1970, 1980; Lerner & Matthews, 1967; and Lerner & Simmons, 1966. See also Wortman, 1976.

18. See, for example, Reisenzein, 1986; Weiner, 1980; and Weiner, Perry, & Magnuson, 1988.

19. Ryan, 1971, p. 28.

20. Fischhoff, 1975, and Fischhoff & Beyth, 1975. See also recent work on counterfactual thinking, which suggests that people's responses to negative events are often based on their ability to imagine alternative outcomes. This leads to a tendency to confuse what might have been with what ought to have been; see, for example, Miller, Turnbull, & McFarland, 1990.

21. Janoff-Bulman, Timko, & Carli, 1985.

22. The hindsight bias may contribute to victims' self-blaming as well, but certainly not to the same extent. The victim was there before the negative outcome was known and therefore had firsthand awareness—experiential awareness—of his or her prior psychological state and choice of behaviors. Although the hindsight bias might operate for victims in their reappraisals of the event, it is likely to operate far more powerfully in the case of the reactions of nonvictims to victims, for nonvictims typically learn of (or reconstruct) the prior behaviors of victims after already knowing about the victimization.

23. There is an entire field of sociology—victimology—that is unfortunately largely premised on the victim's contributory role in crimes.

24. Tavris & Wade, 1984, pp. 6–7.

25. Williams, 1987, pp. 3–4.

26. Rich & Stenzel, 1980.

27. Obeyesekere, 1985.

28. Figley, 1985.

29. See, for example, Frieze, Hymer, & Greenberg's (1984) discussion of the particular problems of rape victims due to their husbands' or lovers' negative reactions.

30. Figley, 1988b, p. 637.

31. Figley, 1983, 1985, 1988a, 1988b, 1989.

32. Emm & McKenry, 1988.

33. Dakof & Taylor, 1990, and Dunkel-Schetter, 1984.

34. Bard & Sangrey, 1979. This is likely to stem not only from protective

feelings towards the victim but also from their own need to make sense of the world in light of their own control beliefs.

35. Lindy, Grace, & Green, 1981.

36. See, for example, Sales French, 1984.

37. Wilson, 1978.

38. See, for example, Frieze, 1986.

39. Wortman & Dunkel-Schetter, 1979

40. See, for example, Dakof & Taylor, 1990, and Dunkel-Schetter, 1984.

41. See, for example, Dakof & Taylor, 1990.

42. See discussion by Wortman & Lehman, 1985. See also Silver, Wortman, & Crofton, 1990.

43. Wortman & Dunkel-Schetter, 1979. See also Silver, Wortman, & Crofton, 1990.

44. This 'conspiracy of silence" has been noted to exist in some families of Holocaust survivors. Children of survivors often report that what happened during the six years of World War II were just not discussed in their family; the Holocaust years were just not there—there was a complete gap. See, for example, Steinitz & Szonyi, 1975–76. See also Danieli's (1985) classification of Holocaust families.

45. Dunkel-Schetter, 1984.

46. Kahana, Harel, & Kahana, 1988. Other variables associated with good psychological functioning were an internal locus of control, altruism, and the belief that being a survivor was somehow beneficial to adjustment to aging.

47. For a review, see Wills, 1987.

48. McCann & Pearlman, 1990, p. 93. In their book, McCann and Pearlman generously cite my work in the evolution of their ideas about therapeutic interventions. Their therapy is largely based on the assumption that the client's core schemas have been disrupted and must be resolved. They present seven schemas that may be disrupted. These schemas can be conceptualized as representing the three fundamental assumptions discussed in this book. Their trust/dependency and intimacy schemas are reflections of assumptions regarding the benevolence of the world; the schemas they label "frame of reference" reflect assumptions about the meaningfulness of the world; and independence, power, and esteem schemas are essentially assumptions about self-worth. The safety schema discussed by McCann and Pearlman has elements of assumptions about the benevolence of the world (i.e., the world is dangerous and threatening) and meaningfulness of the world (i.e., there is nothing I can do to protect myself). In the present conceptualization, a sense of safety and an illusion of invulnerability derive from the maintenance of three fundamen-

tal assumptions and can be shattered by a disruption in any one of the three.

49. Parson, 1988.

50. Kohut, 1971, 1977.

51. See Roth & Cohen, 1986, on approach-avoidance processes in coping with stress.

52. Dye & Roth, 1991.

53. The purpose here is not to discuss the specifics of therapeutic approaches but to provide a general perspective from which to view clinical interventions. For discussion of specific therapies and treatment issues, see, for example, Burgess & Holmstrom, 1974; Dye & Roth, 1991; Figley, 1978, 1988a; Friedman, 1988; Keane, Fairbank, Caddell, Zimering, & Bender, 1985; Keane & Kaloupek, 1982; Marmar & Freedman, 1988; Marmar & Horowitz, 1988; McCann & Pearlman, 1990; Ochberg, 1988, 1991; Parson, 1988; and Scurfield, 1985.

Chapter 8
Recovery: Some Final Thoughts

1. See Figley, 1985, and Ochberg, 1991.

2. Weiss, 1988, p. 44.

3. Garmezy, 1983, p. 77.

4. See results of the community-based studies reported by Kahana, Harel, & Kahana, 1988.

5. These are victims who would be characterized as having chronic PTSD. See also the study of Lehman, Wortman, & Williams (1987) on the effects of losing a child or spouse in an automobile accident. They suggest the need to take a longer-term view of the recovery process than has been typical. Depression and a lack of resolution seemed to characterize the respondents four to seven years after their loss.

6. For a review, see Jones, E. E., 1979.

7. See, for example, Buss & Plomin, 1984.

8. H. Krystal, 1988, p. 31. Affect tolerance is central to Krystal's understanding and conceptualization of trauma.

9. Far more research is needed to provide a finer-grained analysis of the victim's inner world. Although trauma appears to alter our fundamental assumptions, we do not have a sense of how the experience is cognitively represented. Based on the expectation that this decreased absolutism and rigidity will be apparent in survivors' schemas and their general cognitive orientation, we are presently conducting research to explore, for example, whether recovery from trauma is associated with greater cognitive com-

plexity (see, e.g., Linville, 1987) and tolerance for ambiguity (e.g., Budner, 1946).

Further, recent research we've conducted on the long-term effects of divorce on children (Franklin, Janoff-Bulman, & Roberts, 1990) suggests that one way of coping optimally, over time, is to narrowly constrain a negative event's impact on one's cognitive system. Large changes in fundamental assumptions may be avoided by having changes occur primarily in a few lower- or middle-level schema. In order to begin to address these issues, Hillary Morgan and I are presently investigating the pervasiveness and level of schema-change in self-perceptions of trauma survivors.

10. From May Sarton's poem, "Humpty Dumpty."

11. See Breznitz, 1983, on the distinction between denial and hope. See also Janoff-Bulman & Timko, 1987.

12. This phrase is used by May Sarton in her poem, "Nightwatch."

13. This is Kierkegaard's phrase. According to Kierkegaard (1944), one goes through all of the anxiety to arrive at faith. For Kierkegaard, facing up to the terror of existence is ultimately associated with the establishment of religious faith. The new possibility open to an individual educated by dread involves a type of transcendence, a relationship with the "Ultimate Power of Creation." Although a newfound faith might characterize the response of some trauma survivors, this certainly need not define the "new possibility" open to others post-trauma.

References

ABELSON, R. P. 1981. The psychological status of the script concept. *American Psychologist, 36,* 715–29.

ABRAMS, R. D., AND J. E. FINESINGER. 1953. Guilt reactions in patients with cancer. *Cancer, 6,* 474–82.

ABRAMSON, L. Y., AND L. B. ALLOY. 1981. Depression, nondepression, and cognitive illusions: A reply to Schwartz. *Journal of Experimental Psychology, 110,* 436–47.

ABRAMSON, L. Y., L. B. ALLOY, AND R. ROSSOFF. 1981. Depression and the generation of complex hypotheses in the judgment of contingency. *Behavior Research and Therapy, 19,* 35–45.

ABRAMSON, L. Y., M. E. P. SELIGMAN, AND J. D. TEASDALE. 1978. Learned helplessness in humans: Critique and reformulation. *Journal of Abnormal Psychology, 87,* 49–74.

ADLER, G. 1985. *Borderline psychopathology and its treatment.* New York: Aronson.

AFFLECK, G., D. A. ALLEN, H. TENNEN, B. J. McGRADE, AND S. RATZAN. 1985. Causal and control cognitions in parent coping with a chronically ill child. *Journal of Social and Clinical Psychology, 3,* 369–79.

AFFLECK, G., B. J. McGRADE, D. A. ALLEN, AND M. McQUEENEY. 1985. Mothers' beliefs about behavioral causes for their developmentally disabled infant's condition: What do they signify? *Journal of Pediatric Psychology, 10,* 293–303.

AINSWORTH, M. D. S. 1979. Attachment as related to mother-infant interaction. In *Advances in the study of behavior,* vol. 1, ed. J. B. Rosenblatt, R. H. Hinde, C. Beer, and M. Bushell. New York: Academic Press.

AINSWORTH, M. D. S., AND B. WITTIG. 1969. Attachment and exploratory behavior in one-year-olds in a stranger situation. In *Determinants of infant behavior,* ed. B. M. Foss. New York: Wiley.

AINSWORTH, M. D. S., M. C. BLEHAR, E. WATERS, AND S. WALL. 1978. *Patterns of attachment.* Hillsdale, N.J.: Erlbaum.

ALBA, J. W., AND L. HASHER. 1983. Is memory schematic? *Psychological Bulletin, 93,* 203–31.

ALLOY, L. B., AND L. Y. ABRAMSON. 1979. Judgment of contingency in depressed and nondepressed students: Sadder but wiser? *Journal of Experimental Psychology: General, 108,* 441–85.

————. 1982. Learned helplessness, depression, and the illusion of control. *Journal of Personality and Social Psychology, 42,* 1114–26.

ALLOY, L. B., AND A. H. AHRENS. 1987. Depression and pessimism for the future: Biased use of statistically relevant information in predictions for self versus others. *Journal of Personality and Social Psychology, 52,* 366–78.

ALLOY, L. B., AND N. TABACHNIK. 1984. Assessment of covariation by humans and animals: The joint influence of prior expectations and current situational information. *Psychological Review, 91,* 112–49.

ALLPORT, G. W. 1943. *Becoming: Basic considerations for a psychology of personality.* New Haven: Yale University Press.

AMERICAN PSYCHIATRIC ASSOCIATION. 1980. *Diagnostic and statistical manual of mental disorders.* 3rd ed. Washington, D.C.: American Psychiatric Association.

————. 1987. *Diagnostic and statistical manual of mental disorders.* 3rd ed., rev. Washington, D.C.: American Psychiatric Association.

AMIR, M. 1971. *Patterns in forcible rape.* Chicago: University of Chicago Press.

ANDERSON, C. A., M. R. LEPPER, AND L. ROSS. 1980. Perseverance of social theories: The role of explanation in the persistence of discredited information. *Journal of Personality and Social Psychology, 39,* 1037–49.

ANDERSON, N. H. 1974. Information integration: A brief survey. *Contemporary developments in mathematical psychology,* ed. D. H. Krantz, R. C. Atkinson, R. D. Lance, and P. Suppes. San Francisco: Freeman.

ANISMAN, H. L., M. RITCH AND L. S. SKLAR. 1981. Noradrenergic and dopaminergic interactions in escape behavior. *Psychopharmocology, 74,* 263–68.

ANTONOVSKY, A. 1979. *Health, stress, and coping.* San Francisco: Jossey-Bass.

ARIETI, S. 1970. Cognition and feeling. In *Feelings and emotions,* ed. M. B. Arnold. New York: Academic Press.

ARIETI, S., AND J. BEMPORAD. 1978. *Severe and mild depression*. New York: Basic Books.

ARONSON, E. 1968. The theory of cognitive dissonance: A current perspective. In *Advances in experimental social psychology*, vol. 4, ed. L. Berkowitz. New York: Academic Press.

ASCH, S. 1946. Forming impressions of personality. *Journal of Abnormal and Social Psychology, 41*, 258–90.

ATKESON, B. M., K. S. CALHOUN, P. A. RESICK, AND E. M. ELLIS. 1982. Victims of rape: Repeated assessment of depressive symptoms. *Journal of Consulting and Clinical Psychology, 50*, 96–102.

AVERILL, J. 1976. Emotion and anxiety: Sociocultural, biological, and psychological determinants. In *Emotion and anxiety: New concepts, methods and applications*, ed. M. Zuckerman and C. D. Spielberger. New York: Erlbaum-Wiley.

BANDURA, A. 1982. Self-efficacy mechanism in human agency. *American Psychologist, 37*, 122–47.

BARD, M., AND R. B. DYK. 1956. The psychodynamic significance of beliefs regarding the cause of serious illness. *Psychoanalytic Review, 43*, 146–62.

BARD, M., AND D. SANGREY. 1979. *The crime victim's book*. New York: Basic Books.

BARKAS, J. L. 1978. *Victims*. New York: Scribner's.

BARTLETT, F. 1932. *A study in experimental and social psychology*. New York: Cambridge University Press.

BAUM, A., R. FLEMMING, AND J. E. SINGER. 1983. Coping with victimization by technological disaster. *Journal of Social Issues, 39*, 119–40.

BAUM, A., M. K. O'KEEFE, AND L. M. DAVIDSON. 1990. Acute stressors and chronic response: The case of traumatic stress. *Journal of Applied Social Psychology, 20*, 1643–54.

BECK, A. T. 1967. *Depression: Clinical, experimental, and theoretical aspects*. New York: Harper & Row.

BECKER, E. 1973. *The denial of death*. New York: Free Press.

BEM, D. 1970. *Beliefs, attitudes, and human affairs*. Belmont, Calif.: Brooks/Cole.

BLANCHARD, E. B., L. C. KOLB, R. J. GERARDI, P. RYAN, AND T. P. PALLMEYER. 1986. Cardiac response to relevant stimuli as an adjunctive tool for diagnosing post-traumatic stress disorder in Vietnam veterans. *Behavior Therapy, 17*, 592–606.

BLISS, E. L. 1980. Multiple personalities: A report of 14 cases with implications for schizophrenia and hysteria. *Archives of General Psychiatry, 37,* 1388–97.

BORNSTEIN, P. E., P. J. CLAYTON, J. A. HALIKAS, W. L. MAURICE, AND E. ROBINS. 1973. The depression of widowhood after thirteen months. *British Journal of Psychiatry, 122,* 561–66.

BOURNE, P. G., R. M. ROSE, AND J. W. MASON. 1967. Urinary 17-OHCS levels—data on seven helicopter medics in combat. *Archives of General Psychiatry, 17,* 104–10.

———. (1968). 17-OHCS levels in combat—Special Forces "A" team under threat of attack. *Archives of General Psychiatry, 19,* 135–40.

BOWKER, J. 1970. *Problems of suffering in religions of the world.* Cambridge, Eng.: Cambridge University Press.

BOWLBY, J. 1969. *Attachment and loss,* vol. 1: *Attachment.* London: Hogarth.

———. 1973. *Attachment and loss,* vol. 2: *Separation:* New York: Basic Books.

BREZNITZ, S. 1983. Denial versus hope: Concluding remarks. In *The denial of stress,* ed. S. Breznitz. New York: International Universities Press.

BRICKMAN, P. 1978. Is it real? In *New directions in attribution research,* vol. 2, ed. J. H. Harvey, W. I. Ickes, and R. F. Kidd. Hillsdale, N.J.: Erlbaum.

———. 1987. *Commitment, conflict, and caring.* Englewood Cliffs, N.J.: Prentice-Hall.

BRICKMAN, P., AND R. (JANOFF-)BULMAN. 1977. Pleasure and pain in social comparison. In *Social comparison processes: Theoretical and empirical perspectives,* ed. R. L. Miller and J. M. Suls. Washington, D.C.: Hemisphere.

BRICKMAN, P., V. RABINOWITZ, J. KARUZA, D. COATES, E. COHN, AND L. KIDDER. 1982. Models of helping and coping. *American Psychologist, 37,* 368–84.

BROWN, J. D. 1986. Evaluations of self and others: Self-enhancement biases in social judgments. *Social Cognition, 4,* 353–76.

BROWNMILLER, S. 1975. *Against our will: Men, women, and rape.* New York: Simon & Schuster.

BUDNER, S. 1962. Intolerance of ambiguity as a personality variable. *Journal of Personality, 30,* 29–50.

BURGES-WATSON, I. P., L. HOFFMAN, AND G. V. WILSON. 1988. The neuropsychiatry of post-traumatic stress disorder. *British Journal of Psychiatry, 152,* 164–73.

BURGESS, A. W., C. R. HARTMAN, M. P. MCCAUSLAND, AND P. POWERS. 1984. Response patterns in children and adolescents exploited through six rings and pornography. *American Journal of Psychiatry, 141,* 656–62.

BURGESS, A. W., AND L. L. HOLMSTROM. 1974. *Rape: Victims of crisis.* Bowie, Md.: Robert J. Brady.

———. 1978. Recovery from rape and prior life stress. *Research in Nursing and Health, 1,* 165–74.

———. 1979. Adaptive strategies and recovery from rape. *American Journal of Psychiatry, 136,* 1278–82.

BUSS, A. H., AND R. PLOMIN. 1984. *Temperament: Early developing personality traits.* Hillsdale, N.J.: Erlbaum.

CALHOUN, K. S., B. M. ATKESON, AND P. A. RESICK. 1982. A longitudinal examination of fear reactions in victims of rape. *Journal of Counseling Psychology, 29,* 665–61.

CAMPBELL, J. D. 1986. Similarity and uniqueness: The effects of attribute type, relevance, and individual differences in self-esteem and depression. *Journal of Personality and Social Psychology, 50,* 281–94.

CANTOR, N., AND W. MISCHEL. 1979. Prototypes in person perception. In *Advances in experimental social psychology,* vol. 12, ed. L. Berkowitz. New York: Academic Press.

CANTRIL, H. 1966. *The pattern of human concerns.* New Brunswick, N.J.: Rutgers University Press.

CAPLAN, R. D. 1979. Social support, person-environment fit, and coping. In *Mental health and the economy,* ed. L. Furman and J. Gordis. Kalamazoo, Mich.: The Upjohn Institute.

CAREY-TREFZER, C. G. 1949. The results of a clinical study of war-damaged children who attended the Child Guidance Clinic, The Hospital for Sick Children, Great Ormond Street, London. *Journal of Mental Science, 95,* 535–59.

CASSEM, N. H., AND T. P. HACKETT. 1971. Psychiatric consultation in a coronary care unit. *Annals of Internal Medicine, 75,* 9–14.

CHODOFF, P., S. B. FRIEDMAN, AND D. A. HAMBURG. 1964. Stress, defense, and coping behavior: Observations in parents of children with malignant disease. *American Journal of Psychiatry, 120,* 743–49.

CHODOROW, N. 1978. *The reproduction of mothering.* Berkeley: University of California Press.

CIARANELLO, R. D. 1983. Neurochemical aspects of stress. In *Stress, coping, and development in children,* ed. N. Garmezy and M. Rutter. New York: McGraw-Hill.

COATES, D., AND T. WINSTON. 1983. Counteracting the deviance of depression: Peer support groups for victims. *Journal of Social Issues, 39,* 171–96.

COATES, D., AND C. B. WORTMAN. 1980. Depression maintenance and interpersonal control. In *Advances in environmental psychology,* vol. 2: *Applications of personal control,* ed. A. Baum and E. J. Singer. Hillsdale, N.J.: Erlbaum.

COBB, S. 1976. Social support as a moderator of life stress. *Psychosomatic Medicine, 38,* 300–314.

COBB, S., AND S. V. KASL. 1977. Termination: The consequences of job loss. *NIOSH Research Report.* (DHEW Publication 77–224).

COHEN, C. E. 1981. Person categories and social perception: Testing some boundaries of the processing effects of prior knowledge. *Journal of Personality and Social Psychology, 40,* 441–52.

COHEN, S., AND T. A. WILLS. 1985. Stress, social support, and the buffering hypothesis. *Psychological Bulletin, 98,* 310–57.

COLLINS, R. L., S. E. TAYLOR, AND L. A. SKOKAN. 1990. A better world or a shattered vision?: Changes in life perspectives following victimization. *Social Cognition, 8,* 263–85.

COOLEY, C. H. 1902. *Human nature and the social order.* New York: Scribner's.

COYNE, J. C., AND I. H. GOTLIB. 1983. The role of cognition in depression: A critical appraisal. *Psychological Bulletin, 94,* 472–505.

CROCKER, L. G. 1962. Introduction to Voltaire's *Candide & Zadig.* New York: Washington Square Press.

DAKOF, G. A., AND S. E. TAYLOR. 1990. Victims' perceptions of social support: What is helpful from whom? *Journal of Personality and Social Psychology, 58,* 80–89.

DANIELI, Y. 1985. The treatment and prevention of long-term effects and intergenerational transmission of victimization: A lesson from Holocaust survivors and their children. In *Trauma and its wake: The study and treatment of post-traumatic stress disorder,* ed. C. Figley. New York: Brunner/Mazel.

DARLEY, J. M., AND E. ARONSON. 1966. Self-evaluation vs. direct anxiety reduction as determinants of the fear-affiliation relationship. *Journal of Experimental Social Psychology, 27,* 100–108.

DAVIS, F. 1963. *Passage through crisis: Polio victims and their families.* Indianapolis, Ind.: Bobbs-Merrill.

DESOUZA, E. B. 1988. Localization and modulation of brain and pituitary receptors involved in stress responses. *Psychopharmacology Bulletin, 24,* 360–64.

DEUTSCH, H. 1944. *The psychology of women.* New York: Grune & Stratton.

DIMSDALE, J. E. 1980. The coping behavior of Nazi concentration camp survivors. In *Survivors, victims, and perpetrators: Essays on the Nazi Holocaust,* ed. J. E. Dimsdale. Washington, D.C.: Hemisphere.

DOWNEY, G., R. C. SILVER, AND C. B. WORTMAN. 1990. Reconsidering the attribution-adjustment relation following a major negative event: Coping with the loss of a child. *Journal of Personality and Social Psychology, 59,* 925–40.

DRUSS, R. G., AND D. S. KORNFELD. 1967. The survivors of cardiac arrest. *Journal of the American Medical Association, 201,* 291–96.

DUDLEY, D. L., J. W. VERNEY, M. MASUDA, C. J. MARTIN, AND T. H. HOLMES. 1969. Long-term adjustment, prognosis, and death in irreversible diffuse obstructive pulmonary syndromes. *Psychosomatic Medicine, 31,* 310–25.

DUNCAN, S. L. 1976. Differential social perception and attribution of intergroup violence: Testing the lower limits of stereotyping of blacks. *Journal of Personality and Social Psychology, 34,* 590–98.

DUNKEL-SCHETTER, C. A. 1984. Social support and cancer: Findings based on patient interviews and their implications. *Journal of Social Issues, 40,* 77–98.

DUNKEL-SCHETTER, C. A., AND C. B. WORTMAN. 1982. The interpersonal dynamics of cancer: Problems in social relationships and their impact on the patient. In *Interpersonal issues in health care,* ed. H. S. Friedman and M. R. DiMatteo. New York: Academic Press.

DYE, E., AND S. ROTH. 1991. Psychotherapy with Vietnam veterans and rape and incest survivors. *Psychotherapy, 28,* 103–20.

EITINGER, L. 1980. The concentration camp syndrome and its late sequelae. In *Survivors, victims, and perpetrators: Essays on the Nazi Holocaust,* ed. J. E. Dimsdale. Washington, D.C.: Hemisphere.

———. 1983. Denial in concentration camps: Some personal observations on the positive and negative functions of denial in extreme life situations. In *The denial of stress,* ed. S. Breznitz. New York: International Universities Press.

ELLIS, E., B. ATKESON, AND K. CALHOUN. 1981. An assessment of long-term reaction to rape. *Journal of Abnormal Psychology, 90,* 263–66.

EMM, D., AND P. C. MCKENRY. 1988. Coping with victimization: The impact of rape on female survivors, male significant others, and parents. *Contemporary Family Therapy, 10,* 272–79.

EPSTEIN, S. 1967. Toward a unified theory of anxiety. In *Progress in experimental personality research,* vol. 4, ed. B. A. Maher. New York: Academic Press.

———. 1973. The self-concept revisited, or a theory of a theory. *American Psychologist, 28,* 404–16.

———. 1979. The ecological study of emotions in humans. In *Advances in the study of communication and affect,* vol. 5: *Perception of emotions in self and others,* ed. P. Pliner, K. R. Blanstein, and I. M. Spigel. New York: Plenum.

———. 1980. The self-concept: A review and the proposal of an integrated theory of personality. In *Personality: Basic issues and current research,* ed. E. Staub. Englewood Cliffs, N.J.: Prentice-Hall.

———. 1983. Natural healing processes of the mind: Graded stress inoculation as an inherent coping mechanism. In *Stress reduction and prevention,* ed. D. Meichenbaum and M. E. Jaremko. New York: Plenum.

———. 1984. Controversial issues in emotion theory. In *Review of personality and social psychology: Emotions, relationships, and health,* ed. P. Shaver. Beverly Hills, Calif.: Sage.

———. 1985. The implications of cognitive-experiential self-theory for research in social psychology and personality. *Journal of the Theory of Social Behavior, 15,* 283–310.

———. 1991. The self-concept, the traumatic neurosis, and the structure of personality. In *Perspectives on personality,* vol. 3, ed. D. Ozer, J. M. Healy, Jr., and A. J. Stewart. London: Jessica Kingsley.

ERIKSON, E. 1968. *Identity: Youth and crisis.* New York: Norton.

ERIKSON, K. T. 1976. *Everything in its path: Destruction of community in the Buffalo Creek flood.* New York: Simon & Schuster.

FAIRBAIRN, W. R. D. 1952. *An object-relations theory of the personality.* New York: Basic Books.

FARINA, A., C. J. HOLLAND, AND K. RING. 1966. The role of stigma and set in interpersonal interaction. *Journal of Abnormal Psychology, 71,* 421–28.

FARINA, A., J. THAW, R. D. FELNER, AND B. E. HUST. 1976. Some interpersonal consequences of being mentally ill or mentally retarded. *American Journal of Mental Deficiency, 80,* 414–22.

FESTINGER, L. 1954. A theory of social comparison processes. *Human Relations, 40,* 427–48.

———. 1957. *A theory of cognitive dissonance.* Stanford, Calif.: Stanford University Press.

FIGLEY, C. R., ED. 1978. *Stress disorders among Vietnam veterans: Theory, research, and treatment.* New York: Brunner/Mazel.

———. 1983. Catastrophes: An overview of family reaction. In *Stress and the family: Coping with catastrophe,* vol. 2, ed. C. Figley and H. I. McCubbin. New York: Brunner/Mazel.

———. 1985. From victim to survivor: Social responsibility in the wake of catastrophe. In *Trauma and its wake: The study and treatment of post-traumatic stress disorder.* New York: Brunner/Mazel.

———. 1988a. A five-phase treatment of post-traumatic stress disorders in families. *Journal of Traumatic Stress, 1,* 127–41.

————. 1988b. Victimization, trauma, and traumatic stress. *The Counseling Psychologist, 16,* 635–41.

————. 1989. *Helping traumatized families.* San Francisco: Jossey-Bass.

FIGLEY, C. R., AND S. LEVENTMAN, EDS. 1980. *Strangers at home: Vietnam veterans since the war.* New York: Praeger.

FINKELHOR, D. 1984. *Child sexual abuse: New theory and research.* New York: Free Press.

FINKELHOR, D., AND A. BROWNE. 1985. The traumatic impact of child sexual abuse: A conceptualization. *American Journal of Orthopsychiatry, 55,* 530–41.

FISCHER, C. T. 1984. A phenomenological study of being criminally victimized: Contributions and constraints of qualitative research. *Journal of Social Issues, 40,* 161–78.

FISCHHOFF, B. 1975. Hindsight ≠ foresight: The effect of outcome knowledge on judgment under uncertainty. *Journal of Experimental Psychology: Human Perception and Performance, 1,* 288–99.

FISCHHOFF, B., AND R. BEYTH. 1975. "I knew it would happen"—Remembered probabilities of once-future things. *Organizational Behavior and Human Performance, 13,* 1–16.

FISHER, C. 1945. Amnesic states and war neuroses: The psychogenesis of fugues. *Psychoanalytic Quarterly, 14,* 437–68.

FISH-MURRAY, C. C., E. V. KOBY, AND B. A. VAN DER KOLK. 1987. In *Psychological trauma,* ed. B. A. van der Kolk. Washington, D.C.: American Psychiatric Press.

FISKE, S. T., AND S. L. NEUBERG. 1990. A continuum of impression formation, from category-based to individuating processes: Influences of information and motivation on attention and interpretation. In *Advances in experimental social psychology,* vol. 23, ed. M. P. Zanna. New York: Academic Press.

FISKE, S. T., AND M. A. PAVELCHAK. 1986. Category-based versus piecemeal-based affective responses: Developments in schema-triggered affect. In *Handbook of motivation and cognition,* ed. R. M. Sorrentino and E. T. Higgins. New York: Guilford.

FISKE, S. T., AND S. E. TAYLOR. 1991. *Social cognition.* New York: McGraw-Hill.

FOY, D. W., H. S. RESNICK, R. C. SIPPRELLE, AND E. M. CARROLL. 1987. Premilitary, military, and postmilitary factors in the development of combat-related post-traumatic stress disorder. *The Behavior Therapist, 10,* 3–9.

FRANK, E., S. M. TURNER, B. D. STEWART, M. JACOB, AND D. WEST. 1981. Past psychiatric symptoms and the response to sexual assault. *Comprehensive Psychiatry, 22,* 479–87.

FRANK, J. D. 1963. *Persuasion and healing*. New York: Schocken.

FRANKL, V. E. 1963. *Man's search for meaning: An introduction to logotherapy*. New York: Washington Square Press.

FRANKLIN, K. M., R. JANOFF-BULMAN, AND J. E. ROBERTS. 1990. Long-term impact of parental divorce on optimism and trust: Changes in general assumptions or narrow beliefs? *Journal of Personality and Social Psychology*, 59, 743–55.

FRASIER, P. 1990. Victims attributions and postrape trauma. *Journal of Personality and Social Psychology*, 59, 298–304.

FREDERICK, C. J. 1980. Effects of natural vs. human-induced violence. *Evaluation and change: Services for survivors*. Minneapolis, Minn.: Minneapolis Medical Research Foundation.

———. 1986. Psychic trauma in victims of crime and terrorism. In *Cataclysms, crises, and catastrophes: Psychology in action*, ed. G. R. VandenBos and B. K. Bryant. Washington, D.C.: American Psychological Association.

FREUD, S. 1921. *A general introduction to psychoanalysis*. New York: Boni & Liverwright.

———. [1924] 1961. The loss of reality in neurosis and psychosis. *Standard Edition*, Vol. 23. London: Hogarth.

———. 1927. *The future of an illusion*. Garden City, N.Y.: Doubleday.

FREUD, S. [1928] 1959. *Beyond the pleasure principle*. New York: Bantam Books.

———. 1936. The ego and the mechanisms of defense. New York: International Universities Press.

FRIEDMAN, M. J. 1988. Toward rational pharmacotherapy for post-traumatic stress disorders: An interim report. *American Journal of Psychiatry*, 145, 281–85.

FRIEZE, I. H. 1986. The female victim: Rape, wife beating, and incest. In *Cataclysms, crises, and catastrophes: Psychology in action*, ed. G. R. VandenBos and B. K. Bryant. Washington D.C.: American Psychological Association.

FRIEZE, I. H., S. HYMER, AND M. S. GREENBERG. 1984. Describing the victims of crime and violence. In *Victims of crime and violence: Final report of the APA task force on the victims of crime and violence*, ed. S. S. Kahn. Washington, D.C.: American Psychological Association.

FUNCH, D. P., AND J. MARSHALL. 1983. The role of stress, social support and age in survival from breast cancer. *Journal of Psychosomatic Research*, 27, 77–83.

GARBER, J., AND M. E. P. SELIGMAN, EDS. 1980. *Human helplessness: Theory and application*. New York: Academic Press.

GARMEZY, N. 1983. Stressors of childhood. In *Stress, coping, and development in children,* ed. N. Garmezy and M. Rutter. New York: McGraw-Hill.

GHISELIN, B. 1952. *The creative process.* New York: Mentor.

GILLIGAN, C. 1982. *In a different voice.* Cambridge: Harvard University Press.

GLESER, G. C., B. L. GREEN, AND C. WINGET. 1981. *Prolonged psychosocial effects of disaster: A study of Buffalo Creek.* New York: Academic Press.

GLICK, I. O., R. S. WEISS, AND C. M. PARKES. 1974. *The first year of bereavement.* New York: Wiley.

GLUCKMAN, M. 1944. The logic of African science and witchcraft: An appreciation of Evans-Pritchard's "Witchcraft Oracles and Magic among the Azande" of the Sudan. *The Rhodes-Livingstone Institute Journal,* June 1944, 61–71.

GOFFMAN, E. 1963. *Stigma: Notes on the management of spoiled identity.* Englewood Cliffs, N.J.: Prentice-Hall.

———. 1967. *Interaction ritual.* Newport Beach, Calif.: Westcliff.

GOLDBERGER, L. 1983. The concept and mechanisms of denial: A selective overview. In *The denial of stress,* ed. S. Breznitz. New York: International Universities Press.

GOLEMAN, D. 1985. *Vital lies, simple truths: The psychology of self-deception.* New York: Simon & Schuster.

GOODWIN, J. 1980. The etiology of combat-related post-traumatic stress disorders. In *Post-traumatic stress disorders of the Vietnam veterans,* ed. T. Williams. Cincinnati, Ohio: Disabled Veterans National Headquarters.

GOTLIB, I. 1983. Perception and recall of interpersonal feedback: Negative bias in depression. *Cognitive Therapy and Research, 7,* 399–412.

GOULD, R. 1978. *Transformations.* New York: Simon & Schuster.

GREEN, B. L., M. C. GRACE, AND G. C. GLESER. 1985. Identifying survivors at risk: Long-term impairment following the Beverly Hills Supper Club fire. *Journal of Consulting and Clinical Psychology, 53,* 672–78.

GREENBERG, J. R., AND S. A. MITCHELL. 1983. *Object relations in psychoanalytic theory.* Cambridge: Harvard University Press.

GREENBERG, M. S., AND B. A. VAN DER KOLK. 1987. Retrieval and integration of traumatic memories with the "painting cure." In *Psychological trauma,* ed. B. A. van der Kolk. Washington, D.C.: American Psychiatric Press.

GREENWALD, A. G. 1980. The totalitarian ego: Fabrication and revision of personal history. *American Psychologist, 35,* 603–18.

GUNDERSON, J. G. 1984. *Borderline personality disorder.* Washington, D.C.: American Psychiatric Press.

References

HAAN, N. 1977. *Coping and defending.* New York: Academic Press.

HACKETT, T. P., AND N. H. CASSEM. 1974. Development of a quantitative rating scale to assess denial. *Journal of Psychosomatic Research, 18,* 93–100.

HACKETT, T. P., AND A. D. WEISMAN. 1969. Denial as a factor in patients with heart disease and cancer. *Annals of New York Academy of Sciences, 164,* 802–11.

HARLOW, H. 1971. *Learning to love.* San Francisco: Albion.

HARVEY, J. H., B. HARRIS, AND R. D. BARNES. 1975. Actor-observer differences in perceptions of responsibility and freedom. *Journal of Personality and Social Psychology, 32,* 22–28.

HASTIE, R. 1981. Schematic principles in human memory. In *Social cognition: The Ontario symposium,* vol. 1, ed. E. T. Higgins, C. P. Herman, and M. P. Zanna. Hillsdale, N.J.: Erlbaum.

HAYMAN, P. M., R. SOMMERS-FLANAGAN, AND J. P. PARSONS. 1987. Aftermath of violence: Post-traumatic stress disorder among Vietnam veterans. *Journal of Counseling and Development, 65,* 363–66.

HEIDER, F. 1958. *The psychology of interpersonal relations.* New York: Wiley.

HELZER, J. E., L. N. ROBINS, E. WISH, AND M. HESSELBROCK. 1979. Depression in Vietnam veterans and civilian controls. *American Journal of Psychiatry, 136,* 526–29.

HENSLIN, J. M. 1967. Craps and magic. *American Journal of Sociology, 73,* 316–30.

HERMAN, J. L. 1981. *Father-daughter incest.* Cambridge: Harvard University Press.

HERMAN, J. L., AND B. A. VAN DER KOLK. 1987. Traumatic antecedents of borderline personality disorder. In *Psychological trauma,* ed. B. A. van der Kolk. Washington, D.C.: American Psychiatric Press.

HIGGINS, E. T., AND G. KING. 1981. Accessibility of social constructs: Information processing consequences of individual and contextual variability. In *Personality, cognition, and social interaction,* ed. N. Cantor and J. Kihlstrom. Hillsdale, N.J.: Erlbaum.

HILBERMAN, E. 1980. Overview: The "wife-beater's wife" reconsidered. *American Journal of Psychiatry, 137,* 1336–46.

HILBERMAN, E., AND K. MUNSON. 1978. Sixty battered women. *Victimology, 2,* 460–71.

HILGARD, E. R. 1977. *Divided consciousness: Multiple controls in human thought and action.* New York: Wiley.

HINTON, J. 1984. Coping with terminal illness. In *The experience of illness,* ed. R. Fitzpatrick, J. Hinton, S. Newman, G. Scambler, and J. Thompson. New York: Tavistock.

HOBFOLL, S. E. 1989. Conservation of resources: A new attempt at conceptualizing stress. *American Psychologist, 44,* 513–24.

HOFFMAN, L., P. BURGES-WATSON, G. WILSON, AND J. MONTGOMERY. 1989. Low plasma B-endorphin in post-traumatic stress disorder. *Australian and New Zealand Journal of Psychiatry, 23,* 269–87.

HOREVITZ, R. P., AND B. G. BRAUN. 1984. Are multiple personalities borderline: An analysis of 33 cases. *Psychiatric Clinics of North America, 7,* 69–87.

HORNEY, K. 1937. *The neurotic personality of our time.* New York: Norton.

———. 1973. *Feminine psychology.* New York: Norton.

HOROWITZ, M. 1975. Intrusive and repetitive thoughts after experimental stress: A summary. *Archives of General Psychiatry, 32,* 1457–63.

———. 1976. *Stress response syndromes.* New York: Aronson.

———. 1980. Psychological response to serious life events. In *Human stress and cognition,* ed. V. Hamilton and D. Warburton. New York: Wiley.

———. 1982. Stress response syndromes and their treatment. In *Handbook of stress,* ed. L. Goldberger and S. Breznitz. New York: Free Press.

HUERTA, F., AND R. HORTON. 1978. Coping behavior of elderly flood victims. *The Gerontologist, 18,* 541–46.

HURSCH, C. J. 1977. *The trouble with rape.* Chicago: Nelson-Hall.

IRVING, J. 1978. *The world according to Garp.* New York: E. P. Dutton.

IRWIN, F. W. 1944. The realism of expectations. *Psychological Review, 51,* 120–26.

JAFFE, R. 1968. Dissociative phenomena in concentration camp inmates. *International Journal of Psychoanalysis, 49,* 310–12.

JAHODA, M. 1958. *Current concepts of positive mental health.* New York: Basic Books.

JAMES, W. 1985. *The varieties of religious experience.* Cambridge: Harvard University Press.

———. 1962. *Essays on faith and morals.* New York: World Publishing Company.

———. 1907. *Pragmatism.* New York: Longmans, Green, & Co.

JANOFF-BULMAN, R. 1979. Characterological versus behavioral self-blame: Inquiries into depression and rape. *Journal of Personality and Social Psychology, 37,* 1798–1809.

———. 1982. Esteem and control bases of blame: "Adaptive" strategies for victims versus observers. *Journal of Personality, 50,* 180–92.

———. 1985a. Criminal vs. non-criminal victimization: Victims' reactions. *Victimology, 10,* 498–511.

———. 1985b. The aftermath of victimization: Rebuilding shattered assumptions. In *Trauma and its wake: The study and treatment of posttraumatic stress disorder*, ed. C. Figley. New York: Brunner/Mazel.

———. 1989a. Assumptive worlds and the stress of traumatic events: Applications of the schema construct. *Social Cognition, 7*, 113–36.

———. 1989b. The benefits of illusions, the threat of disillusionment, and the limitations of inaccuracy. *Journal of Social and Clinical Psychology, 8*, 158–75.

JANOFF-BULMAN, R., AND P. BRICKMAN. 1982. Expectations and what people learn from failure. In *Expectations and actions: Expectancy-value models in psychology*, ed. N. T. Feather. Hillsdale, N.J.: Erlbaum.

JANOFF-BULMAN, R., AND I. H. FRIEZE. 1983. A theoretical perspective for understanding reactions to victimization. *Journal of Social Issues, 39*, 1–17.

———. 1987. The role of gender in reactions to victimization. In *Gender and stress*, ed. R. Barnett, J. Biener, and R. Baruch. New York: Free Press.

JANOFF-BULMAN, R., AND L. LANG-GUNN. 1989. Coping with disease and accidents: The role of self-blame attributions. In *Social-personal inference in clinical psychology*, ed. L. Y. Abramson. New York: Guilford.

JANOFF-BULMAN, R., M. MADDEN, AND C. TIMKO. 1983. Victims' reactions to aid: The role of perceived vulnerability. In *New directions in helping*, vol. 3: *Applied perspectives in help-seeking and -receiving*, ed. A. Nadler, J. D. Fisher, and B. DePaulo. New York: Academic Press.

JANOFF-BULMAN, R., AND G. MARSHALL. 1982. Mortality, well-being, and control in a population of institutionalized elderly. *Personality and Social Psychology Bulletin, 8*, 691–98.

JANOFF-BULMAN, R., AND S. SCHWARTZBERG. 1991. Toward a general model of personal change: Applications to victimization and psychotherapy. In *Handbook of social and clinical psychology: The health perspective*, ed. C. R. Snyder & D. R. Forsyth. New York: Pergamon.

JANOFF-BULMAN, R., AND C. THOMAS. 1989. Towards an understanding of self-defeating responses following victimization. In *Self-defeating behaviors: Experimental research, clinical impressions, and practical implications*, ed. R. Curtis. New York: Plenum.

JANOFF-BULMAN, R., AND C. TIMKO. 1987. Coping with traumatic life events: The role of denial in light of people's assumptive worlds. In *Coping with negative life events: Clinical and social psychological perspectives*, ed. C. R. Snyder and C. Ford. New York: Plenum.

JANOFF-BULMAN, R., C. TIMKO, AND L. L. CARLI. 1985. Cognitive biases in blaming the victim. *Journal of Experimental Social Psychology, 21*, 161–77.

(JANOFF-)BULMAN, R., AND C. B. WORTMAN. 1977. Attributions of blame

222

and coping in the "real world": Severe accident victims react to their lot. *Journal of Personality and Social Psychology, 35,* 351–63.

JONES, D. R. 1985. Secondary disaster victims: The emotional effects of recovering and identifying human remains. *American Journal of Psychiatry, 142,* 303–307.

JONES, E. E. 1979. The rocky road from acts to dispositions. *American Psychologist, 34,* 107–17.

JONES, E. E., AND S. C. BERGLAS. 1978. Control of attributions about the self through self-handicapping strategies: The appeal of alcohol and the role of underachievement. *Personality and Social Psychology Bulletin, 4,* 200–206.

JONES, E. E., A. FARINA, A. H. HASTORF, H. MARKUS, D. T. MILLER, AND R. A. SCOTT. 1984. *Social stigma: The psychology of marked relationships.* New York: Freeman.

JONES, E. E., AND G. GOETHALS. 1972. Order effects in impression formation: Attribution context and the nature of the entity. In *Attribution: Perceiving the causes of behavior,* ed. E. E. Jones, D. E. Kanouse, H. H. Kelley, R. E. Nisbett, S. Valins, and B. Weiner. Morristown, N.J.: General Learning Press.

JONES, E. E., AND R. E. NISBETT. 1972. The actor and the observer: Divergent perceptions of the causes of behavior. In *Attribution: Perceiving the causes of behavior,* ed. E. E. Jones, D. E. Kanouse, H. H. Kelley, R. E. Nisbett, S. Valins, & B. Weiner. Morristown, N.J.: General Learning Press.

JONES, E. E., L. ROCK, K. G. SHAVER, G. R. GOETHALS, AND L. M. WARD. 1968. Pattern of performance and ability attribution: An unexpected primacy effect. *Journal of Personality and Social Psychology, 10,* 317–40.

JONES, S. C., AND D. PANITCH. 1971. The self-fulfilling prophecy and interpersonal attraction. *Journal of Experimental Social Psychology, 7,* 356–66.

JOSEFOWITZ, N. 1980. *Paths to power.* Reading, Mass.: Addison-Wesley.

JOURARD, S. M., AND T. LANDSMAN. 1980. *Healthy personality: An approach from the viewpoint of humanistic psychology.* New York: Macmillan.

JUDD, C. M., AND J. A. KULIK. 1980. Schematic effects of social attitudes on information processing and recall. *Journal of Personality and Social Psychology, 38,* 569–78.

KAGAN, J., R. B. KEARSLEY, AND P. R. ZELAZO. 1978. *Infancy: Its place in human development.* Cambridge: Harvard University Press.

KAHANA, B., A. HAREL, AND E. KAHANA. 1988. Predictors of psychological well-being among survivors of the Holocaust. In *Human adaptation to extreme stress: From the Holocaust to Vietnam,* ed. J. P. Wilson, Z. Harel, and B. Kahana. New York: Plenum.

KAHNEMAN, D., AND A. TVERSKY. 1973. On the psychology of prediction. *Psychological Review, 80,* 237–51.

KAYLOR, J. A., D. W. KING, AND L. A. KING. 1987. Psychological effects of military service in Vietnam: A meta-analysis. *Psychological Bulletin, 102,* 257–71.

KEANE, T. M., J. A. FAIRBANK, J. M. CADDELL, R. T. ZIMERING, AND M. E. BENDER. 1985. A behavioral approach to assessing and treating post-traumatic stress disorder in Vietnam veterans. In *Trauma and its wake: The study and treatment of post-traumatic stress disoder,* ed. C. Figley. New York: Brunner/Mazel.

KEANE, T. M., AND D. KALOUPEK. 1982. Imaginal flooding in the treatment of a post-traumatic stress disorder. *Journal of Consulting and Clinical Psychology, 50,* 138–40.

KEANE, T. M., B. T. LITZ, AND D. D. BLAKE. 1990. Post-traumatic stress disorder in adulthood. In *Handbook of child and adult psychopathology: A longitudinal perspective,* ed. M. Hersen and C. G. Last. New York: Pergamon.

KEANE, T. M., AND J. WOLFE. 1990. Comorbidity in post-traumatic stress disorder: An analysis of community and clinical studies. *Journal of Applied Social Psychology, 20,* 1776–88.

KEANE, T. M., R. T. ZIMERING, AND J. M. CADDELL. 1985. A behavioral formulation of post-traumatic stress disorder in Vietnam veterans. *Behavior Therapy, 8,* 9–12.

KELLEY, G. A. 1955. *A theory of personality: A psychology of personal constructs.* New York: Norton.

KIERKEGAARD, S. 1944. *The concept of dread.* Princeton, N.J.: Princeton University Press.

KILPATRICK, D. G., B. E. SAUNDERS, L. J. VERONEN, C. L. BEST, AND J. M. VON. 1987. Criminal victimization: Lifetime prevalence, reporting to police, and psychological impact. *Crime and Delinquency, 33,* 479–89.

KILPATRICK, D. G., L. J. VERONEN, AND C. L. BEST. 1985. Factors predicting psychological distress among rape victims. In *Trauma and its wake: The study and treatment of post-traumatic stress disorder,* ed. C. Figley. New York: Brunner/Mazel.

KILPATRICK, D. G., L. J. VERONEN, AND P. A. RESICK. 1979. The aftermath of rape: Recent empirical findings. *American Journal of Orthopsychiatry, 49,* 658–69.

———. 1982. Psychological sequelae to rape: Assessment and treatment strategies. In *Behavioral medicine: Assessment and treatment strategies,* ed. D. M. Doleys, R. L. Meredith, and A. R. Ciminero. New York: Plenum.

KINZIE, J. D. 1986. Severe post-traumatic stress syndrome among Cambodian refugees: Symptoms, clinical course, and treatment approaches. In *Disaster stress studies: New methods and findings,* ed. J. H. Shore. Washington, D.C.: American Psychiatric Press.

KLECK, R. E. 1968. Physical stigma and nonverbal cues emitted in face-to-face interaction. *Human Relations, 21,* 19–28.

KLECK, R. E., H. ONO, AND A. H. HASTORF. 1966. The effects of physical deviance upon face-to-face interaction. *Human Relations, 19,* 425–36.

KLUFT, R. P. 1985. *Childhood antecedents of multiple personality.* Washington, D.C.: American Psychiatric Press.

KOBASA, S. C. 1979. Stressful life events and health: An inquiry into hardiness. *Journal of Personality and Social Psychology, 37,* 1–11.

KOBASA, S. C., S. R. MADDI, AND S. KAHN. 1982. Hardiness and health: A prospective study. *Journal of Personality and Social Psychology, 42,* 168–77.

KOBASA, S. C., AND M. C. PUCETTI. 1983. Personality and social resources in stress resistance. *Journal of Personality and Social Psychology, 45,* 839–50.

KOHUT, H. 1971. *The analysis of the self.* New York: International Universities Press.

———. 1977. *The restoration of the self.* New York: International Universities Press.

KRYSTAL, H. 1968. *Massive psychic trauma.* New York: International Universities Press.

——— 1988. *Integration and self-healing: Affect, trauma, alexithymia.* New York: Analytic Press.

KRYSTAL, J. H. 1990. Animal models for post-traumatic stress disorder. In *Biological assessment and treatment of P.T.S.D.,* ed. E. Giller Washington, D.C.: APA Press.

KUBLER-ROSS, E. 1969. *On death and dying.* New York: Macmillan.

KUHN, T. S. 1962. *The structure of scientific revolutions.* Chicago: University of Chicago Press.

KULKA, R. A., W. E. SCHLENGER, J. A. FAIRBANK, R. L. HOUGH, B. K. JORDAN, C. R. MARMAR, AND D. S. WEISS. 1988. *National Vietnam veterans readjustment study (NVVRS): Description, current status, and initial PTSD prevalence rates.* Washington, D.C.: Veterans Administration.

KUSHNER, H. S. 1981. *When bad things happen to good people.* New York: Schocken Books.

KUSHNER, R. 1975. *Why me?* New York: New American Library.

LANGER, E. J. 1975. The illusion of control. *Journal of Personality and Social Psychology, 32,* 311–28.

———. 1978. Rethinking the role of thought in social interaction. In *New directions in attribution research,* vol. 2, ed. J. H. Harvey, W. I. Ickes, and R. F. Kidd. Hillsdale, N.J.: Erlbaum.

LAPLANCHE, J., AND J. B. PONTALIS. 1973. *The language of psychoanalysis.* London: Hogarth.

LAZARUS, R. S. 1966. *Psychological stress and the coping process*. New York: McGraw-Hill.

———. 1983. The costs and benefits of denial. In *The denial of stress*, ed. S. Breznitz. New York: International Universities Press.

LAZARUS, R. S., AND S. FOLKMAN. 1984. *Stress, appraisal, and coping*. New York: Springer.

LECKY, P. 1945. *Self-consistency: A theory of personality*. Fort Myers, Fla.: Island Press.

LEHMAN, D. R., C. B. WORTMAN, AND A. F. WILLIAMS. 1987. Long-term effects of losing a spouse or child in a motor-vehicle crash. *Journal of Personality and Social Psychology, 52,* 218–31.

LERNER, M. J. 1970. The desire for justice and reactions to victims: Social psychological studies of some antecedents and consequences. In *Altruism and helping behavior*, ed. J. Macaulay and L. Berkowitz. New York: Academic Press.

———. 1980. *The belief in a just world*. New York: Plenum.

LERNER, M. J., AND G. MATTHEWS. 1967. Reactions to suffering of others under conditions of indirect responsibility. *Journal of Personality and Social Psychology, 5,* 319–25.

LERNER, M. J., AND C. SIMMONS. 1966. Observer's reaction to the "innocent victims": Compassion or rejection? *Journal of Personality and Social Psychology, 4,* 203–10.

LEVINE, S. 1983. A psychobiological approach to the ontogeny of coping. In *Stress, coping, and development in children*, ed. N. Garmezy and M. Rutter. New York: McGraw-Hill.

LIFTON, R. J. 1967. *Death in life: Survivors of Hiroshima*. New York: Simon & Schuster.

———. 1980. The concept of the survivor. In *Survivors, victims, and perpetrators: Essays on the Nazi Holocaust*, ed. J. E. Dimsdale. Washington, D.C.: Hemisphere.

———. 1986. *The Nazi doctors: Medical killing and the psychology of genocide*. New York: Basic Books.

———. 1988. Understanding the traumatized self: Imagery, symbolization, and transformation. In *Human adaptation to extreme stress: From Holocaust to Vietnam*, ed. J. P. Wilson, Z. Harel, and B. Kahana. New York: Plenum.

LIFTON, R. J., AND E. OLSON. 1976. Death imprint in Buffalo Creek syndrome: Symptoms and character change after a major disaster. In *Emergency and disaster management*, ed. H. J. Parad, H. L. P. Resnik, and L. G. Parad. Bowie, Md.: Charles Press.

LINDEMANN, E. 1944. Symptomatology and management of acute grief. *American Journal of Psychiatry, 101,* 141–48.

———. 1977. Symptomatology and management of acute grief. In *Stress and coping,* ed. A. Monat and R. Lazarus. New York: Columbia University Press.

LINDY, J. D., M. C. GRACE, AND B. L. GREEN. 1981. Survivors: Outreach to a reluctant population. *American Journal of Orthopsychiatry, 51,* 468–78.

LINVILLE, P. W. 1987. Self-complexity as a cognitive buffer against stress-related depression and illness. *Journal of Personality and Social Psychology, 42,* 193–211.

LINVILLE, P. W., AND E. E. JONES. 1980. Polarized appraisals of outgroup members. *Journal of Personality and Social Psychology, 38,* 689–703.

LITZ, B. T., W. R. PENK, R. J. GERARDI, AND T. M. KEANE. In press. The assessment of post-traumatic stress disorder. In *Post-traumatic stress disorder: A behavioral approach to assessment and treatment,* ed. P. Saigh. New York: Pergamon.

MAGUIRE, M. 1980. Impact of burglary on victims. *British Journal of Criminology, 20,* 261–275.

MANDLER, G. 1964. The interruption of behavior. In *Nebraska Symposium on motivation,* ed. D. Levine. Lincoln: University of Nebraska Press.

———. 1984. *Mind and body: Psychology of emotion and stress.* New York: Norton.

MARKUS, H. 1977. Self-schemata and processing information about the self. *Journal of Personality and Social Psychology, 35,* 63–78.

MARMAR, C. E., AND M. FREEDMAN. 1988. Brief dynamic psychotherapy of post-traumatic stress disorders: Management of narcissistic regression. *Journal of Traumatic Stress, 1,* 323–37.

MARMAR, C. E., AND M. J. HOROWITZ. 1988. Diagnosis and phase-oriented treatment of post-traumatic stress disorder. In *Human adaptation to extreme stress: From the Holocaust to Vietnam,* ed. J. P. Wilson, Z. Harel, and B. Kahana. New York: Plenum.

MARRIS, P. 1975. *Loss and change.* Garden City, N.Y.: Anchor/Doubleday.

MARTIN, L. L., AND A. TESSER. 1989. Toward a motivational and structural theory of ruminative thought. In *Unintended thought,* ed. J. S. Uleman and J. A. Bargh. New York: Guilford.

MASON, J. W., J. V. BRADY, AND W. W. TOLSON. 1966. Behavioral adaptations and endocrine activity—psychoendocrine differentiation of emotional states. In *Endocrines and the central nervous system,* ed. R. Levine. Baltimore: Williams & Wilkins.

MASON, J. W., T. R. KOSTEN, S. M. SOUTHWICK, AND E. L. GILLER, JR. 1990. The use of psychoendocrine strategies in post-traumatic stress disorder. *Journal of Applied Social Psychology, 20,* 1822–46.

MASON, J. W., G. F. MANGAN, J. V. BRADY, D. CONRAD, AND D. RIOCH.

1961. Concurrent plasma epinephrine, norepinephrine, and 17-hydroxy-corticosteroid levels during conditioned emotional disturbances in monkeys. *Psychosomatic Medicine, 23,* 344–53.

MATLIN, M. W., AND D. STANG. 1978. *The Pollyanna principle: Selectivity in language, memory, and thought.* Cambridge, Mass.: Schenkman.

McCANN, I. L., AND L. A. PEARLMAN. 1990. *Psychological trauma and the adult survivor: Theory, therapy, and transformation.* New York: Brunner/Mazel.

McCULLERS, C. 1951. *The ballad of the sad cafe and other stories.* New York: Bantam Books.

McFARLIN, D. B. 1985. Persistence in the face of failure: The impact of self-esteem and contingency information. *Personality and Social Psychology Bulletin, 11,* 153–63.

McGUIRE, W. J. 1964. Inducing resistance to persuasion: Some contemporary approaches. In *Advances in experimental social psychology,* vol. 1, ed. L. Berkowitz. New York: Academic Press.

MEDEA, A., AND K. THOMPSON. 1974. *Against rape.* New York: Farrar, Straus, & Giroux.

MEERLOO, J. 1963. Delayed mourning in victims of extermination camps. *Journal of Hillside Hospital, 12,* 96–98.

MENNINGER, K. A. 1930. What is a healthy mind? In *The healthy-minded child,* ed. N. A. Crawford and K. A. Menninger. New York: Coward-McCann.

MEYER, C. B., AND S. E. TAYLOR. 1986. Adjustment to rape. *Journal of Personality and Social Psychology, 50,* 1226–34.

MILLER, D. T., AND M. ROSS. 1975. Self-serving biases in the attribution of causality: Fact or fiction? *Psychological Bulletin, 82,* 213–25.

MILLER, D. T., W. TURNBULL, AND C. McFARLAND. 1990. Counterfactual thinking and social perception: Thinking about what might have been. In *Advances in experimental social psychology,* vol. 23, ed. M. P. Zanna. New York: Academic Press.

MILLER, R. C., AND J. S. BERMAN. 1983. The efficacy of cognitive behavior therapies: A quantitative review. *Psychological Bulletin, 94,* 39–53.

MOOS, R. H., AND J. A. SCHAEFER. 1986. Life transitions and crises: A conceptual overview. In *Coping with life crises: An integrated approach,* ed. R. H. Moos. New York: Plenum.

NAGAI, T. 1951. *We of Nagasaki.* New York: Duell, Sloan & Pearce.

NASH, R. J. 1976. *Darkest hours.* Chicago: Nelson-Hall.

NATIONAL COMMISSION ON THE CAUSES AND PREVENTION OF VIOLENCE. 1969. *Crimes of violence,* vol. 2. Washington, D.C.: U.S. Government Printing Office.

NEIDERBACH, S. 1986. *Invisible wounds: Crime victims speak.* New York: Haworth Press.

NEISSER, U. 1976. *Cognition and reality.* San Francisco: Freeman.

NIEDERLAND, W. G. 1964. Psychiatric disorders among persecution victims: A contribution to the understanding of concentration camp pathology and its aftereffects. *Journal of Nervous and Mental Diseases, 139,* 458–74.

NISBETT, R. E., AND L. ROSS. 1980. *Human inference: Strategies and shortcomings of social judgment.* Englewood Cliffs, N.J.: Prentice-Hall.

NISBETT, R. E., AND T. D. WILSON. 1977. Telling more than we can know: Verbal reports on mental processes. *Psychological Review, 84,* 231–59.

OBEYESEKERE, G. 1985. Depression, Buddhism, and the work of culture in Sri Lanka. In *Culture and depression,* ed. A Kleinman and B. Good. Berkeley, Calif.: University of California Press.

OCHBERG, F. M., ED. 1988. *Post-traumatic therapy and victims of violence.* New York: Brunner/Mazel.

———. 1991. Post-traumatic therapy. *Psychotherapy, 28,* 5–15.

OEI, T. P. S., B. LIM, AND B. HENNESSY. 1990. Psychological dysfunction in battle: Combat stress reactions and post-traumatic stress disorder. *Clinical Psychology Review, 10,* 355–88.

O'NEILL, E. 1946. *The iceman cometh.* New York: Modern Library.

ORNSTEIN, R. E. 1972. *The psychology of consciousness.* New York: Penguin.

OWENS, M. J., AND C. B. NEMEROFF. 1988. Preclinical and clinical studies with corticotropin-releasing factors: Implications for affective disorders. *Psychopharmacology Bulletin, 24,* 355–59.

PALLMEYER, T. P., E. B. BLANCHARD, AND L. C. KOLB. 1986. The psychophysiology of combat-induced post-traumatic stress disorder in Vietnam veterans. *Behavioral Research Therapy, 24,* 645–52.

PARK, B., AND M. ROTHBART. 1982. Perception of out-group homogeneity and levels of social categorization: Memory for the subordinate attributes of in-group and out-group members. *Journal of Personality and Social Psychology, 42,* 1051–68.

PARKES, C. M. 1971. Psycho-social transitions: A field of study. *Social Science and Medicine, 5,* 101–15.

———. 1975. What becomes of redundant world models? A contribution to the study of adaptation to change. *British Journal of Medical Psychology, 48,* 131–37.

PARKES, C. M., AND R. S. WEISS. 1983. *Recovery from bereavement.* New York: Basic Books.

PARSON, E. R. 1988. Post-traumatic self disorders (PTsfD): Theoretical and practical considerations in psychotherapy of Vietnam war veterans. In

Human adaptation to extreme stress: From the Holocaust to Vietnam, ed. J. P. Wilson, Z. Harel, and B. Kahana. New York: Plenum.

PEARLIN, L. I., AND C. SCHOOLER. 1978. The structure of coping. *Journal of Health and Social Behavior, 19,* 2–21.

PENNEBAKER, J. W. 1990. *Opening up: The healing power of confiding in others.* New York: Morrow.

PENNEBAKER, J. W., AND S. K. BEALL. 1986. Confronting a traumatic event: Toward an understanding of inhibition and disease. *Journal of Abnormal Psychology, 95,* 274–81.

PENNEBAKER, J. W., C. F. HUGHES, AND R. C. O'HEERON. 1987. The psychophysiology of confession: Linking inhibitory and psychosomatic processes. *Journal of Personality and Social Psychology, 52,* 781–93.

PENNEBAKER, J. W., J. K. KIECOLT-GLASER, AND R. GLASER. 1988. Disclosure of traumas and immune function: Health implications of psychotherapy. *Journal of Consulting and Clinical Psychology, 56,* 239–45.

PERLOFF, L. S. 1983. Perceptions of vulnerability to victimization. *Journal of Social Issues, 39,* 41–62.

PERLOFF, L. S., AND B. K. FETZER. 1986. Self-other judgments and perceived vulnerability of victimization. *Journal of Personality and Social Psychology, 50,* 502–10.

PETERSON, C., S. M. SCHWARTZ, AND M. E. P. SELIGMAN. 1981. Self-blame and depressive symptoms. *Journal of Personality and Social Psychology, 41,* 253–59.

PIAGET, J. 1952. *The origins of intelligence in children.* New York: International Universities Press.

———. 1954. *The construction of reality in the child.* New York: Basic Books.

POPPER, K. R. 1963. *Conjectures and refutations: The growth of scientific knowledge.* New York: Harper & Row.

PUTNAM, F. W., R. M. POST, J. J. GUROFF, ET AL. 1986. One hundred cases of multiple personality disorder. *Journal of Clinical Psychiatry, 47,* 285–93.

PYNOOS, R. S., AND S. ETH. 1985. Developmental perspective on psychic trauma in childhood. In *Trauma and its wake: The study and treatment of post-traumatic stress disorder,* ed. C. Figley. New York: Brunner/Mazel.

RACHMAN, S. 1979. Emotional processing. *Behavior Research and Therapy, 18,* 51–60.

RAWLS, J. 1971. *A theory of justice.* Cambridge: Harvard University Press.

REDMOND, D. E., AND J. H. KRYSTAL. 1984. Multiple mechanisms of opiate withdrawal. *Annual Review of Neuroscience, 7,* 443–78.

REISENZEIN, R. 1986. A structural equation analysis of Weiner's attribution-affect model of helping behavior. *Journal of Personality and Social Psychology, 50,* 1123–33.

RICH, R. F., AND S. STENZEL. 1980. Mental health paradigms for victims: Policy paradigms. In *Evaluation and change: Services for survivors*. Minneapolis, Minn.: Minneapolis Medical Research Foundation.

RINSLEY, D. 1982. *Borderline and other self disorders*. New York: Aronson.

ROBERTSON, L. S. 1977. Perceived vulnerability and willingness to pay for crash protection. *Journal of Community Health, 3,* 136–41.

ROGERS, T. B. 1981. A model of the self as an aspect of the human information processing system. In *Personality, cognition, and social interaction,* ed. N. Cantor and J. Kihlstrom. Hillsdale, N.J.: Erlbaum.

ROSCH, E. 1978. Principles of categorization. In *Cognition and categorization,* ed. E. Rosch and B. B. Lloyd. Hillsdale, N.J.: Erlbaum.

ROSENBERG, M. 1979. *Conceiving the self.* New York: Basic Books.

ROSENTHAL, R. 1974. *On the social psychology of the self-fulfilling prophecy: Further evidence of Pygmalion effects and their mediating mechanisms.* New York: MSS Modular Publications (Module 53).

ROSENZWEIG, S. 1943. An experimental study of "repression" with special reference to need-persistive and ego-defensive reactions to frustration. *Journal of Experimental Psychology, 32,* 64–75.

ROSS, L., M. R. LEPPER, AND M. HUBBARD. 1975. Perseverance in self-perception and social perception: Biased attribution processes in the debriefing paradigm. *Journal of Personality and Social Psychology, 32,* 880–92.

ROTH, S., AND L. J. COHEN. 1986. Approach, avoidance, and coping with stress. *American Psychologist, 41,* 813–19.

ROTH, S., AND L. LEBOWITZ. 1988. The experience of sexual trauma. *Journal of Traumatic Stress, 1,* 79–107.

ROTHBART, M., M. EVANS, AND S. FULERO. 1979. Recall for confirming events: Memory processes and the maintenance of social stereotyping. *Journal of Experimental Social Psychology, 15,* 343–55.

ROTHBART, M., AND O. P. JOHN. 1985. Social categorization and behavioral episodes: A cognitive analysis of the effects of intergroup contact. *Journal of Social Issues, 41,* 81–104.

ROTHBART, M., AND B. PARK. 1986. On the confirmability and disconfirmability of trait concepts. *Journal of Personality and Social Psychology, 50,* 131–42.

ROTHENBERG, A. 1979. *The emerging goddess.* Chicago: University of Chicago Press.

ROTTER, J. B. 1966. Generalized expectancies for internal versus external control of reinforcement. *Psychological Monographs, 80,* (1, Whole No. 609).

RUCH, L. O., S. M. CHALDNER, AND R. A. HARTER. 1980. Life change and rape impact. *Journal of Health and Social Behavior, 21,* 248–60.

RUMELHART, D. 1978. *Schemata: The building blocks of cognition*. San Diego: Center for Human Information Processing, University of California at San Diego.

RYAN, W. 1971. *Blaming the victim*. New York: Pantheon.

SACHS, R., J. GOODWIN, AND B. BRAUN. 1986. The role of childhood abuse in the development of multiple personality. In *Multiple personality and dissociation*, ed. B. B. Braun and R. Kluft. New York: Guilford.

SAGAR, H. A., AND J. W. SCHOFIELD. 1980. Racial and behavioral cues in black and white children's perceptions of ambiguously aggressive acts. *Journal of Personality and Social Psychology, 39*, 590–98.

SALES FRENCH, R. 1984. The long-term relationships of marked people. In *Social stigma: The psychology of marked relationships*, ed. E. E. Jones, A. Farina, A. H. Hastorf, H. Markus, D. T. Miller, and R. A. Scott. New York: Freeman.

SARBIN, T. R. 1981. Self-deception, self-esteem, and depression: The adaptive value of lying to oneself. In *Empirical studies of psychoanalytical theories*, vol. 1, ed. J. Masling. Hillsdale, N.J.: Erlbaum.

SCHACHTER, S. 1959. *The psychology of affiliation*. Stanford, Calif.: Stanford University Press.

SCHEPPELE, K. L., AND P. B. BART. 1983. Through women's eyes: Defining danger in the wake of sexual assault. *Journal of Social Issues, 39*, 63–81.

SCHLENKER, B. R. 1980. *Impression management: The self-concept, social identity, and interpersonal relations*. Monterey, Calif.: Brooks/Cole.

SCHWARTZBERG, S. S., AND R. JANOFF-BULMAN. In Press. Grief and the search for meaning: Exploring the assumptive worlds of bereaved college students. *Journal of Social and Clinical Psychology*.

SCURFIELD, F. E. 1985. Post-trauma stress assessment and treatment: Overview and formulation. In *Trauma and its wake: The study and treatment of post-traumatic stress disorder*, ed. C. Figley. New York: Brunner/Mazel.

SECORD, P. F., AND C. W. BACKMAN. 1965. Interpersonal approach to personality. In *Progress in experimental personality research*, vol. 2, ed. B. H. Maher. New York: Academic Press.

SELIGMAN, M. E. P. 1975. *Helplessness: On depression, development, and death*. San Francisco: Freeman.

SHAPIRO, D. A., AND D. SHAPIRO. 1982. A meta-analysis of comparative therapy outcome studies: A replication and refinement. *Psychological Bulletin, 92*, 581–604.

SHONTZ, F. C. 1975. *The psychological aspects of physical illness and disability*. New York: Macmillan.

SILVER, R. L., C. BOON, AND M. L. STONES. 1983. Searching for meaning in misfortune: Making sense of incest. *Journal of Social Issues, 39*, 81–101.

SILVER, R. L., AND C. B. WORTMAN. 1980. Coping with undesirable life events. In *Human helplessness: Theory and application*, ed. J. Garber and M. E. P. Seligman. New York: Academic Press.

SILVER, R. L., C. B. WORTMAN, AND C. CROFTON. 1990. The role of coping in support provision: The self-presentational dilemma of victims of crises. In *Social support: An interactional view*, ed. B. R. Sarason, I. G. Sarason, and G. R. Pierce. New York: Wiley.

SMITH, M. L., G. V. GLASS, AND T. I. MILLER. 1980. *The benefits of psycho-therapy*. Baltimore, Md.: Johns Hopkins University Press.

SMITS, S. J. 1974. Variables related to success in a medical rehabilitation setting. *Archives of Physical Medicine and Rehabilitation, 55*, 449–54.

SNYDER, C. R. 1989. Reality negotiation: From excuses to hope and beyond. *Journal of Social and Clinical Psychology. 8*, 130–57.

SNYDER, C. R., AND R. L. HIGGINS. 1988. Excuses: Their effective role in the negotiation of reality. *Psychological Bulletin, 104*, 23–35.

SNYDER, C. R., R. L. HIGGINS, AND R. J. STUCKY. 1983. *Excuses: The masquerade solution*. New York: Wiley.

SNYDER, M. L., AND S. GANGESTAD. 1981. Hypothesis-testing processes. In *New directions in attribution research*, vol. 3, ed. J. H. Harvey, W. Ickes, and R. F. Kidd. Hillsdale, N.J.: Erlbaum.

SNYDER, M. L., AND W. B. SWANN, JR. 1978. Hypothesis-testing processes in social interaction. *Journal of Personality and Social Psychology, 36*, 1202–12.

SOKOLOV, Y. N. 1963. *Perception and the conditioned reflex*. New York: Macmillan.

SOLOMON, Z. 1990. Does the war end when the shooting stops? The psychological toll of war. *Journal of Applied Social Psychology, 20*, 1733–35.

SONTAG, S. 1978. *Illness as metaphor*. New York: Farrar, Straus & Giroux.

SPOCK, B. 1976. *Baby and child care*. New York: Pocket Books.

SRULL, T. K., AND R. S. WYER. 1979. The role of category accessibility in the interpretation of information about persons: Some determinants and implications. *Journal of Personality and Social Psychology, 37*, 1660–72.

———. 1989. Person memory and judgment. *Psychological Review, 96*, 58–83.

STEINITZ, L., AND D. SZONYI, EDS. 1975–76. *Living after the Holocaust: Reflections by the post-war generation in America*. New York: Bloch.

STERN, D. N. 1985. *The interpersonal world of the infant: A view from psycho-analysis and developmental psychology*. New York: Basic Books.

STONE, E. 1988. Stress and brain neurotransmitter receptors. In *Receptors and ligands in psychiatry*, ed. A. K. Sen and T. Lee. Cambridge, Mass.: Cambridge University Press.

STRAUSS, M. S. 1979. Abstraction of proto typical information by adults and ten-month-old infants. *Journal of Experimental Psychology: Human Learning and Memory, 5,* 618–32.

STROEBE, W., AND M. S. STROEBE. 1987. *Bereavement and health.* Cambridge, Mass.: Cambridge University Press.

SULS, J. M., AND R. L. M. MILLER, EDS. 1977. *Social comparison processes: Theoretical and empirical perspectives.* New York: Wiley.

SUTHERLAND, S., AND D. SCHERL. 1970. Patterns of response among victims of rape. *Journal of Orthopsychiatry, 40,* 503–11.

SWANN, W. B., JR., AND S. J. READ. 1981a. Acquiring self-knowledge: The search for feedback that fits. *Journal of Personality and Social Psychology, 41,* 1119–28.

————. 1981b. Self-verification processes: How we sustain our self-conceptions. *Journal of Experimental Social Psychology, 17,* 351–72.

SYMONDS, M. 1980. The "second injury" to victims. In *Evaluation and change: Services for survivors.* Minneapolis, Minn.: Minneapolis Medical Research Foundation.

TAIT, R., AND R. C. SILVER. 1989. Coming to terms with major negative life events. In *Unintended thought,* ed. J. S. Uleman and J. A. Bargh. New York: Guilford.

TAJFEL, H., AND A. L. WILKES. 1963. Classification and qualitative judgment. *British Journal of Psychology, 54,* 101–14.

TAVRIS, C., AND C. WADE. 1984. *The longest war: Sex differences in perspective.* New York: Harcourt, Brace Jovanovich.

TAYLOR, S. E. 1983. Adjustment to threatening events: A theory of cognitive adaptation. *American Psychologist, 38,* 1161–73.

————. 1990. *Positive illusions: Creative self-deception and the healthy mind.* New York: Basic Books.

TAYLOR, S. E., AND J. D. BROWN. 1988. Illusion and well-being: A social-psychological perspective on mental health. *Psychological Bulletin, 103,* 193–210.

TAYLOR, S. E., R. R. LICHTMAN, AND J. V. WOOD. 1984. Attributions, beliefs about control, and adjustment to breast cancer. *Journal of Personality and Social Psychology, 46,* 489–502.

TAYLOR, S. E., J. V. WOOD, AND R. R. LICHTMAN. 1983. It could be worse: Selective evaluation as a response to victimization. *Journal of Social Issues, 39,* 19–40.

TENNEN, H., AND G. AFFLECK. 1990. Blaming others for threatening events. *Psychological Bulletin, 108,* 209–32.

TENNEN, H., G. AFFLECK, D. A. ALLEN, B. J. McGRADE, AND S. RATZAN. 1984. Causal attributions and coping with insulin-dependent diabetes. *Basic and Applied Social Psychology, 5,* 131–42.

TENNEN, H., G. AFFLECK, AND K. GERSHMAN. 1986. Self-blame among parents of infants with perinatal complications: The role of self-protective motives. *Journal of Personality and Social Psychology, 50,* 690–96.

TERR, L. C. 1979. Children of Chowchilla: A study of psychic trauma. *Psychoanalytic Study of the Child, 34,* 547–623.

———. 1983. Chowchilla revisited: The effects of psychic trauma four years after a school-bus kidnapping. *American Journal of Psychiatry, 140,* 1543–50.

TESSER, A. 1978. Self-generated attitude-change. In *Advances in experimental social psychology,* vol. 11, ed. L. Berkowitz. New York: Academic Press.

TESSER, A., AND J. CAMPBELL. 1983. Self-definition and self-evaluation maintenance. In *Psychological perspectives on the self,* vol. 2, ed. J. Suls and A. G. Greenwald. Hillsdale, N.J.: Erlbaum.

TESSER, A., AND M. C. CONLEE. 1975. Some effects of time and thought on attitude polarization. *Journal of Personality and Social Psychology, 31,* 262–70.

TESSER, A., AND C. LEONE. 1977. Cognitive schemas and thought as determinants of attitude change. *Journal of Experimental Social Psychology, 13,* 340–56.

THOMPSON, S. C. 1985. Finding positive meaning in a stressful event and coping. *Basic and Applied Social Psychology, 6,* 279–95.

THOMPSON, S., AND A. S. JANIGIAN. 1988. Life schemes: A framework for understanding the search for meaning. *Journal of Social and Clinical Psychology, 7,* 260–80.

TIGER, L. 1979. *Optimism: The biology of hope.* New York: Simon & Schuster.

TIMKO, C., AND R. JANOFF-BULMAN. 1985. Attributions, vulnerability, and psychological adjustment: The case of breast cancer. *Health Psychology, 4,* 521–44.

TITCHENER, J. L., F. T. KAPP, AND C. WINGET. 1976. The Buffalo Creek syndrome: Symptoms and character change after a major disaster. In *Emergency and disaster management,* ed. H. J. Parad, H. L. P. Resnik, and L. G. Parad. Bowie, Md.: Charles Press.

TROPE, Y. 1975. Seeking information about one's own ability as a determinant of choice among tasks. *Journal of Personality and Social Psychology, 32,* 1004–32.

ULEMAN, J. S. 1989. A framework for thinking intentionally about unintended thought. In *Unintended thought,* ed. J. S. Uleman and J. A. Bargh. New York: Guilford.

ULEMAN, J. S., AND J. A. BARGH, EDS. *Unintended thought.* New York: Guilford.

ULMAN, R., AND D. BROTHERS. 1988. *The shattered self: A psychoanalytic study of trauma.* Hillsdale, N.J.: Analytic Press.

VAN DER KOLK, B. A. 1985. Adolescent vulnerability to post-traumatic stress. *Psychiatry, 20,* 365–70.

———. 1987. *Psychological trauma.* Washington, D.C.: American Psychiatric Press.

VAN DER KOLK, B. A., P. BROWN, AND O. VAN DER HART. 1989. Pierre Janet on post-traumatic stress. *Journal of Traumatic Stress, 2,* 365–78.

VAN DER KOLK, B. A., AND M. S. GREENBERG. 1987. The psychobiology of the trauma response: Hyperarousal, constriction, and addiction to traumatic reexposure. In *Psychological trauma,* ed. B. A. van der Kolk. Washington, D.C.: American Psychiatric Press.

VAN DER KOLK, B. A., M. S. GREENBERG, H. BOYD, AND J. KRYSTAL. 1985. Inescapable shock, neurotransmitter and addiction to trauma: Towards a psychobiology of post-traumatic stress. *Biological Psychiatry, 20,* 314–25.

VAN DER KOLK, B. A., AND W. KADISH. 1987. Amnesia, dissociation, and the return of the repressed. In *Psychological trauma,* ed. B. A. van der Kolk. Washington, D.C.: American Psychiatric Press.

VAN DER KOLK, B. A., AND O. VAN DER HART. 1989. Pierre Janet and the breakdown of adaptation in psychological trauma. *American Journal of Psychiatry, 198,* 1530–40.

VER ELLEN, P., AND D. P. VAN KAMMEN. 1990. The biological findings in post-traumatic stress disorder: A review. *Journal of Applied Social Psychology, 20,* 1789–1821.

VIORST, J. 1986. *Necessary losses.* New York: Simon & Schuster.

WALKER, L. E. 1979. *The battered woman.* New York: Harper & Row.

WALLSTON, B. S., S. W. ALAGNA, B. M. DEVELLIS, AND R. F. DEVELLIS. 1983. Social support and physical health. *Health Psychology, 2,* 367–91.

WATTS, W., AND L. A. FREE. 1978. *State of the Nation III.* Lexington, Mass.: Lexington Books.

WEGNER, D. M. 1989. *White bears and other unwanted thoughts.* New York: Viking.

WEINER, B. 1980. A cognitive (attributional)-emotion-action model of motivated behavior: An analysis of judgments of help-giving. *Journal of Personality and Social Psychology, 39,* 186–200.

WEINER, B., I. FRIEZE, A. KUKLA, L. REED, S. REST, AND R. M. ROSENBAUM. 1972. Perceiving the causes of success and failure. In *Attribution: Perceiving the causes of behavior,* ed. E. E. Jones, D. E. Kanouse, H. H. Kelley, R. E. Nisbett, S. Valins, and B. Weiner. Morristown, N.J.: General Learning Press.

WEINER, B., R. P. PERRY, AND J. MAGNUSON. 1988. An attributional analysis of reactions to stigma. *Journal of Personality and Social Psychology, 55,* 738–48.

WEINSTEIN, N. D. 1980. Unrealistic optimism about future life events. *Journal of Personality and Social Psychology, 39,* 806–20.

———. 1982. Unrealistic optimism about susceptibility to health problems. *Journal of Behavioral Medicine, 5,* 441–60.

———. 1989. Effects of personal experience on self-protective behavior. *Psychological Bulletin, 105,* 31–50.

WEINSTEIN, N. D., AND E. LACHENDRO. 1982. Egocentrism as a source of unrealistic optimism. *Personality and Social Psychology Bulletin, 8,* 195–200.

WEIS, K., AND S. WEIS. 1975. Victimology and the justification of rape. In *Victimology: A new focus,* vol. 3, ed. I. Drapkin and E. Viano. Lexington, Mass.: Lexington Books.

WEISMAN, A. D. 1972. *On dying and denying.* New York: Behavioral Publications.

———. 1979. *Coping with cancer.* New York: McGraw-Hill.

WEISMAN, A. D., AND J. W. WORDEN. 1975. Psychosocial analysis of cancer deaths. *Omega, 6,* 61–75.

WEISS, R. S. 1988. Loss and recovery. *Journal of Social Issues, 44,* 37–52.

WELLER, S. 1973. Work in progress: Maya Angelou. *Intellectual Digest,* June 1973, 11–12, 14.

WESTEN D., P. LUDOLPH, B. MISLE, S. RUFFINS, AND J. BLOCK. 1990. Physical and sexual abuse in adolescent girls with borderline personality disorder. *American Journal of Orthopsychiatry, 60,* 55–66.

WILDER, T. 1927. *The Bridge of San Luis Rey.* New York: Grosset & Dunlap.

WILKINSON, C. B. 1983. Aftermath of a disaster: The collapse of the Hyatt Regency Hotel skywalks. *American Journal of Psychiatry, 140,* 1134–39.

WILLIAMS, J. H. 1987. *Psychology of women: Behavior in a biosocial context.* New York: Norton.

WILLS, T. A. 1981. Downward comparison principles in social psychology. *Psychological Bulletin, 90,* 245–71.

———. 1987. Help-seeking as a coping mechanism. In *Coping with negative life events: Clinical and social psychological perspectives,* ed. C. R. Snyder and C. E. Ford. New York: Plenum.

WILSON, J. P. 1978. *Identity, ideology, and crisis: The Vietnam veteran in transition,* vols. 1 and 2. Cincinnati, Ohio: Disabled American Veterans.

———. 1988a. Understanding the Vietnam veteran. In *Post-traumatic therapy and victims of violence,* ed. F. Ochberg. New York: Brunner/Mazel.

———. 1988b. Treating the Vietnam veteran. In *Post-traumatic therapy and victims of violence,* ed. F. Ochberg. New York: Brunner/Mazel.

————. 1989. *Trauma, transformation, and healing: An integrative approach to theory, research, and post-traumatic therapy.* New York: Brunner/Mazel.

WILSON, J. P., AND G. E. KRAUSS. 1985. Predicting post-traumatic stress disorders among Vietnam veterans. In *Post-traumatic stress disorder and the war veteran patient,* ed. W. E. Kelly. New York: Brunner/Mazel.

WINNECOTT, D. W. 1965. *The maturational process and the facilitating environment.* New York: International Universities Press.

WITTGENSTEIN, L. 1953. *Philosophical investigations.* New York: Macmillan.

WOLFENSTEIN, M. 1957. *Disaster: A psychological essay.* Glencoe, Ill.: Free Press.

WOOD, J. V. 1989. Theory and research concerning social comparisons of personal attributes. *Psychological Bulletin, 106,* 231–48.

WORTMAN, C. B. 1975. Some determinants of perceived control. *Journal of Personality and Social Psychology, 31,* 282–94.

————. 1976. Causal attributions and personal control. In *New Directions in Attributions Research,* vol. 1, ed. J. H. Harvey, W. J. Ickes, and R. F. Kidd. Hillsdale, N.J.: Erlbaum.

WORTMAN, C. B., AND C. DUNKEL-SCHETTER. 1979. Interpersonal relationships and cancer: A theoretical analysis. *Journal of Social Issues, 3,* 120–55.

WORTMAN, C. B., AND D. R. LEHMAN. 1985. Reactions to victims of life crises: Support attempts that fail. In *Social support: Theory, research, and applications,* ed. I. G. Sarason and B. R. Sarason. Dordrecht, Netherlands: Martinus Nijhoff.

WYLIE, R. C. 1979. *The self-concept,* vol. 1: *Theory and research on selected topics.* Lincoln: University of Nebraska Press.

ZANNA, M. P., AND S. J. PACK. 1975. On the self-fulfilling nature of apparent sex differences in behavior. *Journal of Experimental Social Psychology, 11,* 583–91.

ZIMBARDO, P. G., AND R. FORMICA. 1963. Emotional comparison and self-esteem as determinants of affiliation. *Journal of Personality, 31,* 141–62.

Name Index

Abelson, R. P., 182
Abramson, L. Y., 178, 180, 181,
    190, 200
Adler, G., 193
Affleck, G., 201, 202
Ahrens, A. H., 190
Ainsworth, Mary D. S., 23, 180
Alagna, S. W., 203
Alba, J. W., 182
Allen, D. A., 201
Alloy, L. B., 180, 190
Allport, G. W., 180
American Psychiatric Association,
    49, 53, 54, 184, 189, 195, 196,
    198
Amir, M., 199
Anderson, C. A., 183
Angelou, Maya, 7
Anisman, H. L., 188, 189
Antonovsky, Aaron, 18, 178, 180
Arieti, S., 188, 190
Aristotle, 133
Aronson, E., 181, 199
Asch, Solomon, 37–38, 183
Atkeson, B. M., 188, 190, 193
Auden, W. H., 155
Averill, James, 65, 188

Backman, C. W., 181
Bacon, Roger, 55
Bandura, Albert, 178, 203
Bard, Morton, 58, 63, 78, 127, 128,
    187, 188, 191, 196, 201, 204
Bargh, J. A., 198
Barkas, J. L., 187
Barnes, R. D., 178
Bart, P. B., 202
Bartlett, F., 182
Baum, A., 191, 201
Beall, S. K., 198, 202
Beck, Aaron T., 31–32, 183, 190,
    199
Becker, Ernest, 19, 60–61, 105,
    180, 187, 197
Bem, D., 177
Bemporad, J., 190
Bender, M. E., 188, 206
Berglas, S. C., 181
Berman, J. S., 184
Berscheid, Ellen, 33
Best, Connie L., 185, 194
Beyth, R., 204
Blake, D. D., 184
Blanchard, E. B., 188, 189
Blehar, M. C., 180

239

Subject Index